STRAIT ANSWERS to the
GAY QUESTION
Having Been There...

VICTOR J. ADAMSON

Remnant
Publications
Coldwater MI 49036

Strait Answers to the Gay Question
Having Been There…
by Victor J. Adamson
(Ron Woolsey)

Cover design by David Berthiaume
Text Design by Greg Solie Altamont Graphics

ISBN: 978-1-62913-023-1

STRAIT ANSWERS to the
GAY QUESTION
Having Been There...

I know the questions for this panel are supposed to by anonymous, but if you want to get in contact (if there is any hope), my name is _____.

What do you do when you have tried all the suggestions for overcoming, but you just can't seem to shake it? What do you do when you feel hopeless? What do you do when you feel rejected by your family? What do you do when you feel so discouraged that you never want to try again? What if you have tried counseling, and it didn't work? What if you have been claiming Scripture and memorizing, but it seems futile? What if you want to live, but kill yourself at the same time? What if you have already attempted?

What do you do when it's all you can think about? How do you deal with being molested? How could I ever be changed and happy? I have tried everything. *This is the last time I will ever try again.*

A true Christian, my friend, is not homophobic (fearful of the homosexual issue), but rather "homo-agapic." It is with genuine love and compassion that I reach out to the gay community and to all affected by the homosexual issue in an effort to share with them the blessed hope that I have found for myself in Jesus Christ, inviting and allowing Him to truly be Lord and Master in all dimensions of my life.

"Victor J. Adamson"

WHO IS VICTOR J. ADAMSON?
by Ron Woolsey

I t was the year 2,000 when I was asked to publish my story as a resource for the Christian community faced with the ever-intimidating issue of homosexuality and the church. Upon presenting my manuscript to the publisher, I was advised to use a pen name for my protection.

"Why?" I asked.

"One of our recent authors broaching this subject had his house burned to the ground," I was informed, "and his speaking engagements were hounded by hecklers. We don't want that to happen to you and to your family."

So I labored for weeks to come up with a pen name that would bear the message of victory that I was espousing. Hence, Victor J. Adamson.

Sometime later I was submitting my testimony without a name attached to a global publication that was very interested. However, they soon called me asking for my name.

"Well," I said, "I'm submitting my testimony in anonymity."

"That will never do," came the reply. "How is it a testimony if it is anonymous?!"

"Oh! You're right!" I exclaimed. "What was I thinking?"

What I was thinking was anonymity for my protection.

"Have you not read Psalm 107:2?" they confronted me. " 'Let the redeemed of the LORD say So whom he hath redeemed from the hand of the enemy.' We want to print your testimony in our publication, but we need your name, your picture, and a picture of your family."

So I submitted the pictures and my testimony with the name Victor J. Adamson. However, now emboldened with the Word of God, I have also added my given name, Ron Woolsey.

From that day forward the Lord has empowered me to speak more and more openly and boldly for Him. He is my Protector, my Inspiration, my Confidante, my Friend, and Companion. He is my All in All. I take His words to Jeremiah to heart:

"Thou shalt go to all that I shall send thee, and whatsoever I command thee thou shalt speak. Be not afraid of their faces: for I am with thee to deliver thee, saith the LORD...And the LORD said unto me, Behold, I have put my words in thy mouth" (Jeremiah 1:7–9).

It is my prayer that His expressed will may always shine forth in my presentations, both in writing and in speaking. Only then can I truly be a blessing to others.

"Victor J. Adamson"
(Ron Woolsey)

CONTENTS

PREFACE

At the time of the publication of this manuscript it has been 22 years since turning my back on my old life of homosexuality to begin my new life in and with Jesus Christ. Revelation 12:11 tells us that we overcome the accuser of the brethren (Satan) by the blood of the Lamb and by the word of our testimony.

In Mark 5:19, 20, we read of the "set free" demoniac of Gadara to whom Jesus commissioned:

> Go home to thy friends, and tell them how great things the Lord hath done for thee, and hath had compassion on thee. And he departed, and began to publish in Decapolis how great things Jesus had done for him: and all men did marvel.

I relate well to this young man who was set free indeed by the miracle-working power of Jesus in his life. And, in harmony with this counsel, I have traveled the world, onto every continent (with the exception of the Arctic and Antarctic), telling of the great and wonderful things Jesus has done in my life and how He has shown compassion to me.

One question that always comes up is about my first family: have we been reconciled? So as a little epilogue, I am happy to share that there has been a wonderful reconciliation with my first family. We must realize that there is nothing we can do to change yesterday or yesteryear. However, by God's grace, this day and every day hereafter into eternity can be good, in harmony with God's will, blessed, and blessing.

I'm always thrilled, when I get a phone call on my birthday, to hear my ex-wife and her husband singing "Happy birthday to you…" They are very supportive of what I now stand for and the ministry to which I have been called. We plan to be friends and family in the hereafter forever.

My oldest daughter is married to a wonderful man, and through them I have two handsome grandsons. My oldest son is married to a beautiful young woman, and together they have given me two beautiful granddaughters.

Through my wife Claudia, I have a stepson of whom we both are very proud. He is an officer in the Air Force, and he and his wife have given us yet another grandson.

Together Claudia and I are the proud parents of Zachary and Natalie, now almost grown up. Zachary is off to college next year majoring in business, minoring in music. Natalie will be a senior in high school.

Our "quiver is full." The Lord has blessed us abundantly in harmony with his promise: "As it is written, Eye hath not seen, nor ear heard, neither have entered into the heart of man, the things which God hath prepared for them that love him" (1 Corinthians 2:9).

We do not have to wait for heaven to receive the fulfillment of this promise. Indeed, the kingdom of God begins at the new birth, at conversion. May you, too, receive all that the Lord has prepared for you.

"Victor J. Adamson"

INTRODUCTION

I t was the year 2000 when I was asked to publish my story as a resource for the Christian community faced with the ever-intimidating issue of homosexuality and the church. Upon presenting my manuscript to the publisher, I was advised to use a pen name for my protection.

After publishing my first book *That Kind Can Never Change! Can They...?*, the story of my own personal struggle to understand and overcome homosexuality, I was contracted by the publisher to appear on radio talk shows around the country for three years to tell my story, to be interviewed, and to help promote the book.

The publisher also advised me to create a website in order to further reach out to those seeking assistance in dealing with the homosexual, either for themselves or for their loved ones, friends, acquaintances, or church members. I was told that the book itself would generate questions that would need to be addressed beyond what was covered in just one book.

Thus was born www.victorjadamson.com. Over the ensuing years I have received numerous e-mails from interested readers of the book and visitors to the website. Some have been mildly to extremely hostile, as the origin of hate speech on this issue seems to come from the pro-gay element of society more so than from the Christian element. However, most correspondence has been out of genuine interest in seeking assistance for one's self as a sin-sick gay, or in order to equip one's self to minister to some loved one who is gay.

To many of these questions I have written and posted short to not-so-short responses as a resource for a larger general audience. These postings have been under a web page feature titled "Question of the Week," and "Featured Articles."

Repeatedly, I have been asked to compile these articles into book form as a concise resource for individuals, families, churches, schools, and the general public. Rising to the occasion, I now present this work:

Strait Answers to the Gay Question
Having Been There...

May you be blessed, and may you be better equipped to be a blessing to others, is my hope and prayer.

"Victor J. Adamson"
(Ron Woolsey)

Chapter 1

TRANSFORMED BY THE POWER OF GOD

An interview with the author while in Stenshult, Sweden.
Jay Krueger with "Victor J. Adamson" (Ron Woolsey)

Question: Were you born a homosexual?

Reply: Most of my life I believed I had been born "different" from other people, but I now believe that not to be the case. True scientific research in this area has proven that there is no such thing as a gay gene, that it is impossible for people to be born gay. Homosexuality is a conditioned behavior resulting from any number of many environmental factors.

Question: What factors led to your being a homosexual?

Reply: There were many factors that contributed to my "becoming" homosexual, i.e., being robbed of my innocence through sexual molestation at the tender age of four and repeated such instances as I grew older; misunderstanding and disapproval by the male figures in my life, especially my father who also was emotionally and physically abusive toward me until I left home at the age of 15; my overly sensitive feelings of rejection, real and surmised; my own pride, self-centeredness, and indulged desire (fantasizing) for that which was forbidden by a plain "thus saith the Lord."

No doubt there were other contributing factors as well, but you can see that it is not necessarily any one thing that conditions one's thinking, feelings, emotions, and tendencies into this perversion of God's gift of sexuality, or any other of a number of diversions as well.

Question: Were you ever content with your life as a homosexual?

Reply: On the surface I was content, for I was no longer wrestling against those unwanted feelings, emotions, and tendencies. There is initially a sense of relief when one ceases to fight and just gives in. However, I could never escape the sense of guilt and shame I experienced as one who had given in to a life of perversion. I was not comfortable being open about my homosexuality, but rather attempted to hide that side of myself while in the workplace and in the general public. It was also helpful for me to numb my senses and conscience through the use of alcohol and drugs from time to time, and to fill my life with "busyness" so that I would not have to face myself and my true condition. I drowned out the "still small voice" through nightclubbing and rock music and an acquired addiction to television and movies and all sorts of entertainment.

Question: How did you realize that the homosexual life was not satisfying you?

Reply: Though my life was filled with many distractions to avoid facing my conscience, there was always "the morning after" syndrome, like the hangover from alcohol, or the headache after the caffeine and nicotine wear off, in which I experienced disappointment, loneliness, emptiness, rejection, times of despair and depression, and infidelity by those who were "committed" to me. I began to realize that though my life was filled with much excitement, pleasure, self-gratification, self-glory, and adventure, it was a life with no real and lasting joy, peace, assurance, or the genuine unconditional love offered by God and His true children. There was always the possibility of being replaced by another "Mr. Right," one younger or better looking or more appealing.

The gay life was one of many uncertainties, disappointments, and heartaches. On the rare occasions that I was around genuine Christians, it was also very apparent to me that my life was lacking what they had, that my life was shallow and meaningless, filled with counterfeits of what God really offers His children.

Question: Is it possible to be a homosexual but to not practice the sexual behavior of a homosexual?

Reply: Yes, just as it is possible to be a thief who no longer steals because he is in prison, or a murderer who no longer kills because he is behind bars. Yes, of course, it is possible to suppress one's behavior. Monasteries and convents around the world are filled with people who have taken vows of chastity, poverty, or silence. But that is not an indication of what exists within the heart of man. Sin begins in the heart, or the mind, and can be very active there even though overt behavior is suppressed.

I believe that God's plan for His children results in being born-again spiritually with new motives, new tastes, and new tendencies. I believe that a genuine conversion changes both hereditary and cultivated tendencies to wrong. This is stated clearly in 2 Corinthians 5:17 which reads, "Therefore if any man be in Christ, he is a new creature [creation]: old things are passed away; behold, all things are become new."

Also, if we accept the biblical classification of homosexuality to be that of one of many abominations, a sin issue, then we must acknowledge that it is a form of bondage, or addiction. And to this diagnosis we are given the promise that Jesus "shall save his people *from* their sins" (Matthew 1:21, emphasis added).

We are further encouraged by the promise of complete healing in the words of John 8:36, "If the Son therefore shall make you free, ye shall be free indeed."

One really has no excuse to remain in homosexuality, nor in any other sin condition for that matter, for the apostle Paul tells us that, "It is God which worketh in you both to will and to do of his good pleasure." And that we can be "confident of this very thing, that he which hath begun a good work in you will perform it until the day of Jesus Christ" (Philippians 2:13; 1:6).

Jesus is the Alpha and the Omega, the first and the last, the beginning and the ending, the author and finisher of our faith. He is not a quitter where our salvation from sin is concerned. None have excuse for remaining unchanged, uncleansed, or unsanctified in light of all that God has promised to do for us and in us.

Paul goes on to admonish the homosexual (and other sinners) to not just suppress unwanted feelings and tendencies, but "Be ye transformed by the renewing of your mind, that ye may prove what is that good, and acceptable, and perfect, will of God" (Romans 12:2).

Question: What was the hardest part of leaving your old life?

Reply: I would have to say, just letting go. I was in a long-term relationship, like a marriage, with one in whom I was deeply in love, though it was far from God's ideal of a good relationship. As I looked to Christ, I was faced with a choice—either Him, or him. I could not have both. To believe so would be total self-dishonesty and self-deception, a denial of eternal realities.

Ending that relationship was extremely traumatic as I watched my friend sink into total despair and hopelessness with the experience of yet another rejection in his life. He had been abandoned by his mother at the age of two, and I saw him revert to that two-year-old child going once again through all the horror of being abandoned by one in whom he had placed implicit trust with his life, his love, and his emotions. That experience haunted me for years. But it worked to brace me against ever again putting myself into a situation where I could cause so much pain and heartbreak. The Lord has used that experience in my life, turning a very tragic time around to His glory, as I now live to bring glory to Him rather than to myself, and to be a blessing to others, rather than to seek my own gratification in this life.

Question: What encouragement would you give to someone struggling to overcome homosexuality?

Reply: I could write a book to answer this question. Indeed, I have already! In fact, all of the questions asked in this interview have been addressed in greater depth in my book and with more thorough coverage.

Suffice it to say here, however, that there is power in the Word of God— omnipotent, divine, transforming power. To my gay questions I found my strait answers, yes, straight from the Word of God. I trusted no man with this issue, for

I had been terribly disappointed in the past with counsel. I went to my knees, and to the Word, and asked for enlightenment through the Holy Spirit. In fact, my method of assisting people in this area is to point them to the Word.

There are many exceedingly great and precious promises in the Word, many of which I have compiled into an article (and now a chapter of this book) titled "A Rainbow of Promises." With every promise comes the divine power (grace) to comply with the conditions. As Jesus said to Mary, "Neither do I condemn thee: go, and sin no more" (John 8:11).

In the words of my favorite author, "All His [God's] biddings are enablings" (*Christ's Object Lessons*, 333).

Question: Do you ever desire to go back to your old lifestyle?

Reply: Simply put, No! Why not? "Eye hath not seen, nor ear heard, neither have entered into the heart of man, the things that God hath prepared for them that love him" (1 Corinthians 2:9).

I can testify to the truth of this statement, "Higher than the highest human thought can reach is God's ideal for His children" (*Education*, 18). My new life in Christ is filled with second chances and double portions: reconciliation with God, family and friends, a rich and full spirit-filled ministry, a loving wife and two beautiful children, a music ministry I never thought possible, and the genuine love, joy, peace, and assurance I never really had outside the realm of God's blessing. Truly, our Father knows best.

Chapter 2
THE GAY DILEMMA

The following letter is just a sampling of the gay dilemma that many spiritual people face today, people who want to be right with the Lord, people who want to do right by one another, people who desperately need the intervention of the Lord Jesus Christ, the self-existent eternal One, sent from heaven and anointed to be our personal Savior from sin.

Question: I am a 52-year-old homosexual. I have been attracted to males for as long as I can remember. With total reliance on God and trust in His promise to give me the power to overcome all sin, I married a wonderful girl. We had known each other from childhood and were best friends. She is very beautiful with a character to match. We were married for 20 years and had three children. I was emotionally in love with her but found sex very distasteful; it actually became a nightmare for me. I only found my wife to be attractive to me when she was clothed.

I trusted God completely and prayed constantly for strength and His help to change. Nothing happened and after 20 years of this my wife and I separated. Toward the end of our marriage the stress and struggle had almost destroyed our physical and mental health. She has remarried, but we are still best friends.

I now have a same-sex relationship and feel happy and fulfilled. I still trust God to lead me in my life. My question is, should I have persevered with my marriage until my family and I were totally destroyed? Maybe it is true that only a few are chosen.

I will challenge anyone to dispute the fact that I trusted completely in God's power to change me according to His will.

Reply: Your situation seems to mirror my own past. I, too, gave up on God's ability to save me from homosexuality and brought to an end my own marriage, for all the same reasons you state in your letter to me. Years later, however, I studied my way to an understanding of God's will and methods in regard to this issue. And I studied my own self, acknowledging my own failures, ceasing to blame God and others. I discovered that there is power in the Word, and I studied myself right out of homosexuality. The details are too lengthy to put in an e-mail. It would take a book. But let me tell you the results and then make a recommendation.

I have been married once again, this time for almost 22 years. I am happily married, with 5 children and 5 grandchildren, and I wouldn't change my present situation for the old one for anything in the world. God *is* mighty to save the whosoevers, from whatsoever, even to the uttermost.

Now, the recommendation: All the details are written up in my first book *That Kind Can Never Change! Can They...?* followed up by this sequel, and also on my website: www.victorjadamson.com. It is my prayer that these resources will be a blessing to you as you seek.

Question: I am a gay man who is about to celebrate his 10-year anniversary with his partner. He and I have one adopted son, who is now 6, who is the love of my life. We've had ups and downs, but we are generally very happy with each other and with the life we have, and we aim to be together until we are old and gray for the purpose of our son being happy and successful. Am I on the right path? If not, what do I need to do to get on the right path?

Reply: Many times Jesus answered questions by asking questions in return. Perhaps that method will work here as well. In Isaiah 1:18 God said, "Come now, and let us reason together." So let us try here a little consistent line of questioning and reasoning and see where God leads. And please know that I go this route out of a sincere concern and godly love for you as you honestly seek truth about your situation and your destiny.

I must share with you, however, that sometimes a lifesaving medicine may be found in the form of a "bitter pill," even though administered with inestimable love, occasionally referred to as tough love.

To determine whether or not you are on the right path, we must first determine your destination. Where are you wanting to go? Do you have a road map to guide you successfully to your destination? If you do have a road map, who wrote out the instructions for you? Is the one who has given you directions from point A to point B trustworthy? The road he has directed you to travel may be filled with all kinds of adventures, pleasures, excitement, self-gratification, ups and downs, and general happiness. And you may have been advised that you can expect to travel down that road until you are old and gray and that your adopted son will end up being happy and successful as he travels with you.

But are you certain that you will find at the end of that road your expected destination? Is the one who has directed you down this "right path" the same One who died for you in order to provide for you eternal life? Or could it be possible that the one directing you down this "right path" is the same one who told Eve in the Garden of Eden, "Thou shalt not surely die"? You might want to check out this story in Genesis 3.

If your destination is "eternal life with Jesus Christ our Lord," then you might want to make sure that He is the author of your road map. After all, He has said, "Enter ye in at the strait gate [no pun intended]: for wide is the gate, and broad is the way, that leadeth to destruction, and many there be which go in thereat:

because strait is the gate, and narrow is the way, which leadeth unto life, and few there be that find it" (Matthew 7:13, 14).

In other words, it seems as though the masses of the world are getting their road maps from an impostor, the one who slyly promises, "Ye shall not surely die." While believing and trusting that they are on the right path, they are, in fact, on the broad way that leads to eternal destruction in the end, though they feel very good about it all along the way.

Jesus has told us, "I am the way, the truth, and the life." So if we want to stay on the right path we must make sure we keep our eyes upon Him. Yes? He is our example in life and our substitute in life and in death, as long as we are willing to pattern our lives after His. We are told in Revelation that those who are with Him in heaven are the called, the chosen, and the faithful. In order to follow Him wherever He goes in eternity, we must first learn to follow Him in life here on earth.

Jesus has promised to guide us constantly along the narrow way (for it is easy to lose one's footing if attempting to go it alone). "And thine ears shall hear a word behind thee, saying, This is the way, walk ye in it, when ye turn to the right hand, and when ye turn to the left" (Isaiah 30:21).

He has promised to work in us to will and to do of His good pleasure, and that he which hath begun a good work in you will perform it until the day of Jesus Christ (See Philippians 2:13; 1:6).

When asked, "What shall I do to inherit eternal life?" Jesus confirmed the tempting lawyer in His answer that we are to love God supremely and our neighbor as ourselves. Elsewhere He said, "If ye love me, keep my commandments" (John 14:15).

To the same question, He reminded the rich young ruler that he was expected to live in harmony with the law of God, the Ten Commandments. The young man turned away sorrowfully because in his efforts to keep all Ten Commandments, he did not really love God supremely.

When the jailor of Philippi asked Paul and Silas, "What must I do to be saved?" the answer was given, "Believe on the Lord Jesus Christ, and thou shalt be saved" (Acts 16:31).

"Lord" refers to "Jehovah," the self-existent, eternal God. "Jesus" means Savior. And Jesus came to save His people from their sins (Matthew 1:21), not in their sins. "Sin is the transgression of the law" (1 John 3:4). "Christ" means the Anointed One.

In other words, what Paul was saying was this: Believe on the self-existent, eternal God, who is anointed to be your personal Savior from sin, and you shall be saved, from the power of sin, from the penalty of sin, and from the very presence of sin itself.

This is the same God who has listed homosexuality as one of many abominations throughout the Bible and has offered to save His people from homosexuality as well as from any other sin. Why? For the wages of sin is death, eternal death.

You see, friend, the broad way, which to many seems to be the right path, is in reality the path that leads to destruction, eternal death. But the gift of God is eternal life, and it is the narrow way which leads unto this eternal life. The path of loving obedience is the true path, this narrow way.

The apostle Paul speaks of those who perish at the end of their perceived right path:

> Because they received not the love of the truth, that they might be saved. And for this cause God shall send them strong delusion, that they should believe a lie: that they all might be damned who believed not the truth, but had pleasure in unrighteousness. (2 Thessalonians 2:10–12)

So, you ask if you are on the right path? Do you want the truth? Do you love truth? Are you willing to follow the Way, the Truth, and the Life in loving obedience to all of His 10 commandments, regardless of the sacrifice and the consequences?

> Through all ages, and in all nations, those who believe that Jesus can and will save them personally from sin are the elect and chosen of God, His peculiar treasure. They obey His call. They come out from the world, and separate themselves from every unclean thought and unholy practice. (*The Review and Herald*, August 1, 1893)

My friend, if you are truly honest with yourself and with your God and genuinely love His truth, "Ye shall know the truth, and the truth shall make you free … If the Son therefore shall make you free, ye shall be free indeed" (John 8:32, 36).

Question: As a gay man with a partner and an adopted son, suppose I was willing to follow your advice. How do you suppose it would affect my relationship with my partner and my child? How do you suppose it would affect my family? Also, supposing I was not willing to follow your advice, what would the earthly consequences be?

Reply: In response to your latest questions, if you were willing to follow my advice, which I believe is biblical counsel, then the relationship with your partner would have to come to an end. Your friendship would have to become a distant one, in order to not place yourself in the path of temptation. Your adopted child would still be your child, of course. And, if legally adopted, he would probably be the beneficiary of a joint custody, as with other children of divorced parents.

In the Bible we read of a very difficult separation called for by God Himself, because the marriage was without His sanction. This situation also involved an innocent child, but the Lord required a separation nonetheless. You can read the story of Abraham, Hagar, and Ishmael in the book of Genesis, chapter 21.

There are many gay couples who go through this situation based upon just a desire to separate or divorce apart from following the Lord. If your desire is to separate for spiritual reasons, the Lord will bless you and help you through the difficult issues.

Sooner or later your child will be asking you tough questions, even if you and your partner choose to stay together. I believe he would respect you greatly in the end when he discovers that your decision was based upon a desire to follow the Lord.

Supposing you would not choose to follow my advice, I cannot predict what the earthly consequences might be. It could be that you would not realize any noticeable earthly consequences at all. It could be that your partnership could fall apart down the road for other reasons, leaving you to face the same questions you have posed to me now, but for other than spiritual reasons. Only God knows what your earthly consequences might be.

But, friend, it is the eternal realities that really matter, is it not? This life is but a fleeting moment. There is an eternity to win or lose, and a hell to shun depending upon choices you now face.

All power to you,
Victor

Question: I have a friend who is struggling with his faith because of the following question. If you have any ideas, that would be great!

God is strongly against homosexuality. (This friend has very strong ties with that community, including a little personal experience). Why would God so strongly condemn something that those experiencing it seem helpless to control? One of his friends said it this way (his friend is a homosexual): Why would anyone in his right mind choose homosexuality?

Reply: Yes, God *is* strongly opposed to homosexuality, according to texts in Scripture such as, "If a man also lie with mankind, as he lieth with a woman, both of them have committed an abomination" (Leviticus 20:13). And:

> Wherefore God also gave them up to uncleanness through the lusts of their own hearts, to dishonour their own bodies between themselves… For this cause God gave them up unto vile affections… and likewise also the men, leaving the natural use of the woman, burned in their lust one toward another; men with men working that which is unseemly… And even as they did not like to retain God in their knowledge, God gave them over to a reprobate mind. (Romans 1:24–28)

A number of other texts also bear out this truth. The tragedy we see in these texts is that of unrepentance, defiance, and self-justification. God will not force His will upon the unwilling.

However, God does not condemn the homosexual. He condemns the sin of homosexuality. You asked why God would so strongly condemn something that those experiencing it seem helpless to control.

Mankind has been helpless to control sin, period, since Adam and Eve chose to disobey in the Garden of Eden. It is only by the grace of God (which, by the way, is divine strength and fortitude), that any of us are able to overcome any kind of sin. Homosexuality is simply sin. It is when we reclassify it as an acceptable alternative lifestyle, or a genetic disorder, or a minority status like that of race and gender, that we take it out of the redemptive hand of our Savior.

You see, Jesus did not come to save His people from these things. Jesus came to "save His people from their sins." "Only acknowledge thine iniquity [sin]," says God in Jeremiah 3:13, "and I will heal your backslidings" (Jeremiah 3:22).

Your friends must be able to acknowledge to themselves, as well as to God, that they are struggling with a sin issue. Then, and only then, does God's grace, His divine strength and power, become sufficient. "For my strength is made perfect in [your] weakness" (2 Corinthians 12:9). The sin-sick homosexual must acknowledge his weakness to overcome his sin, taking it to the Lord who promises sufficient grace for him to overcome.

You asked, "Why would anyone in his right mind choose homosexuality?" This was an argument I used for years against those who tried to help me choose to leave the gay lifestyle, for I had struggled against my tendencies and temptations for years before finally giving up and just accepting "who I was born to be."

But think about this for a moment. Why would anyone in his or her right mind choose to disobey God, sin, in any way? "For the wages of sin is death" (Romans 6:23). None of us choose the nature of our temptations, and this is a point I wish to make very clear. The nature of our temptation to sin does not define who we are, nor do our temptations define our orientation. It is our choices that define us.

Let me illustrate. I used to be a pilot in my youth. Sometimes I would be flying with a tail wind, or against a cross wind, or even into a head wind, and sometimes through a violent storm. The wind had its designs for my destination, which were contrary to the course I had charted for myself. As a pilot I had to compensate for the direction of the wind if I was to safely reach the destination of my orientation. My orientation was the destination of *my* choosing, not that of the wayward wind.

Another illustration: occasionally I find myself driving a vehicle with bad alignment. It always pulls to the left, or always to the right. But *I* am driving! The tendency of that vehicle is to ditch itself—always. But when placed in my hands as the driver, the orientation of the vehicle becomes that of following the straight and narrow way that leads to my destination—home! Eventually I am able to adjust the alignment to where it no longer wrestles against me as the driver. But I have one vehicle now that never seems to be correctly aligned. However, it still always gets me safely to my destination, because with my hand always on the wheel, I compensate for its wayward tendency.

Spiritually speaking, the devil is like the contrary wind, and our fallen human nature is like the bad alignment. Satan has designs for you, for your friends, and for me that are contrary to our own choosing—contrary to the plan that God has for us as well. With every tendency and temptation to sin we are faced with a choice. Do we compensate for that contrary wind in order to reach our chosen destination? Or, do we go with the wind, only to crash on some remote mountain of destruction?

Only when we choose to go with the wind, and choose to give in to the tendencies of our fallen natures and go with the temptations of the devil do our orientation, tendencies, and temptations become the same.

The words of a song are so appropriate here: "Jesus, Savior, pilot me over life's tempestuous sea." Only by placing our lives into the hands of the Master Pilot can we be assured of safely reaching the destination He has planned for us—home! Our alignment may be set right, or we may end up with a continuous struggle. Either way, Jesus can guide us safely home.

The great apostle Paul put it this way, "But I keep under my body, and bring it into subjection: lest that by any means, when I have preached to others, I myself should be a castaway." Also, "I die [to self] daily" (1 Corinthians 9:27; 15:31).

"Having therefore these promises, dearly beloved [God dearly loves you and your homosexual friends], let us cleanse ourselves from all filthiness of the flesh and spirit, perfecting holiness in the fear of God" (2 Corinthians 7:1).

Question: How did the term "gay" become associated with homosexuals?

Reply: On a recent radio show, I was asked the question, how did the term "gay" become associated with homosexuals? I had to admit that I really had no idea; and that I, too, had asked that question many times. So I invited anyone with that information to call in to the show and share with us, or to e-mail the answer to me.

A couple days later I received the following reply from Dr. Neil Whitehead, co-author of the book *My Genes Made Me Do It*, published by Huntington House Publishers and Vital Issues Press:

Hi! And good to follow you on the radio again! According to Ruth Tiffany Barnhouse, (*Homosexuality: A Symbolic Confusion*), 'gay' was used in

1940 in NY as a term for effeminate male homosexuals in theaters and nightclubs. Other homosexuals were highly insulted. However, it seems they eventually adopted the term. It had acquired a bad connotation by the 17th century, being a euphemism for "immoral" and those generally addicted to social pleasures and dissipations. Blessings, Neil.

Thank you, Neil Whitehead.
And there you have it.

Chapter 3

GOD'S LOVE FOR THE HOMOSEXUAL

Question: God loves you for who you are. I am a happy gay man who happens to be very close to God. He's gotten me through alcoholism, drug abuse, and losing my partner to cancer. Most importantly, He's helped me accept myself for all that I am. We talk every day, and I don't know about you, but I don't care what anybody else tells me about my relationship with God; I know we're good. I know that you're only trying to help people, and I can't be angry at someone for that, as I'm sure you're dealing with plenty of criticism. I'm sure that the Lord will see you through this.

Reply: I am sorry to hear about the loss of your partner to cancer. And I rejoice with you for your victory over alcoholism and drug abuse. The Lord has certainly begun a good work in you. However, from a biblical perspective, Jesus came not to help people accept themselves, but to save His people from their sins. The Lord does not love us for who we are, but in spite of who we are. He died for His enemies, and for strangers, demonstrating His unconditional love that they might turn to Him for saving grace, which is divine transforming power (according to the Greek dictionary). We are not saved from sin by God's unconditional love alone, but because of His unconditional love we are saved from sin by His grace, His divine, transforming power.

The plan of salvation is all about transformation, re-creation, new motives, new thoughts, new tastes, and new tendencies. We read in 2 Corinthians 5:17 that "if any man be in Christ, he is a new creature [creation]: old things are passed away; behold, all things are become new."

It is never safe to trust our feelings or our own human reasoning when evaluating our stand with Christ. God tells us through His Word in Jeremiah 17:9, 10, "The heart is deceitful above all things, and desperately wicked: who can know it?" Then He answers the question by saying, "I the LORD search the heart, I try the reins, even to give every man according to his ways, and according to the fruit of his doings."

The only safe way to evaluate our standing with Christ is by stepping up to the mirror, His moral law, the Ten Commandments. He says, "If ye love me, keep my commandments" (John 14:15). And, 1 John 5:2, 3 adds, "By this we know that we love the children of God, when we love God, and keep his commandments. For this is the love of God, that we keep his commandments: and his commandments are not grievous."

You might also want to consider His warning in Matthew 7:21–23:

Not every one that saith unto me, Lord, Lord [in other words, professing to be Christians], shall enter into the kingdom of heaven; but he that *doeth* the will of my Father which is in heaven. Many will say to me in that day, Lord, Lord, have we not prophesied in thy name? and in thy name have cast out devils? and in thy name done many wonderful works? And then will I profess unto them, I never knew you [we don't have a saving relationship]: depart from me, ye that work iniquity. (Emphasis added.)

Knowing Jesus and having a good relationship with Him results in allowing Him to transform your life into one of obedience in every area of your life, not just in overcoming alcohol and drugs, but also in overcoming the addiction of homosexuality. If you truly have a good relationship with Jesus, then you will allow Him to truly save you from sin, from disobedience, the result being a life of obedience, living in harmony with His will as expressed in His moral law, the Ten Commandments.

I know we have a difference of opinion, but as a student of the Bible, God's Word, I can come to no other conclusion. I know you are happy. But God's plan for His children far exceeds anything they can think or imagine for themselves.

May you allow Jesus to truly be Lord and Master of your life.

Victor

Question: Will God forgive me? I have been saved since I was a child but have strayed away from the Lord in the last several years and have been confused as to why I have homosexual thoughts. I gave in a couple weeks ago to temptation and had a homosexual interaction. I am ashamed of what I have done and can't do anything without the terrible thought going through my mind. I've prayed every day since then for forgiveness. I'm ready to get back in the right and to live a better life, and I mean it.

Reply: I am sorry that you strayed away from the Lord and had a moral fall, but do not give in to discouragement. "God is love" (1 John 4:8). And He "commendeth his love toward us, in that, while we were yet sinners, Christ died for us" (Romans 5:8). So of course God will forgive you. He says in 1 John 1:9 that "If we confess our sins, he [God] is faithful and just to forgive us our sins, and to cleanse us from all unrighteousness."

Not only will He forgive you, but He will enable you to overcome, to be victorious, to stand up against temptation, for Jesus says in 2 Corinthians 12:9, "My grace [My divine, omnipotent power] is sufficient for thee: for my strength is made perfect in weakness." He also says in 1 John 2:1, "My little children, these things write I unto you, that ye sin not. And if any man sin [if you should stumble and fall], we have an advocate with the Father, Jesus Christ the righteous."

Here Jesus promises to be your friend in court, even when you sin against Him, if you are willing to repent and turn away from your sin. So do not give up on the Lord. He will never give up on you!

God is love!

Victor

———————————

Chapter 4

THE CAUSE OF
HOMOSEXUALITY

Question: How is homosexuality a learned behavior? I grew up in a heterosexual family where gays don't just come out of the closet—they get hung! It took me 18 or 19 years to come out of the closet. I believe I was born this way. I just would like to know more. So how is this a learned behavior?

Reply: For years I believed that I was born gay; for as far back as I could remember I was attracted to the male gender sexually. But I now realize that for young children to have sexual attractions of any kind, like before puberty, is not natural, not normal. The hormones are not yet raging. At the age of four I was not equipped to deal with sexuality. That's why I found myself totally unequipped to deal with the loss of my innocence at the hands of a farmhand at that young age. I was not equipped to process what had happened. I just knew that it wasn't right. But, from that day onward I found myself unable to control my fantasies and attractions. And I found myself to be an easy, repeat victim.

I believe, however, that there may be many, many different factors that play into someone's conditioning to be gay. You see, I personally believe that homosexuality is a conditioned or learned behavior. But I must quickly add that one's perception is his own reality. So I don't like to press hard on that point. If one believes he was born gay, so be it.

The bottom line is, what is to be done about it? If one is drowning in the sea, does it really matter how he found himself to be in that predicament? Does the lifeguard qualify the situation before offering the hand of deliverance? The same goes for one drowning in the sea of sin. Jesus doesn't seem to focus much upon the reasons one is the sinner he is, but rather simply offers him salvation from his sin. In Jeremiah 3, God says, "Only acknowledge thine iniquity… and I will heal your backslidings" (verses 13 and 22).

In my situation, after years of blaming others, especially God Himself, for my homosexuality, I finally came to acknowledge that I was dealing with a sin issue. The Bible makes it clear that homosexuality is abominable behavior, a sin issue along with many other abominations, I might add. And as I decided to deal with my homosexuality in that light, using the Bible formulas for overcoming sin, I was able to walk away from my addictive homosexual behavior and lifestyle. Not without temptation, though.

Please don't misunderstand me here. I continued to struggle with temptation for some time. But then, Jesus was tempted in all points like we are; yet, He didn't sin (see Hebrews 4:15). So temptation, big deal! And Jesus "suffered being tempted" (Hebrews 2:18). That means that He had a tremendous struggle with temptation, urges, desires, and passions, too. But He "resisted unto blood, striving against sin" (Hebrews 12:4). Jesus chose with all of His temptations to die rather than yield to them. He expects no less from us, for He assures us that His grace, His divine transforming power and strength, is sufficient for us. He works in us "both to will and to do of His good pleasure." And we can be confident that He who has "begun a good work in [us] will perform it until the day of Jesus Christ" (Philippians 2:13; 1:6).

Bottom line? Born gay, or conditioned to be gay, no matter, God has a remedy. The question is, will you reach out your hand to His and allow Him to pull you from the sea of homosexuality to safety in His arms? He is not only your Life Giver, but your Life Saver and Life Sustainer as well.

Question: How important is it to find out what happened in my past to justify my perverted sexual outlook today?

Reply: In answer to your question, researching the past can be helpful in understanding the origin of your problems. However, I don't encourage anyone to expend a lot of energy in that direction if the answers don't come too easily. Here's why: picture someone drowning in the sea. Along comes a lifeboat with a lifeguard. Does the lifeguard spend time questioning the drowning victim as to how he came to be in such a desperate condition? Does the drowning victim waste time explaining to himself or to the lifeguard how he came to be in his predicament?

It really doesn't matter how he got there. What matters is that he needs a savior, a lifeguard, and One is there to save him. But he must cooperate with the Lifeguard, the Savior. He must submit to His instructions or risk demise.

So it is with the soul drowning in the sea of sin. You don't need to explain to God all the reasons you are in your lost condition. For one thing, He already knows all that. You don't need to explain to yourself, either. Jesus says simply, "Only acknowledge thine iniquity … and I will heal your backslidings" (Jeremiah 3:13, 22).

In other words, He is saying, stop explaining, blaming, rationalizing, and justifying yourself. I cannot justify you (forgive you), while you are busy justifying yourself. Just admit that you are sinning, that you need a Savior to rescue you *from* your sins (See Matthew 1:21), not *in* your sins, and I can be that Savior, for I came to save My people from their sins.

Friend, there is nothing you can do about yesterday, no way that you can erase it or reverse it. But by your choices today and God's grace, which is sufficient for you today, you can chart an entirely new course for yourself. This requires total submission on your part to His instructions and to His plan for your life. We find that 2 Corinthians 5:17 says, "Therefore if any man be in Christ, he is a new creature: old things are passed away; behold, all things are become new."

This simply and most assuredly means that the new birth consists in having new motives, new tastes, and new tendencies. A genuine conversion changes hereditary and cultivated tendencies to wrong.

Please read on to find much more information that I know will be helpful to you.

————————————

Chapter 5
THE LESBIAN ISSUE

Question: What verses in the Bible show that being a lesbian is sin? And how do I approach my lesbian friends on this subject?

Reply: Regarding your question about lesbian love: in general terms, any intimate, sexual relationship outside of marriage as God ordained it in the Garden of Eden is a violation of the seventh commandment. There are not too many texts in Scripture that make a distinction between the sins of men and the sins of women, for, as the old saying goes, "What is good [bad] for the goose is good [bad] for the gander." So when we read such texts as Leviticus 18:22, "Thou shalt not lie with mankind, as with womankind: it is abomination," we must understand that if intimate, sexual relations between men is abominable in the sight of our holy, creator God, then logically it is just as abominable for intimate, sexual relations to exist between women. Otherwise, our loving God is inconsistent, illogical, unreasonable, and unfair—all charges Satan would love to have stick.

Leviticus 20:13 is an even stronger revelation of how God feels about gay or lesbian love: "If a man also lie with mankind, as he lieth with a woman, both of them have committed an abomination: they shall surely be put to death; their blood shall be upon them." These are God's words, not mine, spoken under a theocracy. But can there be any doubt that God hates this sin?

Now, look with me at Romans 1:26, 27:

> For this cause God gave them up unto vile affections: for *even their women did change the natural use into that which is against nature*: and likewise also the men, leaving the natural use of the woman, burned in their lust one toward another; men with men working that which is unseemly, and receiving in themselves that recompence of their error which was meet. And even as they did not like to retain God in their knowledge, God gave them over to a reprobate mind, to do those things which are not convenient [or, becoming]. (Emphasis added.)

This text clearly states that women had begun to indulge in sexual activity that is not the natural activity between a man and a woman in marriage. In other words, anything and everything goes—perversion of all kinds, with women, with men, and even with animals. The text goes on to say *"Likewise* also the men ... men with men." The word "likewise" indicates then "women with women." Right?

Anyone who has the mind of Christ (Philippians 2:5) will clearly be able to discern the inappropriateness of lesbian love as well as gay love in the context of Scripture as well as in the context of nature itself.

- Is idolatry by a woman okay while that of a man is not?

- Is the taking of the Lord's name in vain by a woman okay while by a man it is not?

- Is a woman's Sabbath breaking excusable while that of a man is condemned?

- Is it okay for a woman to dishonor her parents while it is wrong for a man?

- Is murder by a woman okay while murder by a man is not?

- Is it okay for a woman to steal but criminal for a man?

- Is it okay for a woman to bear false witness while for a man it is perjury and sin?

- Is coveting okay for the woman but sinful for the man?

We don't accept that kind of logic in our court system today, so why would we expect God to be so illogical in His expectations of men and women?

Probably the best way to approach questions like this is to inquire, "Where in God's word can we find God's blessing, or approval for this kind of behavior or activity? We know He approves of marriage between one man and one woman based on Eden and the wedding of Cana, as well as His own love language toward His people likening them to His bride.

But nowhere, absolutely nowhere, in the Bible can we find His blessing over intimate, sexual relations between two or more men, or two or more women, even though some use the very weak argument of the love between Ruth and Naomi and that of David and Jonathan. In both cases, both were married to spouses of the opposite sex and bore or sired children. On the contrary, the biblical language quite strongly condemns it.

You must be very careful in how you approach your gay and lesbian friends on this issue, because unless they are looking for answers, they may be offended by even your broaching of the subject. Sometimes God's hands are even tied, for He cannot go where He is not invited. Therefore, He paints the word picture, "Behold, I stand at the door and knock." He won't just go in.

If you have a burden to approach your gay or lesbian friends on this issue, pray that God will give you an opening, an invitation, an inquiry that will open the door for you.

Question: How can a lesbian fall out of love with another lesbian?

Reply: By truly falling in love with Jesus Christ, your Creator and Re-Creator, your Sustainer in life, your Savior from sin, your Substitute in the wages of sin (death), your Redeemer, your Advocate in the judgment, your Friend who wants to be your Companion and Confidante for now and for all eternity, the One who promises to work within you to will and to do of His good pleasure, if you will but submit to His lordship in your life, the One whose plan for your life far exceeds anything you can even imagine for yourself.

Jesus loves you unconditionally with an infinite, incomprehensible love. However, His acceptance of the lesbian, or the gay, or any other sinner is not unconditional. It is conditional upon the entire surrender of the will to Him. (Have you ever done a study on "if, then" in the Bible?) His work in you goes far beyond love, even beyond acceptance, for He wants to transform your life into one of nobility and purity, like that of His own. "Be ye transformed," the apostle Paul says, "by the renewing of your mind" (Romans 12:2).

"If any man [person] be in Christ, he [she] is a new creature [a new creation]: old things are passed away; behold, all things are become new" (2 Corinthians 5:17). This promise assures us that a genuine conversion results in new motives, new tastes, and new tendencies, though it is a process, of course. When one is truly born-again, he (or she) can overcome every inherited and cultivated tendency to wrong.

When Jesus says, "My grace is sufficient for you" (2 Corinthians 12:9), we need to make sure we understand the definition of "grace" as it is given in the Greek dictionary. Grace is the divine influence working upon the heart and reflecting in the life. In other words, grace is the transforming power of God. It is not a license to continue in sin, sin being the transgression of the law of God (see 1 John 3:4).

This is just a sampling of the information I share on my website to assist gays and lesbians in their endeavors to live in harmony with biblical principles. I hope this is helpful to you, and I invite you to spend time going through this material which has been posted especially for you.

By the way, in my book I chronicle my own experience of ending my long-term "lover" relationship in exchange for accepting Jesus Christ. I have to tell you that it was the most traumatic experience in my life, for I truly was in love with my partner. I continued to love him, but I loved Jesus more. I made the tough decision to follow Jesus and end my gay "lover" relationship which I knew to be out of sync with God's ideal for my life. And my new life has proven to be just what I stated above—far more than I could ever have imagined for myself. I truly believe that our Father knows best.

Question: Why are you promoting bigotry and prejudice against gays and lesbians? I am a proud lesbian, and God loves and accepts me just as I am. Where do you get off saying that homosexuality is a sin? Prove to me that the Bible says that it is sin!

Reply: First of all, my efforts are not meant, in any way, to offend you or anyone else. But I must ask, can you point to one thing that I have ever written or said that promotes bigotry and prejudice against gays and lesbians? It sounds to me like your main concern is my use of my freedom of speech, which I use to help those who recognize their need and want help. It is not my purpose to debate with those content with their alternative lifestyle. I respect your freedom of choice, as long as it does not impose itself upon mine and that of others.

By the way, have you read in the Bible how God feels about pride?

It is true that God loves you unconditionally, but His acceptance of you is conditional upon an entire surrender of your will to His. As He told Mary, "Neither do I condemn thee: go, and sin no more" (John 8:11).

Can you present even one text of Scripture that shows God's approval of lesbian/homosexual behavior?

It is true that the King James Bible does not use the labels "homosexuality" and "lesbian," though other translations do. God knows that we are likely to change the labels from one generation to another, so He just spells out the behavior. Rather than the term "sin" however, He uses the term "abomination," as He does for a number of other sins as well: "If a man also lie with mankind, as he lieth with a woman, both of them have committed an abomination" (Leviticus 20:13; see also 18:22).

That does not sound like acceptance to me. But notice that the Bible does not isolate homosexuality as the only abomination. Apparently, all sin is abomination in His sight. Notice other abominations:

- Idolatry (Deuteronomy 13:13, 14)
- An impure sacrifice (Deuteronomy 17:1)
- Occult practices (Deuteronomy 18:10–12)
- Wearing that which pertaineth to the opposite sex (Deuteronomy 22:5)
- Certain re-marriages to former spouses (Deuteronomy 24:4)
- Dishonesty (Deuteronomy 25:13–16)
- Perverse behavior (Proverbs 3:32)
- A proud look, a lying tongue, murder, wicked imaginations, mischief, false witness, and he that sows discord (Proverbs 6:16–19)
- Justifying evil, condemning the just (Proverbs 17:15)
- Adultery (Ezekiel 22:11)

It should especially be noticed in this line up of abominations that adultery of *any kind* is included. The heterosexual sinner need not look down his nose with condescension upon the homosexual sinner, for *any* sexual behavior outside the marriage institution as designed and created by God is sin—abomination. In short, we all need a Savior from sin, from abomination of one kind or another.

Read also Romans 1:24–28, 32. It is very clear here how God feels about lesbianism and homosexuality. Don't look for the labels, just read the descriptions of behavior.

The following is a response posted on my website to the reckless statement from a gay pamphlet that the Bible never mentions homosexuality or sexual orientation:

In this you are correct, but only if the King James Version of the Bible is your rule of faith and practice. Those words and terms are not used in the King James Version, the version of my own personal preference. However, the behavior and practice are spelled out quite in detail in several places in the Bible, with all of which you are familiar. Might I point out other words or terms that also are not mentioned in the Bible as they randomly come to my mind: bisexual, masturbation, incest, pornography, pedophilia, Sunday, cuss words, drug abuse, alcohol, smoking, marijuana, pot, heroin, cocaine, child abuse, sex, sex addict, addiction, sexual abuse, spousal abuse, immaculate conception, purgatory, rapture, secret rapture, homicide, genocide, infanticide, abortion, ad infinitum.

However, if you use other Bible translations such as the NIV (which is quoted in your cover text), you will see clearly that "homosexuals" unfortunately are listed among those who shall not inherit the kingdom of God. And please note that this is not based upon my own opinion, criticism, judgment, prejudice, or bias, for I myself was once one like you.

For example, the 1984 *New International Version* (NIV), the one used in your own flier, says, 'Do not be deceived: Neither … male prostitutes nor homosexual offenders … will inherit the kingdom of God. And that is what some of you were …' (Note: "homosexual offenders" are those who offend the law of God in at least one point, that of homosexuality. They are not those who offend the 'gift of homosexuality.' James 2:10 reads, 'For whosoever shall keep the whole law, and yet offend in one point, he is guilty of all').

The New American Standard Bible, for example, says clearly, 'Do you not know that the unrighteous will not inherit the kingdom of God? Do not be deceived; neither fornicators … nor adulterers, nor effeminate, nor homosexuals… will inherit the kingdom of God. Such were some of you; but you were washed, but you were sanctified, but you were justified in the name of the Lord Jesus Christ, and in the Spirit of our God' (1 Corinthians 6:9–11 NASB). (Effeminate: catamite, a boy used in sodomy. Sodomy: unnatural sexual relations, especially between male persons. Standard College Dictionary)

The Living Bible paraphrase says, 'Don't fool yourselves. Those ... who are idol worshipers, adulterers or homosexuals—will have no share in his Kingdom ... There was a time when some of you were just like that but now your sins are washed away'(1 Corinthians 6:9–11 TLB).

The New King James Version says, "Do not be deceived. Neither ... homosexuals, nor sodomites ... will inherit the kingdom of God" (1 Corinthians 6:9, 10 NKJV).

The problem I see with your line of reasoning, that homosexuality is not mentioned in the Bible, is the same problem I see with many theologians who can talk about sin all day long and make lists of sins all day long and never acknowledge the authority of the law of God, especially in relation to the fourth commandment. They never get to the root of the sin issue. Why? Because they ignore the one text of Scripture that defines sin as 'the transgression of the law' (1 John 3:4). One can quibble over words forever and never address the real issue, which is the principle of the Word. Languages change from generation to generation, and word meanings change. For example, the word 'gay' today means something entirely different than it did in previous generations. 'Bad' means good today. And 'good' is something to be mocked. Slang words mean something totally different from what they originally meant. But God never changes. His standards remain the same. His Word is infallible.

Now, I would refer you to 2 Thessalonians 2:8–12 where Paul talks about those who receive not the love of the truth but have pleasure in unrighteousness, the resulting "strong delusion" that God allows, and the unfortunate consequences that result.

Think on these things! And remember, God truly loves you, and is not willing that any should perish, but that all should come to repentance.

Victor

Chapter 6

A SAMPLING OF
MYTHS VS. FACTS

Question: What is the percentage of men who have successfully come out of the gay lifestyle and have gone into the heterosexual lifestyle by means of forgiveness of their sins, and walking into this new life with Him? I hope this makes some sense.

Reply: I'm sorry to say that I do not have that figure for you presently. Perhaps I could best answer your question by asking a few questions.

What is the number of people living at the time of the flood in Noah's day who took advantage of the invitation to life? Eight people.

How many spies returning from Canaan trusted that God could deliver the land into the hands of His people? Two spies.

How many of the adult Israelites who left Egypt to enter the Promised Land actually lived to enter it? Only two of the original adults because of the rebellion of the remainder.

What percentage of the 32,000 soldiers initially answering the call of Gideon were the 300 that actually went through with that call? Ninety-four hundredths of one percent.

In the days of Elijah, what amount of the population had not bowed the knee to Baal? God said to Elijah, "I have reserved to myself seven thousand men, who have not bowed the knee to the image of Baal. Even so then at this present time also there is a remnant according to the election of grace" (Romans 11:4, 5).

What percentage of Israel accepted and followed their Messiah Jesus? Except for a relative few, the entire nation rejected Him.

What percentage of the world's population will be ready to meet Jesus when He comes in the clouds of glory?

> And the kings of the earth, and the great men, and the rich men, and the chief captains, and the mighty men, and every bondman, and every free man, hid themselves in the dens and in the rocks of the mountains; and said to the mountains and rocks, fall on us, and hide us from the face of him that sitteth on the throne, and from the wrath of the Lamb: for the great day of his wrath is come; and who shall be able to stand? (Revelation 6:15–17)

An amazing study in the Word of God is the subject of "few." God has never had the majority on His side in this world. The majority of the citizens of this world, both Christian and non-Christian, will be lost in the end; not for lack of

God's mercy and grace, but for lack of man's acceptance of His forgiveness and redemption, and His offer of deliverance from the bondage of sin.

In Matthew 22:14, Jesus tells us, "For many are called, but few are chosen."

In another place Jesus said to his few, chosen disciples, "Have not I chosen you twelve, and one of you is a devil?" (Speaking of Judas.)

Also, Matthew 7:13,14:

Enter ye in at the strait gate: for wide is the gate, and broad is the way, that leadeth to destruction, and many there be which go in thereat: because strait is the gate, and narrow is the way, which leadeth unto life, and few there be that find it.

Matthew 7:21–23 says:

Not every one that saith unto me, Lord, Lord, shall enter into the kingdom of heaven; but *he that doeth the will of my Father* which is in heaven. *Many* will say to me in that day, Lord, Lord, have we not prophesied in thy name? and in thy name have cast out devils? and in thy name done many wonderful works? And then will I profess unto them, *I never knew you: depart from me, ye that work iniquity.*" (Emphasis added.)

In Revelation 12:17 we read:

And the dragon was wroth with the woman, and went to make war with the *remnant* of her seed, *which keep the commandments of God*, and have the testimony of Jesus Christ. (Emphasis added.)

Joel 2:31, 32 reads:

The sun shall be turned into darkness, and the moon into blood, before the great and the terrible day of the LORD come. And it shall come to pass, that whosoever shall call on the name of the LORD shall be delivered: for in mount Zion and in Jerusalem shall be deliverance, as the LORD hath said, and in the *remnant* whom the LORD shall call". (Emphasis added.)

The remnant of Israel shall not do iniquity. (Zephaniah 3:13).

Esaias also crieth concerning Israel, *Though the number of the children of Israel be as the sand of the sea, a remnant shall be saved.* (Romans 9:27, emphasis added.)

Thou hast a *few* names even in Sardis which have not defiled their garments; and they shall walk with me in white: for they are worthy. (Revelation 3:4, emphasis added.)

Who makes up this remnant of saved? Revelation 17:14, speaking of the Lord of Lords and King of Kings, says, "And they that are with him are *called*, and *chosen*, and *faithful*" (emphasis added).

The danger I see in your question is that you might be looking to the success or failure of man in order to determine the likelihood of your own success or failure in dealing with the sin of homosexuality. We must not look in that direction, but look to Jesus Christ, the author and finisher of our faith, who promises that His grace is sufficient for you. The failures we see in the world around us are due to the poor choices and lack of faith of our fellow man. We do not have to fail. We have only to look to Jesus, for by beholding Him we become changed.

"Therefore if any man be in Christ, he is a new creature: old things are passed away; behold, all things are become new" (2 Corinthians 5:17). A genuine conversion, my friend, results in new motives, new tastes, and new tendencies. When you are truly born-again, you can and will go forth to overcome every inherited and cultivated tendency to wrong. "But as many as received him, to them gave he power to become the sons of God, even to them that believe on his name" (John 1:12).

"According to your faith," my friend, "be it unto you" (Jesus, in Matthew 9:29). Victor

---

More Myths vs. Facts

Myth #1: Science indicates that homosexuality is genetic.
- In 2002 Bearman and Brueckner studied tens of thousands of adolescent students in the U.S. The same-sex attraction concordance between identical twins was only 7.7% for males and 5.3% for females—lower than the 11% and 14% in the 2,000 Australian study by Bailey et al.

- Twins studies have overall debunked the possibility of homosexuality being exclusively genetic.

- Despite vast amounts of funding, no credible science to date has confirmed any solid genetic factor in the development of homosexuality.

Myth #2: Homosexuality is unchangeable.
- A study published in the peer-reviewed *Journal of Human Sexuality* found that sexual orientation can be changed, and that psychological

care for individuals with unwanted same-sex attractions is generally beneficial. Research has not found any significant risk of harm.

- The researchers examined more than 100 years of professional and scientific literature from 600-plus studies and reports from clinicians, researchers, and former clients principally published in professional and peer-reviewed journals.

- Further confirmed in a 2007 study by Jones and Yarhouse.

- In 2002, Bearman and Brueckner found that among 16- and 17-year-old young people with romantic attractions to the same sex, almost all had switched one year later.

- Sexual preference is especially fluid in females, particularly adolescents.

- Neutral academic surveys show there is substantial change. About half of the homosexual/bisexual population (in a non-therapeutic environment) moves toward heterosexuality over a lifetime. About 3 percent of the present heterosexual population once firmly believed themselves to be homosexual or bisexual, and… Sexual orientation is not set in concrete, according to Dr. Neil Whitehead, PhD in biochemistry and statistics.

- "Numbers of people who have changed toward exclusive heterosexuality are greater than current numbers of bisexuals and homosexuals combined. In other words, ex-gays outnumber actual gays." (www.hollanddavis.com/?p=3647, referencing Identical Twin Study by Dr. Neil Whitehead, accessed 5/8/2014.)

MYTH #3: Homosexual behavior is a healthy and safe alternative to heterosexual behavior. Or, homosexuals are generally just as well-adjusted as heterosexuals psychologically and socially.

- Despite knowing the AIDS risk, many/most homosexuals repeatedly and pathologically continue to indulge in unsafe sex practices.

- Homosexuals represent the highest number of STD cases.

- More than one-third of homosexual men and women are substance abusers.

- Forty percent of homosexual adolescents report suicidal histories.

- Homosexuals are more likely than heterosexuals to have mental health concerns such as eating disorders, personality disorders, paranoia, depression, and anxiety.

- Homosexual relationships are statistically recognized to be more violent than heterosexual relationships.

- There is significantly greater medical, psychological, and relational pathology in the homosexual population than the general population. Overall, many of these problematic behaviors and psychological dysfunctions are experienced among homosexuals at about three times the prevalence found in the general population—and sometimes much more … No other group of comparable size in society experiences such intense and widespread pathology." (www.narth.com, accessed 5/8/2014.)

Myth #4: Homosexuality is not correlated with promiscuity or addiction. Or homosexual marriage is pretty much like heterosexual marriage.

- In 1978 in San Francisco, Bell and Weinberg reported evidence of widespread sexual promiscuity among homosexual men. Of the homosexual men surveyed, 83% estimated they had sex with 50 or more partners in their lifetime, 43% estimated they had sex with 500 or more partners, and 28% with an astonishing 1,000 or more partners! Only 1% of the sexually active men had had fewer than five lifetime partners.

- In 2003, Urban Men's Health Study reported that over 30% of US homosexual men studied frequented bathhouses with an average of 27 partners per year. In a 2003 study, Amsterdam "singles" averaged 22 casual partners per year, while those with a "steady partner" averaged eight. The average duration of partnerships was 1.5 years. In a 2005 Canadian vaccine trial, homosexual individuals reported seven partners in the last six months.

- "Experts believe syphilis is on the rise among gay and bisexual men because they are engaging in unprotected sex with multiple partners, many of whom they met in anonymous situations such as sex clubs, adult bookstores, meetings through the internet, and in bathhouses." (*San Francisco Chronicle, October 26, 2001*)

- A 2010 Center for Disease Control data analysis reveals that the rate of primary and secondary syphilis among MSM (men who have sex with men) is more than 46 times that of other men and more than 71 times that of women. Promiscuity is the factor most responsible for the extreme rates of these and other sexually transmitted diseases.

- A survey conducted in 1996 by a New York homosexual magazine known as *Genre* found that 24% of the gay respondents had sexual encounters with more than 100 partners in their lifetime. The magazine noted that several respondents suggested including a category for those who had more than 1,000 sexual partners.

- According to Dr. Robert Kronemeyer, author of *Overcoming Homosexuality*, "Nearly two-thirds of gay men are *constantly* on the hunt for instant sex." A typical attitude is expressed in the statement, "If I don't score in 20 minutes after hitting the bar, I start to fall apart." Kronemeyer indicates further that "30% of homosexual men have never had a relationship that survived a one-night stand." This stands in stark contrast with the average heterosexual male who has on average five to nine sexual partners throughout his life, and who would thus appear considerably more monogamous by comparison.

- In one recent study of gay male couples, 41.3% had open sexual agreements with some conditions or restrictions, and 10% had open sexual agreements with no restrictions on sex with outside partners. One-fifth of participants (21.9%) reported breaking their agreement in the preceding 12 months, and 13.2% of the sample reported having unprotected anal intercourse in the preceding three months with an outside partner of unknown or discordant HIV-status.

- The gay community has long walked a thin public relations line, presenting their relationships as equivalent to those of heterosexual married couples. But many gay activists portray a very different cultural ethic. Michelangelo Signorile describes the campaign as a "fight for same-sex marriage and its benefits and then, once granted, redefine the institution completely—to demand the right to marry not as a way of adhering to society's moral codes, but rather to debunk a myth and radically alter an archaic institution."

- The same study revealed that homosexual men have to a great extent separated sexuality from relationships. The survey showed 79% of the respondents saying that over half of their sexual partners were strangers, and 70% said that over half of their sexual partners were people with whom they had sex only once.

- William Aaron's autobiographical book *Straight* draws similar conclusions: "In the gay life, fidelity is almost impossible. Since part of the compulsion of homosexuality seems to be a need on the part of the homophile to 'absorb' masculinity from his sexual partners, he must be constantly on the lookout for [new partners]. Constantly the most successful homophile 'marriages' are those where there is an agreement between the two to have affairs on the side while maintaining the semblance of permanence in their living arrangement.

"Gay life is most typical and works best when sexual contacts are impersonal and even anonymous. As a group the homosexuals I have known seem far more preoccupied with sex than heterosexuals are, and far more likely to think of a good sex life as many partners under many exciting circumstances" (pp. 208, 209).

- "In the gay world the only real criterion of value is physical attractiveness… The young homosexual will find that his homosexual brothers usually only care for him as a sexual object. Although they may invite him out to dinner and give him a place to stay, when they have satisfied their sexual interest in him, they will likely forget about his existence and his own personal needs… Since the sole criterion of value in the homosexual world is physical attractiveness, being young and handsome in gay life is like being a millionaire in a community where wealth is the only criterion of value" (Hoffman 1968, pp. 58, 153, 155).

- Promiscuity among lesbians is less extreme, but it is still higher than among heterosexual women. Overall, women tend to have fewer sex partners than men. But there is a surprising finding about lesbian promiscuity in the literature. Australian investigators reported that lesbian women were 4.5 times more likely to have had more than 50 lifetime male partners than heterosexual women (9 percent of lesbians versus 2 percent of heterosexual women), and 93 percent of women who identified themselves as lesbian reported a history of sex with men. Other studies similarly show that 75–90 percent of women who have sex with women have also had sex with men. (Factsaboutyouth.com, accessed 5/8/2014.)

- When McWhirter and Mattison published *The Male Couple* in 1984, their study was undertaken to disprove the reputation that gay male relationships do not last. The authors themselves were a homosexual couple, one a psychiatrist, the other a psychologist. After much searching they were able to locate 156 male couples in relationships that had lasted from 1 to 37 years. Two-thirds of the respondents had entered the relationship with either the implicit or the explicit expectation of sexual fidelity.

  Of those 156 couples, only seven had been able to maintain sexual fidelity. Furthermore, of those seven couples, none had been together more than 5 years. In other words, the researchers were unable to find *a single male couple that was able to maintain sexual fidelity for more than five years.*

- Outside affairs, the researchers found, were not damaging to the relationship's endurance, but were in fact essential to it. "The single most important factor that keeps couples together past the ten-year mark is the lack of possessiveness they feel," say the authors. (D. McWhirter and A. Mattison, *The Male Couple: How Relationships Develop, 256*)

Question: Is the "born gay" concept a Myth, a Fact, or a Hoax?

Reply: To answer this question, I am simply going to share excerpts from the abridged article "The 'Born Gay' Hoax Exposed" by www.liveleak.com.

The "born gay" hoax was invented in 1985 by Marshall Kirk (field of Psychology) and Dr. Hunter Madsen (PhD in Politics) when they co-authored an article titled "The Gay Agenda" in a pro-sodomy magazine called *Christopher Street*, emphasizing the strategic importance of shifting the central issue in the debate over "homosexuality" away from sodomy and toward a sexual pseudo-identity called "gay."

The goal of The Gay Agenda was to force opponents of sodomy into a position where they would be seen as attacking the civil rights of so-called "gay" citizens, rather than opposing a specific antisocial behavior. "The Gay Agenda" also briefly outlined the strategy that would eventually be used to convince the public that individuals are "born gay."

Initially... many activists considered the proposed strategy degrading because they viewed "rights related to sexuality as analogous to the constitutional rights to association, expression, or religion." [1]

... However, these initial reservations would not last for long.

In 1986 the pro-sodomy [gay] movement lost... the United States Supreme Court case which upheld the rights of individual states to criminalize sodomy... Desperate, angry, and galvanized [gay] activists learned that if they could make a compelling case that they were "born gay," they could become eligible for "Minority Status" as a "Suspect Class" under the 1964 Civil Rights Act. If Minority Status were granted, it would force the courts to overturn [the ruling], thus legalizing sodomy. It must be noted however, that the Civil Rights Act recognizes Minority Status only for those groups who:

1) Have suffered a long history of discrimination

2) Are powerless to help themselves as a community

3) Are born that way

The legalization of sodomy by way of "Minority Status" is the secret to understanding why [gay] activists adopted the strategy... claim[ing] that people are "born gay."

Wasting little time, Marshal Kirk and Hunter Madsen... published a follow-up to "The Gay Agenda" titled "The Overhauling of Straight America." This article, which appeared in the pro-sodomy publication *Guide* in November of 1987, outlined a point-by-point strategy that could be used to convince "straight America" that men and women who develop same-sex attractions are born "gay."

---

1   *The Advocate*, March 24, 1992, 62 quotation (Pat) mine

In 1988, a "War Conference" of 175 leading Gay activists, from every part of the United States convened in Warrenton, Virginia to establish an official agenda for the newly conceived "gay" movement. At this conference Gay activists adopted the political strategy outlined in "The Gay Agenda" and "The Overhauling of Straight America," and the "born gay" hoax was born.

In 1989, Marshal Kirk and Hunter Madsen expanded their article "The Overhauling of Straight America" into a book titled *After the Ball: How America Will Conquer Its Fear and Hatred of the Gays in the 90s*, declaring their intent to "get tough" on straights. "… It is time to learn from Madison Avenue and to roll out the big guns … We are talking about propaganda."

Kirk and Madsen explained the central tenant of their strategy: "The public should be persuaded that gays are victims of circumstance, that they no more chose their sexual orientation than they did, say, their height, skin color, talents, or limitations. (We argue that, for all practical purposes, gays should be considered to have been 'born gay'—even though sexual orientation, for most humans, seems to be the product of a complex interaction between innate predispositions and environmental factors during childhood and early adolescence.)" [2]

Here, the authors admit that human sexuality "seems to be the product of a complex interaction between innate predispositions and environmental factors," yet they urge readers to abandon the truth for "practical purposes," i.e., furthering "The Gay Agenda." The propagandists could not have been clearer about their plan to deceive Americans. The following excerpts from *After the Ball* will exemplify the manipulative tactics Marshall Kirk and Hunter Madsen enticed Gay activists to employ.

"The first order of business is desensitization of the American public concerning gays… To desensitize the public is to help it view homosexuality with indifference instead of with keen emotion. Ideally we would have the straight register differences in sexual preference the way they register different tastes for ice cream…" [3]

"The masses should not be shocked and repelled by premature exposure to homosexual behavior itself… the imagery of sex should be downplayed…" [4]

"… Gays must be cast as victims in need of protection so that straights will be inclined by reflex to assume the role of protector …" [5]

"… Make use of symbols which reduce the mainstream's sense of threat, which lower its guard…" [6]

---

2   Kirk and Madsen, *After the Ball: How America Will Conquer Its Fear and Hatred of the Gay's in the 90s,* 184

3   Ibid., 7

4   Ibid., 8

5   Ibid., 8

6   Ibid., 8

"... Replace the mainstream's self-righteous pride about its homophobia with shame and guilt... "[7]

"Talk about gays and gayness as loudly and as often as possible... " "The principal behind this advice is simple: almost all behavior begins to look normal if you are exposed to enough of it at close quarters and among your acquaintances."[8]

"Constant talk builds the impression that public opinion is at least divided on the subject... "[9]

Madsen and Kirk explain their scheme in greater depth when they write:

"Where we talk is important. The visual media, film and television, are plainly the most powerful image-makers in Western civilization. The average American household watches over seven hours of TV daily. Those hours open up a gateway into the private world of straights, through which a Trojan horse might be passed. As far as desensitization is concerned, the medium is the message—of normalcy. So far, gay Hollywood has provided our best covert weapon in the battle to desensitize the mainstream."[10]

"Not so many years ago, all of these statements would have been unbelievably offensive to most Americans, even if they contained no reference to 'homosexuality,' precisely because they all advocate coercive tampering with peoples most private domain, their thoughts, opinions, and beliefs. Kirk and Madsen call it 'transforming the social values of straight America...'"[11]

Let's look at the mechanics of their strategy for 'transforming' society into what they feel would be a more acceptable form. The authors continue:

"Would a desensitizing campaign of open and sustained talk about gay issues reach every rabid opponent of homosexuality? Of course not! While public opinion is one primary source of mainstream values, religious authority is the other. When conservative churches condemn gays, there are only two things we can do to confound the homophobia of true believers. First, we can use talk to muddy the moral waters. This means publicizing support for gays by more moderate churches, raising theological objections of our own about conservative interpretations of biblical teachings, and exposing hatred and inconsistency.

"Second, we can undermine the moral authority of homophobic churches by portraying them as antiquated backwaters, badly out of step with the times and with the latest findings of psychology. Against the mighty pull of institutional Religion one must set the mightier draw of Science & Public Opinion (the shield and sword of that accursed "secular humanism"). Such an unholy alliance has worked well against churches before on such topics as divorce and abortion. With

---

7 Ibid., 10

8 Ibid., 7

9 Ibid., 8

10 Ibid., 8

11 Ibid., 14

enough open talk about the prevalence and acceptability of homosexuality, that alliance can work again here."[12]

"... The campaign should paint gays as superior pillars of society. Yes, yes, we know—this trick is so old it creaks."[13]

"... It will be time to get tough with remaining opponents. To be blunt, they must be vilified."[14]

"...We intend to make anti-gays look so nasty that average Americans will want to dissociate themselves from such types... "[15]

"Each sign will tap patriotic sentiment; each message will drill a seemingly agreeable position into mainstream heads..."[16]

"The public should be shown images of ranting homophobes whose secondary traits and beliefs disgust middle America... the Ku Klux Klan demanding that gays be burned alive or castrated; bigoted southern [sic] ministers drooling with hysterical hatred to a degree that looks both comical and deranged; menacing punks, thugs and convicts... Nazi concentration camps..."[17]

"These images (of anyone opposed to homosexual behavior) should be combined with those of their gay victims by a method propagandists call the 'bracket technique.' For example, for a few seconds an unctuous beady-eyed Southern preacher is seen pounding the pulpit in rage about 'those sick, abominable creatures.' While his tirade continues over the soundtrack, the picture switches to pathetic photos of gays who look decent, harmless, and likable; and then we cut back to the poisonous face of the preacher, and so forth. The contrast speaks for itself. The effect is devastating."[18]

A group called Parents and Friends of Lesbians and Gays (PFLAG) actually used this technique in an advertising campaign in the fall of 1995 against Pat Robertson, Jesse Helms, and Jerry Falwell. As reported in the San Francisco Examiner, Sunday, November 12, 1995... "a new television ad campaign [portrays scenes of] a teenage girl contemplating suicide with a handgun, [and] a young man being beaten by a gang as his attackers shout slurs... interspersed with actual clips of the Rev. Pat Robertson and other conservatives deploring homosexuality. Most stations turned down the ads, but they ran in Tulsa, and Washington D.C. A print version of the ad (much less emotionally effective) was run in USA Today, November 21, 1995."

It is absolutely appalling to hear the tactics promoted by Kirk and Madsen. The Gay activists who have employed these techniques have nothing to be proud

12 Ibid., 9

13 Ibid., 9

14 Ibid., 10

15 Ibid., 10

16 Ibid., 11

17 Ibid., 10

18 Ibid., 13, 14

of. These self-styled propagandistic tactics represent a twisted and fascist, deceitful and degrading approach to the winning of American public opinion.

In specialized press, Gay activists speak candidly about the movement's practical purposes for promoting the idea that people are "born gay." In doing So they admit that public "born gay" rhetoric is fabricated propaganda, contrived and carried out for specific political ends; mainly, the overturning of court ruling and the normalization of sodomy.

Dr. Lillian Faderman, states: "And we continue to demand Rights, ignoring the fact that human sexuality is fluid and flexible, acting as though we are all stuck in our category forever." She further states, "The narrow categories of identity politics are obviously deceptive."

It becomes obvious later in the article that Dr. Faderman sees a political threat from the truth, from the fluidity of human sexuality. "I must confess that I am both elated and terrified by the possibilities of a bisexual moment. I'm elated because I truly believe that bisexuality is the natural human condition. But I'm much less happy when I think of the possibility of huge numbers of homosexuals (two-thirds of women who identify as lesbian for example) running off to explore the heterosexual side of their bisexual potential and, as a result, decimating our political ranks."

Later in the article Dr. Faderman writes, "The concept of gay and lesbian identity may be nothing but a social construct, but it has been crucial, enabling us to become a political movement and demand the rights that are due to us as a minority. What becomes of our political movement if we openly acknowledge that sexuality is flexible and fluid, that gay and lesbian does not signify 'a people' but rather a 'sometime behavior'? [19]

Psychologist Dr. John DeCecco, Director of the Center for Research and Education in Sexuality at San Francisco State University, and Editor of The Journal of Homosexuality, calls himself "gay" but insists that such attractions are a *changeable preference not an orientation.* He explains in his book that the whole "born gay" and immutable characteristic idea is just "gay and lesbian politics" and is aimed at achieving "gay" rights. [20]

Female homosexual writer Jennie Ruby admits, "I don't think lesbians are born… I think they are made… The gay rights movement has (for many good, practical reasons) adopted largely an identity politics." [21]

Jan Clausen, female homosexual author of the book "Apples and Oranges" writes, "What's got to stop is the rigging of history to make the either/or look permanent and universal."

19   *The Advocate*, September 5, 1995, 43

20   *If You Seduce A Straight Person You Can Make Them Gay*, John DeCecco, 17, 18

21   *Off Our Backs*, October 1996, 22

Later, Clausen quotes the popular lesbian poet Audre Lorde, who admits the lies associated with the born "gay" hoax as well, when she writes, "I do not believe our wants have made all our lies holy." [22]

Female homosexuals Lyne Harne and Elaine Miller explain their feelings regarding the "born gay" hoax: "There's nothing natural in lesbianism, 'it's a positive choice,' and a political one." [23]

Yet another admission appeared in the homosexual magazine "Girlfriends". It states, "No wonder lesbians are so nervous. What makes the lesbian movement strong is the formation of a collective identity, unified behind sexual orientation as a category. If bisexuality undoes that, it kicks the lesbian movement where it really hurts: in the heart and soul of identity politics." [24]

The National Center for Lesbian Rights (NCLR) is one of the homosexual activist organizations that pressured the American Psychiatric Association to reject homosexual reparative therapy. The NCLR claims that the "gay" identity is innate and unchangeable. JoAnne Loulan, one of the psychotherapists who served on the board of directors, made hypocritical headlines on the February 18, 1997 edition of the homosexual magazine The Advocate because she reportedly changed her own sexual orientation when she fell in love with a man...?

Further, Kate Kendall, Director of the NCLR, argued that the so-called "gay" person was endowed with a fixed, innate, and unchangeable, "sexual orientation" and commanded the American Psychiatric Association to halt all forms of reparative therapy for all people, including those desperately looking for help. She actually wrote an article for Frontiers Magazine arguing that sexual orientation is fluid, not fixed. [25]

Kendall and Loulan stood before the American Psychiatric Association with straight faces declaring reparative therapy to be the dangerous equivalent of pouring bleach on a black person's skin to make them white. Then, one of these self-proclaimed "gays" went out and changed her own so-called "sexual orientation" by falling in love with a man, and the other took the time to write an article for an insiders' magazine arguing that sexuality is changeable. Is it possible, for us to continue to trust these activists when they say that they are "born gay?"

The bottom line truth is that beginning in 1985, The Gay Agenda was sold to the American public by Gay propagandists. The carefully calculated lies of these propagandists are blatant, and have been admitted in numerous Gay publications. It is obvious however, that "born gay" propagandists from Kirk and Madsen on, keep the fact of sexual fluidity secret from the straight community for political reasons. Gay activists however, as evidenced by their

---

22 *Apples and Oranges*, Jan Clausen, quoting the popular lesbian poet Audre Lorde.

23 Lambda Book Report, October 1996, 11, "Commenting on All the Rage: Reasserting Radical Lesbian Feminism"

24 *Girlfriends*, May/June, 1996, p. 40

25 *Frontiers*, April 19, 1996, 31

own articles, talk about the "born gay" hoax and the realities of sexual choice regularly amongst themselves.

Note: Kirk's and Madsen's Homosexual Agenda scripted hate tactic is called "Jamming", vilifying all those who dissent from the homosexual script.

This full article can be found at:
http://www.liveleak.com/view?i=927_1345510160

Read more at:
http://www.liveleak.com/view?i=927_1345510160#6Fp3sOhwicmF4ETl.99

www.liveleak.com

———————————

Chapter 7

RESPONSES TO JUSTIFICATION OF HOMOSEXUALITY

Responding to Gay Pride

Question: Of what exactly is it that homosexuals are proud?

Reply: Around the country for years now, homosexuals en masse have conducted gay pride parades. I used to attend them every summer in Los Angeles. Thousands of homosexuals and friends and curious onlookers would line the streets of Hollywood Boulevard to watch the "proud" homosexuals put themselves on display in all their variant and deviant personas for the world to see. And in the year 2,000, then-President Bill Clinton actually declared the month of June to be gay pride month! More recently, President Obama has declared the month of June to be National Pride for LGBTs, Lesbians/Gays/Bisexuals/Transgenders.

But for many people, the question comes to mind, "Of what exactly is it that homosexuals are proud? The embarrassment, pain, confusion, frustration, and despair they cause their parents, spouses, children, and other family members? For bringing upon themselves the same? For the loneliness, helplessness, and hopelessness that so many of them experience daily? For the disease that is associated so closely, though not exclusively, with their lifestyle? For their freedom of choice to live in defiance and rejection of God's plan for their lives—the very God who created them with the power of choice in the first place? For their bringing to an end a 6,000 year old line of seed?"

Granted, there is much beauty, talent, creativity, education, intelligence, and ambition demonstrated within the gay community. However, an honest look at homosexuality will reveal it to be a dead-end street. The self-admiration, self-exaltation, self-advancement, self-seeking, self-serving, self-gratification is but for a fleeting moment. "Woe to the crown of *pride* ... whose glorious beauty is a fading flower" (Isaiah 28:1, emphasis added).

Just think of all the great talents of our time, and the thousands not so well known, who have died so prematurely from AIDS. The average life expectancy of the homosexual is a low 40-something, about half that of the heterosexual. Homosexuality also tends to greatly diminish the *reproduction* of life. Just think, if all the world were homosexual, life would come to a screeching halt within one generation!

So what is gay pride all about? Pride of rebellion? Pride of defiance? Pride of separation from the will of their creator God?

Perhaps we should ask, What is God's view of pride, of gay pride? After all, it is He who holds in His hands our eternal destiny.

Interestingly, it was pride (gay pride, perhaps?) that helped bring about the destruction of Sodom. "Behold, this was the iniquity of thy sister Sodom, *pride*, fullness of bread, and abundance of idleness was in her and in her daughters, neither did she strengthen the hand of the poor and needy. And they were haughty, *and committed abomination* before me: therefore I took them away as I saw good" (Ezekiel 16:49, 50, emphasis added).

It was pride that drove Nebuchadnezzar to insanity.

But when his heart was lifted up, and his mind hardened in *pride*, he was deposed from his kingly throne, and they took his glory from him: and he was driven from the sons of men; and his heart was made like the beasts, and his dwelling was with the wild asses: they fed him with grass like oxen, and his body was wet with the dew of heaven; till he knew that the most high God ruled in the kingdom of men, and that he appointeth over it whomsoever he will.

Now I Nebuchadnezzar praise and extol and honour the King of heaven, all whose works are truth, and his ways judgment: and those that walk in *pride* he is able to abase. (Daniel 5:20, 21; 4:37, emphasis added.)

It was pride that brought about the fall of Israel, mentioned above as the sister of Sodom. "And the *pride of Israel* doth testify to his face: therefore shall Israel and Ephraim fall in their iniquity; Judah also shall fall with them" (Hosea 5:5, emphasis added).

It was pride that made a devil out of Lucifer, God's highest created being, which resulted in his ultimate destruction (Isaiah 14:12–17; Ezekiel 28:19).

Surely, "Pride goeth before destruction, and an haughty spirit before a fall" (Proverbs 16:18). In Malachi 4:1 God warns very clearly:

For, behold, the day cometh, that shall burn as an oven; and *all the proud*, yea, and all that do wickedly, shall be stubble: and the day that cometh shall burn them up, saith the LORD of hosts, that it shall leave them neither root nor branch. (Emphasis added.)

From the story in Luke of the Pharisee and the Publican we can learn that it is not the proud who find favor and mercy with God, but the humble. The proud will surely meet with God's justice. The humble will be justified by God's grace and mercy.

Two men went up into the temple to pray; the one a Pharisee, and the other a publican. The Pharisee stood and prayed thus with himself, God, I thank thee, that I am not as other men are, extortioners, unjust, adulterers, or even as this publican. I fast twice in the week, I give tithes of all that I possess. And the publican, standing afar off, would not lift up so much as his eyes unto heaven, but smote upon his breast, saying, God be merciful to me a sinner. I tell you, this man went down to his house justified rather than the other: *for every one that exalteth himself shall be abased*; and he that humbleth himself shall be exalted. (Luke 18:10–14, emphasis added.)

Better it is to be of an humble spirit with the lowly, than to divide the spoil with the proud. (Proverbs 16:19)

In light of all this, we must remember, however, that God is love (1 John 4:8). It is not His choice that His wayward children should be destroyed. Oh, no!

The Lord is not slack concerning his promise, as some men count slackness; but is longsuffering to us-ward, not willing that any should perish, but that all should come to repentance. (2 Peter 3:9)

But He cannot and will not force the will. Therefore He invites you, dear friend:

Enter ye in at the strait gate: for wide is the gate, and broad is the way, that leadeth to destruction, and many there be which go in thereat: because strait is the gate, and narrow is the way, which leadeth unto life, and few there be that find it. (Matthew 7:13, 14)

Here are some other references to contemplate from the Word of God (emphasis added):

- "There they cry, but none giveth answer, because of the *pride* of evil men. Surely God will not hear *vanity*, neither will the Almighty regard it" (Job 35:12, 13).

- "The wicked, through the *pride* of his countenance, will not seek after God: God is not in all his thoughts" (Psalms 10:4).

- "The fear of the LORD is to hate evil: pride, and *arrogancy*, and the evil way, and the froward mouth, do I hate" (Proverbs 8:13).

- "When *pride* cometh, then cometh shame" (Proverbs 11:2).

- "Only by *pride* cometh contention" (Proverbs 13:10).

- "A man's *pride* shall bring him low: but honour shall uphold the humble in spirit" (Proverbs 29:23).

- "The *pride* of thine heart hath deceived thee, thou that … saith in his heart, Who shall bring me down to the ground? Though thou exalt thyself as the eagle, and though thou set thy nest among the stars, thence will I bring thee down, saith the LORD" (Obadiah 1:3, 4).

- "And he said, That which cometh out of the man, that defileth the man. For from within, out of the heart of men, proceed evil thoughts, adulteries, fornications, murders, thefts, covetousness, wickedness, deceit, lasciviousness, an evil eye, blasphemy, *pride*, foolishness: all these evil things come from within, and defile the man" (Mark 7:20–23).

- "Lest being lifted up with *pride* he fall into the condemnation of the devil" (1 Timothy 3:6).

- "For all that is in the world, the lust of the flesh, and the lust of the eyes, and the *pride* of life, is not of the Father, but is of the world. And the world passeth away, and the lust thereof: but he that doeth the will of God abideth for ever" (1 John 2:16, 17).

Amen! And God's blessings upon you as you seek His will for your life.

Response to a Letter Justifying Homosexuality
Excerpt from the letter: "I don't feel that there is someone, anyone, who has 'changed his orientation.' A leopard cannot change his spots. A person cannot change the color of his skin. A person cannot change his sexual orientation. Just as God could change the spots on the leopard, or the color of someone's skin, He can also change the orientation of someone. But He doesn't. He doesn't need to. He created us just as we are. He loves us, and I think it makes Him sad to see us trying to be who we aren't."

Reply: In reading your letter, I noted that not one word of Scripture was quoted to authorize your position on homosexuality. Rather, throughout your letter you use such terms as:

"I *think*," "I *feel*," "the orientation scale," "having *feelings* of orientation," "true *feelings* of the gay spouse," "marriage doesn't change the *feelings* and orientation," (No, but Jesus does; see 2 Corinthians 5:17), "honest about one's sexual *attractions*," "no cure for homosexuality because it is not an illness, *nor do I believe* that it is a sin," "All the burdens of life *felt like*, and *continue to feel like*," "I at last *feel good* about myself," "the '*human' viewpoint* and about life," "*I am happier* than I have ever been in my life. *I am happy*," "*I don't feel* that there is someone who has changed their orientation," "*Truth is what our core being feels and is*."

But truth is what is factual. It is not based upon feeling. Many people die while hallucinating under the influence of drugs, thinking that what they feel is reality and truth. Interestingly, the mind does not always need drugs to play tricks on us, for it is carnal by nature since the fall of man.

It is written, "Sanctify them through thy truth: *thy word is truth*" (John 17:17 emphasis added). "The Spirit is truth" (1 John 5:6). And "he will guide you into all truth" (John 16:13). In other words, He (the Spirit) will guide us in our study of God's Word to discern and know all truth.

We cannot trust "our core being feelings," because as it is written:

The heart is deceitful above all things, and desperately wicked: who can know it? I the LORD search the heart, I try the reins, even to give every man according to his ways, and according to the fruit of his doings. (Jeremiah 17:9)

One commentator spoke very well to this issue when stating:

Many make a serious mistake in their religious life by keeping their attention fixed upon their *feelings*, thus judging of their advancement or decline. *Feelings are not a safe guide*. We are not to look within for evidence of our acceptance with God. (*Pacific Union Recorder,* June 5, 1902, "Words to Christians," emphasis added.)

The Pharisees of old *felt* no need of a Savior from sin. They *felt* righteous and thanked God that they weren't like someone else. Jesus Himself could do nothing for them in their lost condition, for they did not and would not recognize or acknowledge their need.

Sadly, Jesus Himself had to say, "I am not come to call the righteous, but sinners to repentance" (Matthew 9:13). Again it is written, "They that are whole have no need of the physician, but they that are sick: I came not to call the righteous, but sinners to repentance" (Mark 2:17). This is, of course, referring to those who *think* themselves righteous, for again, "As it is written, There is none righteous, no, not one" (Romans 3:10).

It is also written, "Knowing this, that the law is not made for a righteous man, but for the lawless and disobedient, for the ungodly and for sinners ... for them that defile themselves with mankind [the homosexual]" (1Timothy 1:9, 10).

If one is content with his life and behavior, Jesus Himself can do nothing. I try to follow His example. My ministry and my website are for those who do recognize their need and want to walk in newness of life, and there are many. There is little time to get caught up in debate with those who are content and militant, for the time demands are great in assisting those who *do* acknowledge their need. However, I am taking the time to address some of your comments, but time will not permit in-depth discussion and debate.

You state that, "*the Bible is less conclusive on the subject than most try to portray*." But the Bible is very clear upon this subject, describing it in detail, both in the New as well as the Old Testaments. My question to you is this, "Do you know of any texts of Scripture that condone homosexuality in any terms whatsoever? Are there any that give you assurance of salvation in your homosexuality specifically?"

As a Seventh-day Adventist homosexual you refer to the writings of Ellen G. White and say, *"I also find that Ellen White never mentions this subject."*

Oh, but she does! She quotes 1 Corinthians 6:9–11, which clearly speaks of those "abusers of themselves with mankind," and "effeminate" (or catamites, those who play the woman's role in sexual behavior). Many Bible translations just come right out and say "homosexuals" and "sodomites." The text speaks of victory over these sins. Then Ellen White comments:

> It is a matter of rejoicing that some have subjected their will to the will of God; have cast off the works of darkness, and have consented to walk in the light as Christ is in the light. But even to these the testing of God will continue until probation ceases. He wants to determine whether we will endure hardness as good soldiers of Jesus Christ. (*Signs of the Times*, February 4, 1897)

Temptation, by the way, is not sin. Neither does it define one's 'orientation.'

Ellen White also has a lot to say about and against "self-abuse," or masturbation, which is a major behavior among homosexuals.

You stated, *"I know that I believe in an all-powerful God. One who can and does work miracles every day. I know the miracle He worked in my life was helping me to accept my sexuality as I was created and that it isn't sinful or less of His perfection than if I were heterosexual."*

How can you, without being informed, *know* that to be a miracle of God rather than a deception of Satan? And how can you be informed except through the Word of God? We are to "try the spirits whether they are of God" (1 John 4:1). "To the law and to the testimony: if they speak not according to this word, it is because there is no light in them" (Isaiah 8:20).

Homosexual thoughts and behavior initially bring upon one a sense of guilt. Guilt is associated with sin. Guilt can eventually be drowned, or suppressed, as the Holy Spirit is grieved away. Children who are prone to homosexuality do not initially flaunt their feelings, emotions, and behavior, but rather struggle with them, and not because of society, but because of the sense of guilt that comes from sin.

Interestingly, I never felt any sense of guilt in having sex while married. Frustration? Yes! Because I was gay. But guilt? Never. Why? Because there was nothing wrong with my having sex within my marriage. And this understanding I have is confirmed in the Bible in Romans chapter 1.

Another statement of yours, "Just as God could change the spots on the leopard, or the color of someone's skin, *He can also change the orientation* of someone.

But He doesn't. He doesn't need to. He created us just as we are. He loves us, and I think it makes Him sad to see us trying to be who we aren't."

Who we are not is Jesus Christ. We are all sinners; we are not perfect. Yet, it is written, "Be ye therefore perfect, even as your Father which is in heaven is perfect" (Matthew 5:48); "Let this mind be in you which was also in Christ Jesus" (Philippians 2:5); "Be ye transformed by the renewing of your mind" (Romans 12:2). There are many such verses. The whole plan of salvation is about becoming what we are not. We are born with a bent toward evil, with a carnal nature not of God, totally focused upon self, since the fall of man in Eden.

Jesus came to show us a better way and to lead us into it. He wants us to be born-again and to walk in newness of life. The first birth we cannot choose. If any of us remain the way we were born, we are lost. We are to choose to be born-again into the kingdom of God and His righteousness, denying self, dying to self, putting "the old man" of self to death, dying daily as we choose to follow Jesus against our nature.

You go on to say, "I don't like the term 'lifestyle' because the gay person doesn't have any different lifestyle than a straight person. Everyone sleeps, eats, works, pays bills, and basically the lives, and the lifestyles are the same. Lifestyle is more appropriate for economic differences and comparisons than for sexual attractions."

I respectfully disagree. Lifestyle involves much more than sleeping, eating, working, and paying bills. The gay lifestyle can be very convoluted and includes many things different from the Christian straight lifestyle: anilingus and anal intercourse, oral sex with same gender, masturbation, for example, just to name a few of the milder practices. Gays often wear certain colors to indicate what sexual perversion is their preference and give other signals to prospects by accessorizing on the right or on the left ear, or pocket, etc.

The straight Christian lifestyle ideally involves saving one's self for a lifelong commitment sexually and otherwise to one and only one person of the opposite gender as God intended with His creation. The gay lifestyle involves multiple sexual encounters and partners prior to commitment. And the incidence of honest monogamy among those involved in the gay lifestyle is very rare, if not totally non-existent. I would be very surprised if there is a homosexual saving himself sexually for the one and only love of his life and consummating that love only after a public commitment before God and man. There might be, but I doubt it.

There is much sexual experimentation and promiscuity within the gay lifestyle. Many things other than sleeping, eating, working, and paying bills define one's lifestyle: the way one dresses and accessorizes sends signals, i.e., the right and left ears and pockets to indicate dominance or passivity preferences, and the colors one chooses to wear to indicate a particular sexual perversion of preference. There are also mannerisms, and the use of code words and actions. There is gay specific recreation and entertainment.

Sexual behavior is a part of a lifestyle. Gays tend to have sex outside of marriage and outside of commitment, recreational sex, far and away more than straights in general. It is not uncommon for a homosexual to have hundreds of sex partners within a lifetime. According to research, homosexual men are disproportionately vulnerable to a host of serious and sometimes fatal infections caused by the entry of feces into the bloodstream such as hepatitis B, shigellosis, and giardia lamblia (known as the gay bowel syndrome, amebiasis, campylobacteriosis, and anorectal infections with Neisseria gonorrhoeae, Chlamydia trachomatis, Treponema pallidum, herpes simplex virus, human papilloma viruses, and AIDS. I could go on with paragraphs. The gay lifestyle results also in a life expectancy 20 to 30 years lower than that of straights. It's because of lifestyle.

What one chooses as entertainment is a part of lifestyle: music, television, plays, movies, restaurants, theaters, beaches, clubs, and resorts. The gay lifestyle incorporates largely gay bars, gay resorts, gay restaurants, gay beaches, gay churches, gay organizations such as Seventh-day Adventist Kinship International, gay cruises, gay parades, gay nights at amusement parks. "Gayness," homosexuality, is flaunted and celebrated. Lifestyle is a very appropriate term, and I make no apologies for using it.

You referred to someone who failed in his "change ministry" as well as personally, which I agree is a sad testimony of an ex-gay or of a ministry assisting in this area. But since when do we allow one man's failure to discredit the Word of God, the work of God, and the power of God? This person had nothing to do with my conversion. I went to the Word of God, to my knees, to the Holy Spirit, and found deliverance and victory that no one can refute. I walked away by God's all-sufficient grace, His divine power, and intervention, and never turned back for over two decades now.

You stated, "I have yet to meet anyone who can honestly say he has actually changed his orientation."

Well, you have met me. And I am one of thousands who have done the same. Let me explain something about orientation. I used to be a pilot. I have flown my plane in tailwinds, crosswinds, headwinds, and violent storms. Yet, by God's grace, I always made it safely to my destination.

You see? I did not allow the tail wind or crosswind to determine my orientation, neither the head wind, nor the violent storm. My orientation was my chosen charted course. I made whatever adjustments necessary to stay on course. Homosexual temptation is like that wind or violent storm sometimes. It is the course that the enemy has charted for my life in order to lead me to a crash landing and eternal destruction. The crosswind of temptation does not define my orientation, neither is it sin. Temptation simply reveals the will of the enemy of souls.

Jesus was tempted in all points like as we are, yet He was without sin (Hebrews 4:15). And who would dare say that His orientation was homosexual, or bisexual, or toward sexual addiction?

Satan knows every circumstance of our family and personal history, and he custom makes his plan for each of us. It does not matter what sin he is successful in leading us into, the final wages of all sin is death. That is his goal for your life, friend, and mine. But I have cooperated with God and changed my orientation. I have charted a new course for myself, and by God's grace I will stay on that course. "Being confident of this very thing, that he which hath begun a good work in you will perform it until the day of Jesus Christ" (Philippians 1:6). And, "It is God which worketh in you both to will and to do of his good pleasure" (Philippians 2:13).

Sorry for the epistle, but I do *feel* passionate about my newly found walk with the Lord and His miracle working in my life over the past two decades. Let me just leave you with this thought, for all God's biddings are enablings, and there is power in the Word: "Therefore if any man be in Christ, he is a new creature: old things are passed away; behold, all things are become new" (2 Corinthians 5:17).

In other words:

The old nature, born of blood and the will of the flesh, cannot inherit the kingdom of God. The old ways, the hereditary tendencies, the former habits, must be given up, for grace is not inherited. *The new birth consists in having new motives, new tastes, new tendencies …*

A genuine conversion changes hereditary and cultivated tendencies, to wrong …

[God] requires the whole heart. No part of it is to be reserved for the development of hereditary or cultivated tendencies to evil. (Seventh-day Adventist Bible Commentary Vol. 6, 1101, emphasis added).

Homosexuality by description is listed in the Bible as evil, an abomination, along with many other abominations. It can be renounced, and it can be overcome.

"Exhibit A – Victor J. Adamson"

Question: My son says he's gay. He was married, an academy teacher, an amazingly talented tenor soloist, has his master's degree [from a prominent Christian university], and has now quit it all saying he doesn't believe in a God who condones murder as stated in the Bible. Therefore, the Bible is not true, either. Now where's the argument for him?

Reply: I have not found any place in the Bible where God condones murder. But I have seen where God Himself, who is perfectly just as well as merciful, has ordered the carrying out of His judgments after much, much patient longsuffering toward the rebellious sinner. We do not have His perfect wisdom and understanding, and that's why He tells us not to judge one another. But He certainly is qualified to judge, for all His judgments are righteous.

We find that 1 John 4:8 tells us that "God is love." And we, as His children, must trust that all He does is through the heart and eyes of love. We may have many questions as to why He has executed His judgments toward some people, even races of people, but we have this assurance found in the second commandment that He visits "the iniquity of the fathers upon the children unto the third and fourth generation of them that hate [Him]" (Exodus 20:5).

This is why he told Abraham that his children could not inherit the land of Canaan for 400 years, or four generations, because the cup of the Amorites was not yet full, the cup of their iniquity. But after Israel came out of Egypt, the patience of the Lord had reached its limit, four generations, and He ordered Israel to destroy the entire race of the Amorites. It's really no different than the lake of fire at the end of the millennium. When God acts, it is out of love and mercy as well as perfect justice. We must trust Him in all this.

I hope that is helpful to you. But what I have found to be true in so many instances with gay people, having been one myself for many years, is that guilt will cause one to go to great lengths to justify and rationalize away his own bad behavior. The Bible refers to them as those who wrest the Scriptures (wrestle with them, twist them, distort them), to their own destruction.

God's perfect justice toward the wicked does not justify for one instant our own bad choices and behavior. We are self-deluded and deceived if we go that route. As our Creator, God knows best what is good for His children when it comes to sexual behavior as with any other issue. He's the one who created us with the capacity to enjoy intimacy. But along with that gift came an instruction book. If the gift is abused, there will be consequences that will cause great grief for God as well as the disobedient child. God takes no delight in the wages or consequences of our sins. He is "not willing that any should perish, but that all should come to repentance" (2 Peter 3:9). But the natural result of disconnecting from God, the Source of life, is ultimately the loss of that life—death.

Again, I hope my insights prove to be helpful to you and your son.

Keep looking up.

Victor

Question: I wish that anti-gay Christians and accepting Christians would start a constructive dialogue instead of each questioning the very faith of the other.

I wish we both could free ourselves from the noise generated by the respective radical fringe groups and just try to communicate based on mutual respect.

Do you think that a moderated round table with strict rules of discussion for both sides would be possible? I don't think a free flowing discussion group would work since emotions are quite high on both sides of the argument.

Reply: Honestly, I do not think that a moderated round table with strict rules of discussion for both sides would be of much benefit to anyone. Here is the basis of my thinking. I see the Christian world divided into two camps: those of the great majority who want salvation *in* their sins, and those of a minority who, with the promise of Genesis 3:15 in their hearts, despise their unworthiness and sinfulness and want salvation *from* their sins, as promised in Matthew 1:21.

While one group refuses to acknowledge homosexuality to even be a sin issue, the other group accepts the Bible definition of sin to be "the transgression of the law" (1 John 3:4), and homosexuality to be one of the abominations listed by God Himself in the Bible. One group seems to rationalize away all the Bible texts relating to homosexuality as referring to something else, and the other group accepts the plain "thus saith the Lord" regarding the very explicit description of homosexuality in the Bible and how God feels about it.

These two groups are very polarized, and God Himself cannot bring everyone to the same consensus, for He will not force His will upon anyone. Generally, nothing positive is accomplished through a debate, which I see this to be. Both sides just become emboldened in their positions. Republicans don't become Democrats as a result of debates. They just hope for a majority of the votes. And how often has the majority, biblically, ever been in the right with God? True Christianity is much more like a republic, rather than a democracy, basing its standards upon the expressed will of God, which are very clearly revealed in His unchangeable law. All the democratic votes in the world cannot alter one jot or one tittle of this law, for it is an expression of His very character.

In fact, we read a very solemn warning in the book of Revelation that:

> If any man shall add unto these things, God shall add unto him the plagues that are written in this book: And if any man shall take away from the words of the book of this prophecy, God shall take away his part out of the book of life, and out of the holy city, and from the things which are written in this book. (Revelation 22:18, 19)

God's Word and expressed will regarding homosexuality is not up for a vote. We have a choice, to either accept it, or reject it, and to live with the consequences.

I have to ask myself, What if the gay-accepting Christian is right in his position? If so, then I am still okay, for surely God will not punish me for being straight, will He? There's nothing in the Bible that indicates being married to a woman is out of harmony with the will of God.

But, what if "Victor" and the anti-gay-theology Christian is right in his position? If so, then one side of this issue is going to have a rude awakening on the Day of Judgment, based upon a plain "thus saith the Lord."

"God is love" (1 John 4:8). And it is with great sorrow that He proclaims: "Say unto them, As I live, saith the Lord GOD, I have no pleasure in the death of the wicked; but that the wicked turn from his way and live: turn ye, turn ye from your evil ways; for why will ye die, O house of Israel?" (Ezekiel 33:11). By the way, the whole 23rd chapter of Ezekiel is very interesting reading.

Please don't think of my message as one of hate speech and dogmatism. It is a loving God who warns His wayward children of the coming consequences of their misguided choices and un-Christlike behavior. Just as loving parents lament the behavior and certain consequences of their children hooked on drugs, crime, or other self-destructive behavior, so our heavenly Father grieves over the choices of His beloved, yet wayward children. He knows the certain end result, His eternal separation from those He loves, from those for whom He gave His only begotten Son to die that they might have eternal life with Him.

Thanks for your "ear."

Sincerely,

Victor

Question: I am not homosexual, but these days it seems that even straight people are practicing homosexual sex. Isn't it hypocritical to condemn homosexual behavior while partaking of the same practice? It seems that married or straight people do partake of this behavior.

Reply: You make a very interesting point in your statement. It has been said that homosexual behavior has become the experimental drug of this age. In other words, it seems that in the never-ending, thrill-seeking attempts of this generation that it has finally come around to playing with the fire of homosexual experimentation and overt behavior. In seeking freedom *from* the law of God rather than freedom *in* the law of God, it seems that there are no limits to rebellion, defiance, and perversion. But there is a limit with God. He says that "As it was in the days of Lot ... even thus shall it be in the day when the Son of man is revealed" (Luke 17:28–30).

But let's face the facts. If someone is fascinated by the excitement of perverted sex, then he or she is a sexual pervert. If someone enjoys having homosexual encounters, then he or she is a homosexual. Some people like to play with words and say that they are "bisexual," that they enjoy sexual behavior with either or both genders. Perhaps we could coin a new phrase and call them "straight gays."

In the eyes of God, participating in sexual activity outside of marriage to one spouse is a violation of the seventh commandment. It doesn't matter if it is same-sex, bi-sex, homo-sex, self-sex (masturbation), or bestiality (with an animal); it is all a violation of the same seventh commandment and a perversion in the eyes of God. I've known people to excuse their persistent sexual immorality with the opposite sex as a "sexual addiction," as though it were some medical condition. They thus deny responsibility for their behavior.

But God asks us only to acknowledge our iniquity, and then He will heal our backsliding (Jeremiah 3). All these games with words are mere excuses, rationalization, and self-justification for bad behavior. God is unable to justify those who are busy justifying themselves.

In Romans 1, the apostle Paul gives a strong warning to such as you describe where he speaks in particular about homosexual behavior. "Who knowing the judgment of God, that they which commit such things are worthy of death, not only do the same, but have pleasure in them that do them" (Romans 1:32). In other words, even if they are not actually involved in the overt behavior, but they do take pleasure in it through involvement in pornography and lust and suggestive television programming and movies; they are still guilty. Knowing that God does not approve and will judge accordingly, they persist anyway.

Yes, it is hypocritical to condemn someone else's breaking of the seventh commandment while indulging in lustful practices and overt behavior that is in violation of the same commandment, whether it be homosexual or heterosexual.

Question: Some Christian homosexuals use Bible texts to support their homosexuality. One passage describes the wonderful friendship between David and Jonathan, which they say were gay. I find the idea repulsive. How do you show them that David and Jonathan were sharing a deep friendship?

Reply: David and Jonathan were not gay, contrary to popular gay opinion. They both were married and fathered children. Jonathan loved David as his own soul according to 1 Samuel 18:1–3 and 20:17, which simply means they were the very best of friends, like brothers, so much so that Jonathan was willing to die for David. Their love for each other transcended that of the love of a man for a woman (2 Samuel 1:26), but that does not equate to sexual or erotic love. To believe so is to believe in pure speculation, based upon one's own perverse fantasies and desires.

In 2 Samuel 1:26, David laments the loss of his friend, his "brother," not his lover: "I am distressed for thee, my brother Jonathan: very pleasant hast thou been unto me: thy love to me was wonderful, passing the love of women."

Note: This love was like to that of a brother, not a lover. It surpassed the love of women; it was not the same as love toward a woman. This word "love" in Hebrew was used toward friends as well as in other relationships and contexts, just as our word in English.

David was so heterosexual that he married not once, but several times. He was so heterosexual that he totally lost control when he saw Bathsheba, another man's wife. He stooped to premeditated murder to get her for himself. There is no indication in the Bible that David loved Jonathan in any such way.

A basic principle used for coming to a clear understanding of any subject in the Bible is to take everything found on that subject and study it all out to get the full picture, "precept upon precept… ; line upon line… ; here a little, and there a little" (Isaiah 28:10). One cannot study the entire life of David in sincerity and truth and possibly come to a logical conclusion that he or Jonathan was gay.

Thanks, for your great question. I hope this explanation is of some help to you.
Victor

A Response to a Pro-Gay Flier Justifying Homosexuality at a Christian Convention

Dear Friends:

I have received your *Come As You Are* flier with the cover text, "Come to me, all you who are weary and burdened, and I will give you rest" (Matthew 11:28, NIV). I trust that a response on my part will be well taken.

This text speaks to all who are weary and burdened with the weight of sin and guilt. Jesus invites you to come to Him for "rest" (Gr. Anapauo), the root words "Ana" and "Pauo" meaning "reversal," "to stop," "restrain," "quit," "desist," "come to an end," "cease," "leave," "refrain," "recreation" (re-creation). As one through the grace of God (through His divine power) *ceases* his practice of sinful thought, word, and behavior, he finds rest and repose from that burden of sin, guilt, and consequences. He allows Jesus to be Lord of his thoughts, Lord of his desires, and Lord of his behavior.

"Recreation" in the dictionary is defined in one sense as "refreshment of body and mind" and comes from the word "recreate," meaning, "to create anew."

Your cover text quoted from the New International Version speaks with great clarity of the power of Jesus to personally save His people *from* their sins of homosexuality as well as from any other sin, not *in* their sins.

The inside cover statement reads, "You ARE Loved! Gay Christians are wholly loved and accepted by God."

You are quite correct on this point. I could not agree with you more. However, the truth of your statement is not the whole truth. We need to know and teach the truth, the *whole* truth, and nothing but the truth. Let me clarify my point:

In my mission work in Romania, I am repeatedly confronted by scenes of the street children who have been put out of their homes as young as five and six years of age because of poverty. They scavenge the streets and garbage containers at night for food. They are dirty, ragged, and appear to be miserable. I struggle with the urge to adopt one of them. Why? Because I love them and accept them just the way they are. My heart goes out to them and aches for them.

Should I ever be able to satisfy my urge to adopt one, I would bring him or her home to a new way of life. I would burn the clothes, shave the head to rid it of lice, and soak them in a tub of hot, soapy water for a week. I would give them a new diet, new clothes, new environment, new friends, and new family. I would give them the best possible education. And why would I do all this? So that I could come to love and accept them? Or because I already love and accept them? The answer is clear. Because of my love and acceptance of them in their miserable condition, which, by the way, he or she is used to and quite comfortable with. I want to transform the little street urchin into a noble and respectable human being with a bright and glorious future, both for now and for eternity.

Therefore, I believe our message should go farther than love and acceptance to include transformation. After all, we expect that in regards to the other nine commandments. Why should we doubt the grace (divine power) of God to transform one in regard to the seventh commandment as well?

One of my favorite texts of Scripture reads: "Therefore if any man be in Christ, he is a new creature (a new creation): old things are passed away; behold, all things are become new" (2 Corinthians 5:17).

In other words, "The old ways, the hereditary tendencies, the former habits, must be given up ... The new birth consists in having new motives, new tastes, new tendencies" (*The Review and Herald*, April 12, 1892). "God makes no compromise with sin. A genuine conversion changes hereditary and cultivated tendencies to wrong" (*Seventh-day Adventist Bible Commentary* Vol. 6, 1101).

Later in your pamphlet the statement is made, "The Bible never mentions homosexuality or sexual orientation."

In this you are correct, if you are referring to the words "homosexuality" and "sexual orientation," but only if the King James Version of the Bible is your point of reference. However, the behavior and practice are spelled out quite in detail in several places in the Bible, all of which you are familiar. Might I point out other words or terms that also are not mentioned in the Bible as they randomly come to my mind: bisexual, masturbation, incest, pornography, pedophilia, Sunday, cuss words, drug abuse, alcohol, smoking, marijuana, pot, heroin, cocaine, child abuse, sex, sex addict, addiction, sexual abuse, spousal abuse, immaculate conception, purgatory, rapture, secret rapture, homicide, genocide, infanticide, abortion, ad infinitum.

However, if you use other Bible translations, such as the NIV (which is quoted in your cover text), you will see clearly that "homosexuals," unfortunately, *are* listed among those who shall not inherit the kingdom of God. And please note that this is not based upon my own opinion, criticism, judgment, prejudice, or bias, for I myself was once one like you.

For example, the *New International Version* (NIV), the one used in your own flier, says, "Do not be deceived: Neither the sexually immoral nor idolaters nor adulterers nor men who have sex with men… will inherit the kingdom of God" (1 Corinthians 6:9, 10, NIV, 2011 edition). "Neither… male prostitutes nor homosexual offenders… will inherit the kingdom of God (Ibid. 1984 edition). "And that is what some of you were" (1 Corinthians 6:11, NIV, 2011 edition).

(Note: "homosexual offenders" are those who offend the law of God in at least one point, that of homosexuality. They are not those who offend the "gift of homosexuality," as many gays like to claim. James 2:10 reads, "For whosoever shall keep the whole law, and yet offend in one point, he is guilty of all.")

The New American Standard Bible, for example, says clearly, "Do you not know that the unrighteous shall not inherit the kingdom of God? ***Do not be deceived:*** neither fornicators … nor adulterers, nor effeminate, nor **homosexuals** … will inherit the kingdom of God. Such **were** some of you; but you **were washed,** but you **were sanctified,** but you **were justified** in the name of the Lord Jesus Christ and in the Spirit of our God" (1 Corinthians 6:9, 11, NASB, 1963 edition, emphasis added).

The marginal reference in my King James Bible for the word "effeminate" is "catamite," which is defined as a boy used in sodomy, or unnatural sexual relations between male persons.

The Living Bible paraphrase says, "Don't fool yourselves. Those … who are… adulterers or homosexuals—will have no share in his kingdom … There was a time when some of you were just like that but now your sins are washed away."

The New King James Version says, "Do not be deceived. Neither … homosexuals, nor sodomites … will inherit the kingdom of God."

The problem I see with your line of reasoning that homosexuality is not mentioned in the Bible is the same problem I see with many theologians who can talk about sin and make lists of sins all day long and never acknowledge the authority of the fourth commandment. They never get to the root of the sin issue. Why? Because they ignore the one text of Scripture that defines sin as "the transgression of the law" (1 John 3:4). One can quibble over words forever and never address the real issue, which is the *principle* of the Word. Languages change from generation to generation, and word meanings change. For example, the word "gay" today means something entirely different than it did in previous generations. "Bad" means good today. And "good" is something to be mocked. Slang words mean something totally different from what they originally meant. But God never changes. His standards remain the same. His Word is infallible.

Finally, I would like to address your statement, "Research tells us that one in 10 people find themselves attracted to members of their own sex.… There are over 12 million baptized adults [within your denomination].… This means that there are 1.2 million gay [members in your church]!"

This truly is a preposterous statement. Your "research" is neither identified nor documented. And there is other research that shows this to be a very inflated, exaggerated number put forth by the homosexual community to suit their own purposes and agenda. For example, "Four researchers with the Alan Guttmacher Institute conducted a *scientific* survey involving 3,321 American men in their twenties and thirties. Only 1 percent of the men surveyed claimed to be exclusively homosexual; 2.3 percent of the men claimed to have ever had same-sex experience within the past 10 years. Similar studies conducted by France in 1992 concur with these most recent findings. [Cf. Jerry Adler, "Sex In the Snoring '90s," *Newsweek*, (April 26, 1993), 55; Kim Painter, "Only 1 Percent of Men Say They Are Gay," *USA Today*, April 15, 1993), 1D.]

The above *scientific* research was not conducted within a special interest group such as a church denomination. Therefore, its numbers would most likely be higher than those within a denomination teaching the identity of sin as the transgression of the law and how to have victory as overcomers.

It was also suggested to me by a member of your organization that since I had been married and fathered children before going into the gay lifestyle that I had not been truly gay, but rather bisexual. If that is true, then the number of gays must be discounted for every gay who has ever been married and had children or has had sex with someone of the opposite gender. I also know of a number of the members and leaders of your own organization who have been previously married and fathered children. So by this type of reasoning, then they, too, can be transformed, even as I have been for they must not truly be "gay" either.

The very fact that this 10-percent claim is so recklessly made and passed out in a flier for the public clearly indicates that an agenda is being given higher priority than truth, and that study of God's Word is being made to support one's already clearly established opinion rather than to honestly search out truth. Let us never forget that:

All scripture is given by inspiration of God, and is profitable for doctrine, for reproof, for correction, for instruction in righteousness: That the man of God may be perfect, thoroughly furnished unto all good works. (2 Timothy 3:16, 17)

In Christian love and understanding I leave you with these words of the apostle Peter:

Wherefore, beloved, seeing that ye look for such things, be diligent that ye may be found of him in peace, without spot, and blameless. And account that the longsuffering of our Lord is salvation; even as our beloved brother Paul also according to the wisdom given unto him hath written unto you; As also in all his epistles, speaking in them of these things; in which are some things hard to be understood, *which they that are unlearned and unstable wrest, as they do also the other scriptures, unto their own destruction.* Ye therefore, beloved, seeing ye know these things before, beware lest ye also, being led away with the error of the wicked, fall from your own steadfastness. But grow in grace, and in the knowledge of our Lord and Saviour Jesus Christ. To him be glory both now and for ever. Amen. (2 Peter 3:14–18, emphasis added.)

Response to a Pro-Gay "Christian" Petition

The bold petition below was posted online June 28, 2010 by anewcommand.com. Responses will be intermittent throughout.

Petition: *Of all the distinctives that might define Christians, Jesus identified only one thing that will distinguish his followers:*

A new command I give you: Love one another. As I have loved you, so you must love one another. By this everyone will know that you are my disciples, if you love one another." (John 13:34, 35)

Response: Yes, this is a beautiful and powerful text of Scripture, but nowhere in the context is the word "only" used. Actually, there are a number of "distinctives" given by Jesus Himself that define Christians. To point out just a few:

Thou shalt love the Lord thy God with all thy heart, and with all thy soul, and with all thy mind. This is the first and great commandment. And the second is like unto it, Thou shalt love thy neighbour as thyself. On these two commandments hang all the law and the prophets. (Matthew 22:37–40)

If ye love me, keep my commandments [including the seventh one]. (John 14:15)

In answer to the question, "What must I do to be saved?" (Acts 16:30), or, "to inherit eternal life" (Luke 10:25), three answers are given in Scripture, two by Jesus Himself. First, He refers to the two commandments of loving God supremely and your neighbor as yourself in Luke 10. Second, in Luke 18 He requires living in harmony with the Ten Commandments. The first to which Jesus refers is the seventh commandment, "Do not commit adultery," Luke 18:20). The third answer is given by the apostle Paul to the Jailor of Philippi: "Believe on the Lord Jesus Christ, and thou shalt be saved" (Acts 16:31).

To rephrase Paul's condition of salvation using definitions: Believe on Him who claims, I AM Jehovah, the self-existent, eternal One, your Creator, anointed to be your personal Savior from sin, and thou shalt be saved." Saved from sin, sin being the transgression of the law, including the seventh commandment forbidding sexual intimacy outside of marriage as created and ordained by God.

Being saved *from* sin involves coming out from the world and separating one's self from every unclean thought and unholy practice.

Petition: *We recognize, however, that we have fallen short of Jesus' vision for his followers—particularly with respect to our lesbian and gay sisters and brothers. We confess that as a church, we have failed to demonstrate Jesus' love in our interactions with the LGBTI* [Lesbian, Gay, Bi-sexual, Trans-sexual, Intersexual] *members of our community.*

Response: First of all, "intersexual" is a birth abnormality that does not involve behavior and, therefore, does not meet with condemnation in the Bible. On the other hand, lesbian, gay, bi-sexual, and trans-sexual all involve thoughts, feelings, emotions, and behavior, all of which *are* to be brought into captivity unto the obedience of Christ (2 Corinthians 10:5).

This linking of "LGBT" with "I" is akin to linking homosexuality with skin color in order to claim minority status, and therefore privilege. But skin color does not involve thoughts, feelings, emotions, and behavior. Neither, therefore, does it find condemnation in the Bible.

On the next point, Jesus' love in interacting with sinners does not embrace or overlook the sin. Jesus' love for the sinner was demonstrated in His taking the guilt, consequence, and punishment for the sin upon Himself in an effort to free the sinner from his or her bondage to sin. In His own words to Mary, guilty of living in violation of the seventh commandment (as do LGBT members of our community), "Neither do I condemn thee: go, and sin no more" (John 8:11). In other words, stop committing adultery. Stop breaking the seventh commandment. Stop having lustful thoughts and sexual intimacy outside of marriage as Jesus created it to be!

Petition: *For that reason, we, the undersigned, call on our fellow [denomination] to extend the love and grace of Jesus to the homosexual individuals in our [denominational] family in the following ways:*

Response: I must here interject these two points:

1) Jesus' love toward the LGBT sinner is unconditional, as should be the Christian's love. Like Christ's love, it leads the way to the foot of the cross,

to hatred for the sin (Genesis 3:15), to contrition, to confession, to repentance, to victory over sexual sin.

2) God's grace is defined in the Greek dictionary as "the divine influence working upon the heart and reflecting in the life." In other words, grace is the divine, omnipotent, transforming power of God. Yes, it is also unmerited favor, but we miss the significance of Jesus' words, "My grace is sufficient for you" (2 Corinthians 12:9), if we do not understand it to also refer to His transforming and sustaining power in overcoming sin.

Back to the Petition: *We, the undersigned, call on our [denomination] to extend the love and grace of Jesus to the homosexual individuals in our [denominational] family in the following ways:*

1. Acknowledging that a homosexual orientation is most often determined before birth and/or very soon after, by a complex combination of physiological and environmental factors that are beyond the individual's control.

Response: This is a broad, sweeping generalization that is simply not true. There is much credible scientific information refuting such a claim that can be reviewed under other postings on my website: www.victorjadamson.com.

The very word "orientation" is defined to involve choice. And wherever orientation exists "reorientation" is also available. (See dictionary definitions of "orientation" and "reorientation." Also see the article "Temptation and Orientation" on the website.)

Petition: *2. Rejecting as a form of violence any programs that attempt to change or redirect one's sexual orientation, recognizing that orientation is highly unlikely to change and that such attempts have caused deep trauma, even leading some to become suicidal.*

Response: The mission of the church is *not* a form of violence! This is a very unfortunate claim to make in light of the commission given by Christ Himself:

> All power is given unto me in heaven and in earth. Go ye therefore, and teach all nations… Teaching them to *observe* all things whatsoever I have commanded you: and, lo, I am with you alway, even unto the end of the world. (Matthew 28:18–20)

The mission of the church is one of seeking the lost, pointing them to Christ and His righteousness as a pattern to follow. For His offered salvation is *from* sin, not *in* sin. Many gay people the world over recognize and acknowledge their need to reorient themselves into harmony with the will of God. It is not a form of violence to meet them where they are and show them the way out. It would be a form of heartless negligence and indifference to *not* minister to the needs of the sin-sick soul.

Petition: *3. Acting deliberately and decisively to prevent judgmental and condemning attitudes and actions against homosexual individuals.*

Response: We here need to clarify that the loving work of redemption should not be portrayed as "judgmental and condemning attitudes and actions against homosexual individuals" lest we so label the infinite sacrifice of Christ Himself, our Savior from sin and our High Priest, currently working to sanctify His people.

Petition: *4. Providing our homosexual sisters and brothers not only a place in our pews, but also a space on our platforms, allowing all of the gifts God has given them to be used to honor and serve God.*

Response: I find no biblical basis whatsoever for such a demand upon God's church. The church is a place for sinners to find redemption and salvation from sin, not sanctuary in sin. The pew is therefore available. It is not, however, to be a place for tolerating, palliating, coddling, promoting, nor celebrating open sin. It is certainly not a place to give platform to open sin. If faithful to our calling, the church will lovingly "Cry aloud, spare not, lift up [her] voice like a trumpet, and shew my people their transgression, and the house of Jacob their sins" (Isaiah 58:1).

People seeking baptism and membership in the body of Christ are to "Bring forth therefore fruits meet for repentance" (Matthew 3:8). Furthermore, the gifts of the Spirit do not include homosexuality, no matter how talented the individual may be. (See 1 Corinthians 12 and 14.)

Petition: *5. Fully integrating lesbian, gay, bisexual, transgender and intersex members of the [denomination] into the life of the church community. These things we resolve to do in Jesus' name, for the sake of the Body of Christ.*

Response: The result and consequence of fully integrating homosexuality into the culture is frightfully revealed through the tragic demise of Sodom and Gomorrah, and the kingdoms of Greece and Rome. We are lovingly warned by the pen of inspiration, "We have nothing to fear for the future, except as we shall forget the way the Lord has led us, and His teaching in our past history" (*Testimonies for the Church*, vol. 9, 10).

Secondly, to make such a resolution in the name of Jesus is to ask His blessing upon that which He has irrefutably condemned as an abomination, to ask the church to go directly against the Word of God upon which it is supposed to base all doctrine, rule of faith, and practice.

Petition: *Add your name to this resolution! Click here.*

Response: Can any true and genuine Christian, disciple of Christ, student of the Word of God add his name to such a resolution? God forbid! And may He have mercy upon His church.

Victor J. Adamson

———————————————

Chapter 8
GAY MARRIAGE, MONOGAMY, AND DIVORCE

Question: Don't gays have the same right to marry as straight people? Isn't forbidding gays to marry a violation of their human rights?

Reply: To answer your questions: No, and no again. I know that's simplistic, but it's correct.

Gays do have legitimate human rights, but they do not have the right to demand legislation to support them in something not approved of by society at large and that is clearly condemned in the Bible. Gays do have the right to be left alone to live as they choose. But what I have observed is that the gay agenda is never satisfied.

First they wanted to be tolerated. They are tolerated.

Then they wanted to be accepted. They are accepted.

Next they wanted to be celebrated. Thanks to Presidents Bill Clinton and Barack Obama, they now have the entire month of June every year to celebrate their Gay Pride, while all the presidents are lumped into one Presidents Day. Mothers and fathers get only one day. Jesus gets three days: Easter, Thanksgiving, and Christmas. But homosexuals get an entire month! (By the way, Sodom and Gomorrah were destroyed for their pride, among other issues, see Ezekiel 16:49.)

Gays then pushed for promotion of homosexuality. It's now promoted throughout the media and the education system and in various ways and means.

Gays want to be privileged and now classify themselves as a minority based upon the "born gay" hoax (See the above chapter, A Sampling of Myths vs. Facts, The Born Gay Hoax Exposed), which was conjured up in the mid-1980s, now being given special protections and privileges above society at large.

But that's not enough! Gays now want control and are lobbying for hate speech and hate crime laws to prevent others from exercising their rights of free speech while gays boldly and openly say and do anything they want, insensitive at times to the feelings and beliefs of others around them in public, and claim that crimes against gays are something more appalling than crimes against any other person in society. That's elitism!

Finally, the gay agenda is now globally seeking legislation to sanction their lifestyle through marriage. Marriage was created by God in Eden to be between one man and one woman for, among other things, the purpose of procreation, to populate the planet. "Be fruitful and multiply," God said in Genesis 1:28. It seems presumptuous and preposterous that the gay agenda would be so bold as to now seek the blessing of God upon a union that He so plainly condemns in the Bible by seeking legislation that would allow them to marry.

You see, it appears to me that the gay community is never to be satisfied; no, not until they have taken control. If you will read Isaiah 14 and Ezekiel 28, you will read about another character who had the same mindset and how God had to deal with him.

Please don't think me callous because I have expressed my view here. For years I lived in a gay relationship like marriage, with joint checking accounts, co-ownership of a home, visitation rights at the hospital, the ability to include my lover in my will, etc. Legalized marriage would have given me nothing I did not already have. Gay marriage today is nothing more or less than political posturing and publicity. As I said, I used to be gay, and it was my study of God's Word that helped me see how blind I had been all those years, living in prideful defiance of society and in prideful rebellion against and defiance of God's expressed will for mankind and for my life in particular.

Now, as Jesus said to Mary, "Neither do I condemn thee: go, and sin no more!" (John 8:11).

Victor

Gay Monogamy—What's Wrong With It?

Question: What difference does it make whether one establishes a same-sex relationship instead of one with the opposite sex as long as the relationship is based upon love and loyalty?

What about the gay (homosexual) who is loyal to a monogamous relationship, the one who does not commit adultery by cheating on his/her spouse, partner, or significant other? Is he not in harmony with the spirit of the law by being faithful to the one and only love of his life, though of the same sex?

Reply: Before we law-abiding Christians hasten to shoot down this rationale, we must recognize this question as being very legitimate and worthy of careful examination. Interestingly, the above question happens to reflect the same reasoning as that used by Christians in general who take the same position about other aspects of God's moral law, the Ten Commandments. In order to help the homosexual see the weakness of his stance, his logic, we must first make sure that our own logic on this principle is sound. We must first make sure that we ourselves are standing upon a sure foundation, upon the solid Rock.

Brothers and sisters in Christ, let us be perfectly honest with ourselves on this point. It is easy for us to see the mote in the eye of our homosexual brothers and sisters while we may be looking around a beam in our own. We ask the homosexuals to take an honest look at themselves in the light of eternal realities. On this question, maybe we, too, should make an honest, introspective self-check.

And before we use our spiritual discernment to analyze and respond to the gay logic in the above sincere and legitimate question, let us make sure that our own logic is sound.

Our loving God invites each of us, "Come now, and let us reason together" (Isaiah 1:18). This is one of those points upon which He calls for us to reason. So let us use our God-given capacity to think and reason with consistency and follow this line of logic to see where it goes when we apply it to all of God's Ten Commandments.

Are you ready?

We Christians need to own up to the possibility that we may be responsible for initiating this line of reasoning when it comes to moral rationalization. Has not Christianity in general taken the official position that it doesn't really matter about God's law? That He's really not that particular?

This gay logic, expressed in the above question, is the same used by those who say, and pardon my saying So but we must be honest, "Oh, it really doesn't matter what day of the week we observe as a holy day for worship, just so I keep one out of seven." Or, we might even say, "I keep every day holy."

Oh, really? How can that possibly be?

Now, bear with me on this point for a moment, and let us reason together. If we keep every day holy, are we not like the homosexual who "loves" everyone he has relationships with? The commandment that speaks to this issue, the fourth commandment, does not allow for us to keep every day holy. It commands, "Six days shalt thou labor." And labor is not a part of God's holy day, for, "in it thou shalt not do any work, thou, nor thy son," etc.

This commandment (found in Exodus 20:8–11) says, "Remember the sabbath day, to keep it holy." Notice, "the sabbath day," one day, one specific day.

It then sets this one, specific day apart from the secular ones by saying:

Six days shalt thou labor... but the seventh day is the Sabbath of the LORD thy God: in it [the seventh day] thou shalt not do any work ... For in six days the LORD made heaven and earth, the sea, and all that in them is. (Exodus 20:9–11)

Six days the Lord labored in His work of creation. And "Six days shalt thou labor." You know. Like Father, like son. He wants us to follow His example in all things. He wants us to grow up to be like Him.

Continuing on, "For in six days the Lord made [created, labored] ... and rested the seventh day." Then again the differentiating statement, "Wherefore the Lord blessed the Sabbath day and hallowed it [made it, and it only, holy]."

You see, dear reader, for us to say that it really doesn't matter on this point of God's law only adds credence to the logic of the dear homosexual and others who also believe it really doesn't matter, but on different points of the same law of God.

1) It doesn't matter whom I worship, just so I worship something or somebody.

2) It doesn't matter if I bow down to images, as long as they represent the true God.

3) It doesn't matter if I cuss a little, as long as it is in good humor.

4) It doesn't matter upon which day I worship, just so long as I do worship.

5) It doesn't matter if I dishonor my parents, if they haven't earned my respect.

6) It doesn't really matter if I kill, if someone really deserves to die.

7) It doesn't matter if we have premarital sex; we're going to get married anyway. Or, it doesn't matter who or what I "marry," as long as I am loyal to that one.

8) It doesn't matter if I steal from the rich, as long as it is for a worthy cause.

9) It doesn't matter if I tell a lie, just so long as it is a "little white lie."

10) It doesn't matter if I lust over pornography (covet). It's private and hurts no one.

Here we should be able to clearly see that if we consistently rationalize that "it doesn't really matter," then the end result of society will someday be total anarchy.

If we as Christians practice and teach that it is okay to live in violation of any one of God's Ten Commandments, then how can we in all honesty and consistency judge homosexuality to be sin? We must accept the Creator's definition of sin as "the transgression of the law" (1 John 3:4), the law of Ten Commandments. And the practice of breaking any one of these Ten Commandments, according to James 2:10, is to be guilty of breaking them all. "For whosoever shall keep the whole law, and yet offend in one point, he is guilty of all."

We Christians will have much more success with helping gays understand the sinfulness of homosexuality, the futility of "gay monogamy," and how to overcome the same if we ourselves come to understand the simple principle of trusting obedience, and if we are consistent in our own reasoning, logic, faith, doctrine, and practice.

Another important point to consider is that apart from Jesus Christ, according to Romans 7, we cannot keep the law of God, no matter how diligent our efforts. Therefore, gays, even though practicing monogamy, cannot truly be in harmony with the seventh commandment in spirit, in the heart and mind where Christ promises to write it, because they are not in harmony with the will of God. Obedience is more than outward compliance. It is a condition of the heart. Even "monogamous" gays would still have to deal with the temptations of lust, pornography, fantasy, and the pull of attractions that only Christ could supply grace (divine strength and power) to overcome. And without submission to His will in this matter, the grace of Christ is unavailable.

Now, you might be thinking at this point that we're not considering a point of the law of Ten Commandments when discussing the issue of homosexuality, but that we are dealing with one of the "abominations" listed in the Bible. This point is discussed elsewhere. (See www.victorjadamson.com, Featured Article, "You, Too, Can Be Made Whole," part 1, #4.)

However, suppose we forget for the moment God's law of Ten Commandments. Instead, let us just visit the Garden of Eden in the beginning. Two institutions were created there. On the sixth day of the week God instituted marriage, the ultimate, highest of all relationships possible between any two of His created children. On the seventh day of creation He instituted the Sabbath, a day He set aside for weekly, quality time with the children of His creation. It is a family day with God, a day for relationship enhancement and growth with Him.

The ever-vigilant enemy of God has labored tirelessly to destroy both of these beautiful relationship institutions since the beginning of time. Homosexuality is nothing less than a breakdown of that sacred institution of marriage as created and designed by our loving Father.

And what has happened to the Sabbath institution?

Now that we have done a little self-check to verify the consistency of our own method of spiritual reasoning, let us address the specific question at hand: What difference does it make whether one establishes a same-sex relationship instead of a relationship with someone of the opposite sex as long as the relationship is based upon love and loyalty—a monogamous one?

Now, suppose we determine gay monogamy to be acceptable as an alternative lifestyle. How many homosexuals could honestly lay claim to monogamy? How many wait until "marriage" before becoming sexually active? How many wait until commitment before having sexual encounters with prospective lovers? God's plan does not allow for sex outside of the marriage institution, either pre-marital or extra-marital. Most homosexuals tend to shop around sexually before settling into a relationship. Therefore, such gay marriages, or unions, even if eventually monogamous, are built upon the sand.

Still, there are those who sincerely believe that it really does not matter who, or what, they marry as long as they stay faithful. Others don't bother to commit through marriage at all. They justify a sexual relationship simply on the basis of being "lovers," or upon having a "meaningful relationship," or upon being "sexually fulfilled," or upon a commitment to one another regardless of gender. Such relationships outside the favor and blessing of the Creator of marriage quite often end up on the rocks as lovers get traded in on newer models, not much unlike divorce and remarriage in the heterosexual lifestyle, which God also hates, according to Malachi 2:15, 16. However, the incidence of turnover among homosexuals is quite a bit higher than among heterosexuals. But at what point should the line be drawn for "meaningful relationships"? God's standard is for the union of one man with one woman, for life. "Therefore shall a man leave his father and his mother, and shall cleave [stick fast; adhere; be faithful] unto his wife: and they shall be one flesh" (Genesis 2:24, in Eden).

> And [Jesus] answered and said unto them, Have ye not read, that he which made them at the beginning made them male and female, And said, For this cause shall a man leave father and mother, and shall cleave to his wife: and they twain [the two of them] shall be one flesh? Wherefore they are no more twain [two], but one flesh. What therefore God hath joined together, let not man put asunder. (Matthew 19:4–6)

If we do not accept this standard of our Creator, then what should be the criterion for sexual behavior? Upon what basis do we even make a standard? Should it be left up to our own feelings and emotions? If not, then whose standard do we accept? Who has the right to set this standard? Would it not be the Creator of sexuality Himself?

If homosexual relationships are to be looked upon as an acceptable alternative lifestyle, by what authority do we accept this standard outside of marriage as created and designed by God? And where are the boundaries to be placed for other acceptable relationships beyond gays and lesbians? What about man/boy relationships? What about pedophiles with consenting children? What about incest? How far down do we go if we do not accept an authoritative standard? God's authoritative standard?

God says, "Thou shalt have no other gods before me" (Exodus 20:3). May I suggest that whoever is allowed to set our standards, besides our creator God, has then assumed a higher position of authority than God whose standard we ignore? Does he not then become another god before the true God?

What's wrong with gay monogamy?

The Creator of sexuality and marriage simply says, "No."

Victor

Question: How do you answer the argument that homosexual marriage will not affect or threaten the traditional institution of marriage, having no designs on interfering with such unions between one man and one woman?

Reply: First of all, I would simply quote journalist Masha Gessen, a radical homosexual activist in an interview readily seen on YouTube. As the ultimate goal of the women's liberation movement seems to be the eradication of the difference between men and women, that of the Gay Agenda is the eradication of marriage altogether. Notice her words from the YouTube video, *Gay Marriage is a Lie: Destruction of Marriage, Masha Gessen*:

> Fighting for gay marriage generally involves lying about what we're going to do with marriage when we get there. The institution of marriage should not exist ... We lie that the institution of marriage is not going to change. That is a lie. [What we want] is not compatible with the institution of marriage.

Beyond this revelation, a legalization and acceptance by society of homosexual marriage is in essence a redefining of the marriage institution as God created it in the beginning in Eden. It is a further attempt to exalt the mind and will of man over the mind and will of man's Creator. It is a promotion of self-determination over moral accountability. This is a most certain violation of the first commandment as well as open defiance against and rejection of the seventh commandment.

The redefining of marriage will lead to a redefining of our culture and, if consistent, a redefining of any other (if not every other) point of God's moral law of Ten Commandments. The end result upon society in general will be a further deterioration of family values, defiance against authority, rebellion against God, and anarchy.

Will this have a negative effect on traditional marriage and family? Absolutely! It is an uprooting of God's protective hedge with the idea of relocating the parameters God has established for the protection of our families. And once uprooted, by what authority do we determine where to relocate that protective hedge? Where are the new boundaries, the new moral parameters, to be placed? Once homosexual marriage is established as an acceptable alternative lifestyle, how do we say "No" to polygamy, to incest, to pedophilia, or to bestiality? How much more difficult will it be to convincingly answer the inevitable questions of our children about the facts of life and to guide them in the ways of righteousness with this new "morality" foisted upon their tender and impressionable psyches?

A legalization and acceptance of a moral evil, homosexual marriage, will expand an already confused social environment for our children and youth, pitting society against Christian families, placing terrible temptation in the way of our youth, inciting more cause for rebellion among youth against their parents' moral values. They will tend to question why their Christian parents oppose something that is legal and accepted by society at large.

The conditioning of society, and the overt recruiting of youth to accept homosexuality as an alternative lifestyle, becomes much easier through all levels of society: government and politics, the education system, entertainment, the media, the sports world, social services, and, yes, even through the church, once gay marriage is legalized and condoned.

Follow-up Question: But what about Gay Rights? Some argue that gays and lesbians just want the same rights as other people living in a de facto relationship, such rights as health coverage, acceptance as families, next of kin rights, and so forth.

Further Reply: All choices, by definition, are a process of elimination of other options. All choices have results and consequences. However, like sinners in general, homosexual activists want choice without elimination and without consequences. They are not satisfied with society's tolerance; they want acceptance. They want protection. They want the special privileges of a minority status. They will not be satisfied until their perversion is celebrated and promoted. There seemingly is no end to their desires and demands. Why?

The roots of homosexuality, like those of all other sins, are pride, selfishness, and covetousness. These are the three sins that are especially offensive to God; they are the three sins that made a devil out of the covering cherub Lucifer, and the three sins that can never be satisfied.

All choices require submission to certain parameters and a giving up of certain other rights. This applies to most aspects of life: selecting a vehicle, ordering a meal, choosing a major in education, choosing a career, getting licensed, getting married, having children, and becoming a Christian. All of these choices require discipline and self-denial, and selection to the exclusion of many other fine options.

Choosing the homosexual lifestyle also automatically results in the exclusion of other rights and privileges. Choosing sin over obedience is choosing the wages of sin over the gift of God.

> No man can serve two masters: for either he will hate the one, and love the other; or else he will hold to the one, and despise the other. Ye cannot serve God and mammon. (Matthew 6:24)

Becoming a true Christian results in a life of self-discipline, self-sacrifice, self-denial, and self*less*-ness. It is a rejection of the wages of sin, and a joyful acceptance of the gift of God, which is eternal life!

In light of eternal realities, may we choose to follow the example of Moses who, by faith:

> When he was come to years, refused to be called the son of Pharaoh's daughter; Choosing rather to suffer affliction with the people of God, than to enjoy the pleasures of sin for a season; Esteeming the reproach of Christ greater riches than the treasures in Egypt: for he had respect unto the recompense of the reward. (Hebrews 11:24–26)

Victor

Question: I just received the following e-mail from my gay son. How can I handle this foursome making a baby? Help! I know I have to hold on to God, and I am, but there are so many practical things. I don't have a clue!

Dear Dad and Mom,

I have some news that is rather important, and, considering the subject matter, I have put a lot of thought into how I was going to share it with you. For about two years D____ and I have talked about having children, how many we wanted, who would be the biological father, or should we adopt, etc.

Two months ago a lesbian couple that we have been friends with for about a year approached us and asked if we would have a child with them. B___ comes from a similar background to mine. She was raised a Christian and wanted me to be the father to help co-parent because I would have similar values. The four of us carefully considered everything and decided to go ahead and try and put the rest in God's hands.

I am ecstatic to spread the news. In approximately eight and a half months you will be grandparents, God willing, and nothing happens during pregnancy. I know this is huge news that will evoke a strong opinion. However, this is something that we have put a lot of thought into, and we are very happy to be moving forward with this dream or ours. We both hope and pray you will share in our excitement.

Love,
S & D

Reply: I know your heart is breaking for your son and his present choices. It is cases like this that help us to understand how we ourselves have caused our heavenly Father so much grief over the years. God Himself must stand back and let us make our choices and suffer the consequences when we do not seek His guidance, approval, and confirmation.

So, perhaps it is best to deal with this situation with your son in the same way that God has to deal with him, and with us, and with countless other people who are determined to do their own will and have their own way, not considering His will.

First of all, your son has not asked for your advice or consent. And as he is an adult, you are in the difficult position of not being able to give unsolicited advice and counsel. Regrettably, it seems that your role now is to love him unconditionally, pray for him without ceasing, and be there for him when he does need

STRAIT ANSWERS TO THE GAY QUESTION

you and does recognize that need. He truly is creating a nightmare scenario for himself and for his "family," but you must step back and let him make his own decisions and reap his own consequences.

As he has said, the act is already done, the baby is in the works, and now everyone is waiting, some with excitement, and some with trepidation.

So what is your role to be when the baby does come? Well, regardless of the circumstances, you are the true grandparents of this child. I would suggest that you make every effort to bond with this little one from the get-go. Why? Because the baby's circumstance is none of his or her doing. The baby will be an innocent child brought into this world, into a very confused and difficult environment.

God loves this little one, and so should you. Your influence in the young life could be a determining factor for the eternal outcome of this child. You and your husband can be the stable force in this new life. You don't want to do anything to lessen the opportunity for this little one to have eternal life. I would advise you to love this child as your own. This action on your part could also be a very positive influence upon your son. It does not indicate that you condone what he has done, only that you are willing to do your part to make the best of an unfortunate situation.

I know this must all be very difficult for you, for it is not what you were looking forward to as grandparents when you were raising your own children. But God can bless your efforts to eternal good, if you will trust in Him and lean not upon your own understanding.

Now, you have the next eight months to get yourselves ready for this. Take a deep breath (many of them, perhaps), and try to begin getting used to the whole situation. You can do this, by God's grace. And you can still be wonderful grandparents. I would strongly advise you to not miss out on this opportunity. It still falls under the principle of loving the sinner while hating the sin. Jesus was able to do it, and, therefore, so can you.

Be of good courage!

Victor

Follow-up Questions: Thank you for your support and advice in this past note. Now, I'm in need of advice again. Because of the Supreme Court decision to allow gay marriage in CA, my son and his partner are now getting married. I felt that I could not attend this "wedding" as I know that it is an abomination to God.

However, I have had two different individuals tell me that I should go to the wedding, that it is a way to show my son that I love him, and that otherwise I may close the possibility of a relationship with him in the future. I really want to do the right thing. I was really shocked that my son even wanted me there, but I really don't know what to do. Please, I would really appreciate your advice and input.

Reply: There are many ways in which you can show your son that you love him. It is very inconsiderate of him, I believe, to ask you to participate in the sanctioning of a union that he knows is in violation of your core religious, moral, social, and ethical standards. A wedding is a ceremony in which the blessing of the Lord, society, and family is sought for the union of two people. Is it appropriate to ask such a blessing upon that which the Lord has already condemned? No, I am certain it is not.

I know this must be very difficult for you. But I sincerely believe that it would be wrong to affirm this union by your presence at the ceremony. Of course you can love your son, and you can love his partner, and you can show it in many, many ways. You can socialize with them, and visit with them in their home, babysit your grandchild, etc. But I think it would be fundamentally wrong to take part in the ceremony that binds these two together as God meant for only one man and one woman.

Does this make sense to you?

What I would suggest is that you write to your son the reasons that you cannot attend, but very plainly reiterate that you love him immensely and unconditionally. That will never change. It is the ceremony that you cannot attend, for that would be a betrayal of your strongly held religious convictions of which he is very familiar, having been raised with them himself.

I know this is very difficult for you, but I do believe it is the right thing to do.

Hang in there, and be of good courage once again!

Victor

Chapter 9
"CHRISTIAN HOMOSEXUALITY"

Q **uestion:** Does God accept and love us where we are and then just leave us there?

Reply: Let us consider what it means for the homosexual to "convert" to Christianity. The definition of "convert, the verb: 1. To change into another state, form, or substance; transform. 2. To apply or adapt to a new or different purpose of use. 3. To change from one belief, doctrine, or course of action to another. 4. To cause to change in character; to turn from a sinful to a righteous life [a life of doing what is right according to the Word]" (from *Standard College Dictionary*; Harcourt, Brace & World).

I believe the Christian world at large, sadly, is guilty of "having a form of godliness, but denying the power thereof" (2 Timothy 3:5). The whole purpose of the plan of salvation is to reconcile fallen man to the will of his creator God. We really short change the omnipotence of our loving God when we teach and believe that God Himself is helpless to redirect, to reorient, to recreate, to convert (or, change) the homosexual.

After all, the Word says, "Let [or, allow] this *mind* be in you, which was also in Christ Jesus" (Philippians 2:5, emphasis added). Jesus rendered unquestioning obedience to His Father, according to the context of Philippians 2, and practiced total self-denial when tempted to deviate from God's plan for His life. So should we.

Also, "be ye *transformed* by the *renewing of your mind*, that ye may prove what is that good, and acceptable, and perfect, will of God" (Romans 12:2, emphasis added).

Recognizing there is power in the Word, we should further accept the counsel of the apostle Paul:

Casting down imaginations, and every high thing that exalteth itself against the knowledge of God, and bringing into captivity *every thought* to the obedience of Christ" (2 Corinthians 10:5, emphasis added).

In light of this admonition, I believe that "even the [homosexual's] thoughts must be brought into subjection to the will of God, and the feelings under the control of reason and religion. Our imagination was not given us to be allowed to run riot and have its own way, without any effort at restraint and discipline. If the thoughts are wrong, the feelings will be wrong; and the thoughts and feelings combined make up the moral character." (*Review and Herald*, April 21, 1885)

So as we truly accept Christ as Lord and Master, we must submit to His conversion process and go through a transformation of character under the influence of the Holy Spirit. That transformation of character will not only be a *change* of behavior, but it must also include a transformation of even our thoughts and feelings.

Here, however, we must differentiate between "temptation" and "sin." Implanted, or spontaneous thoughts may be temptation, but not sin. Lingering thoughts or meditating thoughts become lust, which is sin. Notice this text: "But I say unto you, That whosoever looketh on a woman [or a man] to lust after her [him] hath committed adultery with her [him] already in his heart" (Matthew 5:28).

But some may argue, "There's nothing I can do to change myself. God will do that in His own way and time, and He hasn't chosen to change me yet."

Does this reasoning not then leave God responsible for our continued thoughts, feelings, emotions, and actions that are not in harmony with His Word and His will? I would like to suggest that there *is* something we can do to make the change in our lives. God says in Jeremiah 3:13 to only acknowledge your sin, your need, and He will heal you.

First, we must acknowledge homosexuality to not be in harmony with God's will. (Homosexuality being: "1. The condition of being sexually attracted to persons of the same sex. 2. Sexual relations between those of the same sex" *Standard College Dictionary*; Harcourt, Brace & World)

Isn't knowing this really the cause of the homosexual's mental anguish and struggle, even though he may be living a celibate life? If he didn't feel before God that something was wrong with his thoughts, feelings, and emotions, then why would he not be comfortable with them, both in private and in public?

After acknowledging the sinfulness of homosexuality, then he can choose to allow Jesus to be Lord and Master. This means trusting and obeying Him with a complete surrender of his own will, in spite of his thoughts, feelings, and emotions.

It was not until I stopped blaming God for my homosexuality, not until I stopped saying that He created me "that way," not until I recognized and acknowledged my helplessness in my struggle to be set free, not until I turned to Him with complete surrender of my will and feelings and emotions, not until then was He able to arrest me in my mad career (as He did Saul of Tarsus on the road to Damascus) and take me by the hand, leading me to victory over my addictive sin of homosexuality, which includes thoughts, feelings, and emotions, as well as behavior.

"All power is given unto me in heaven and earth," Jesus says. Believing this, "Go … and teach all nations … teaching them to observe all things whatsoever I have commanded you." And, never forget! Jesus says, "I am with you always, even unto the end of the world" (Taken from Matthew 28:18–20).

"According to your faith be it unto you" (Matthew 9:29).

Jesus is limited only by our lack of faith. But our faith increases by hearing and studying His word, His promises.

In my own experience, my thoughts, feelings, and emotions did not change overnight. They began to change as I decided to trust Him and obey Him in spite of my gay feelings and emotions. I terminated my gay behavior and closed all possible doors to that area of my life and practiced guarding well these avenues to my soul. This included what I read, looked at, watched, listened to, and whom I associated with.

I then attempted to fill my life with everything I could that was in harmony with His will. "Of these ye may freely eat," He says, "But, these things, for your own well-being are off limits." I simply try to accept that and to not even consider anything outside of His will as an option for my life any longer.

And His grace is sufficient. Let us stop shortchanging our Omnipotent Re-Creator! He longs to set us each one free—even in our thoughts, feelings, and emotions!

These are just a few suggestions, and not meant to be comprehensive at all. But we do have our part to play, mainly to surrender the will and make the right choices. He then can work in us to will and to do what is right.

Through the right exercise of the will, an entire change may be made in your life. By yielding up your will to Christ, you link up with all the power in heaven and earth, and you will have strength from above to succeed. Through constant surrender to God you will be enabled to live the new life, the life of faith. (See *Steps to Christ*, p. 48.)

Question: Though I have totally given my heart to Jesus, I have attractions to the same sex and find myself being with other men. I really don't understand it. What does this mean about my relationship with Christ?

Reply: Regarding your relationship with Jesus, I can only say that I do not know your heart, and neither do you, according to Jeremiah 17:9, 10. But Jesus does, and He loves you unconditionally. You are His child, even though you are struggling. What would we think of a parent who would terminate his relationship with his child because of a struggle with habitual sin? Jesus loves you more than your parents could ever think to. Just look at the cross and you will see, though not comprehend, His infinite love and compassion for you.

However, those who consecrate their all to God will not be left unmolested by the enemy of souls. Satan will come to you with his specious temptations, designed to lure you from your loyalty to God. He will present to you his bribe, as he did to Christ in the wilderness of temptation, saying, "All these things will I give thee, if thou wilt fall down and worship me" (Matt. 4:9). Of course, you don't have to fall on your face before Satan to end up worshipping him. All you need to do is let go of Christ, and you are automatically under the supervision of Satan.

But what should your answer be to all the temptations of the evil one? You should say, "I will not lend my influence in any way to the advancement of anything except the cause of Christ. *I am not my own; I have been bought with a price. I am not to live to please myself; for I have been purchased, ransomed by the blood of Christ. It is not possible for me to give to Christ more than that which belongs to Him; for every moment of my life belongs to Him. I am His possession, a servant employed to do the will of my Master."*

This is the only position that is safe for you to occupy when struggling with this or any other habitual sin, and if you will feel this way, what a power you will exert to draw and win other struggling souls to Christ.

Question: Can a homosexual be a Christian? Can there truly be such a thing as Christian homosexuality or homosexual Christianity?

Response: Around the world today, there are thousands of homosexuals who are members of Christian churches who love the Lord and who practice many of the tenets of Christianity. Perhaps they are living up to all the light they presently have and they sincerely want to follow Jesus. But if they will truly look to Him, they will inevitably be changed. For by beholding Him we do become changed into His likeness.

However, and I say this kindly toward the gay community, practicing homosexuality is, in essence, a rejection of Jesus Christ as Lord and Master. Many gays profess Christ. They do "believe." After all, the Bible says only believe in the Lord Jesus Christ, and thou shalt be saved. So the gay "Christian," or the "Christian gay," may attempt to practice religion and perversion side by side. But, as *Lord* and *Master*, Jesus says: "Not every one that saith unto me, Lord, Lord, shall enter into the kingdom of heaven; but he that *doeth* the will of my Father which is in heaven." (Matt. 7:21–23) The apostle James concurs, "Thou believest that there is one God; thou doest well: *the devils also believe*, and tremble. But wilt thou know, O vain man, that *faith without works is dead*?" (James 2:19, 20). Apparently belief without a corresponding lifestyle change is a dead belief that amounts to deception!

There really can be no such thing as "Christian homosexuality," for the same reason that there can be no such thing as Christian adultery, Christian murder, Christian drunkenness, Christian drug addiction, Christian lying, Christian rock 'n' roll, or Christian idolatry, ad infinitum. Attaching the label "Christian" to one's belief, practice, or perversion does not make it so. The word "Christian" connotes discipleship, following after, in belief *and* practice.

A good test of what is Christian would be asking, "Is there any indication in God's Word that Jesus condones or would participate in this belief, behavior, or practice?" As the popular saying goes, "What would Jesus do?"

By beholding Him you will become changed into His likeness … You may have a theoretical knowledge of the truth, but this will not save you. You must know by experience how sinful sin is and how much you need Jesus as a personal Saviour. Only thus can you become sons and daughters of God. Your only merit is your great need. (*Medical Ministry*, 217).

In light of all this, many "Christian homosexuals" will still want to insist that they are just as much saved by grace as any other Christian. But grace, according to the Greek dictionary, is "the divine influence upon the heart, and its reflection in the life." It is the divine power that facilitates *change*.

Paul warns us in 2 Thessalonians 2:10–12 about those who are deceived in their unrighteousness and thus led to perish:

Because they received not the **love** *of the truth*, that they might be saved. And for this cause God shall send them strong delusion, that they should believe a lie: That they all might be damned who believed not the truth, but had pleasure in unrighteousness. (Emphasis added.)

Again in his letter to the Romans he stated:

Wherefore God also gave them up to uncleanness through the lusts of their own hearts, to dishonour their own bodies between themselves: Who changed the truth of God into a lie, and *worshipped and served the creature more than the Creator*, who is blessed for ever. Amen. For this cause God gave them up unto vile affections: for even their women did change the natural use into that which is against nature: And likewise also the men, leaving the natural use of the woman, burned in their lust one toward another; men with men working that which is unseemly, and receiving in themselves that recompense of their error which was meet. *And even as they did not like to retain God in their knowledge, God gave them over to a reprobate mind*, to do those things which are not convenient. (Romans 1:24–28, emphasis added.)

In essence, once the homosexual comes to know Christ, he is faced with a decision, a choice. Will he serve the Creator—trust and obey Him? Or, will he worship the created, and continue in his life of servitude, in bondage to sin and Satan—Satan being the perverter of all that God created to be holy?

The "Christian homosexual," if truly Christian, will submit himself to the divine reconditioning, therapy, reprogramming, and re-creation process of the Creator who loves him unconditionally.

Remember:

The Lord is not slack concerning his promise, as some men count slackness; but is longsuffering to us-ward, not willing that any should perish, but that all should come to repentance. (2 Peter 3:9)

Truly, "God is love" (1 John 4:8).

———————————

Question: What do you think of the "gay church" that actually approves of the gay lifestyle?

Reply: Any gay church that presumes to think that God can accept their worship and their lifestyle of open sin and rebellion is only deceiving itself and its members, basically claiming "peace and safety" when sudden destruction is upon them (see 1 Thessalonians 5:3). It is a religion based upon presumption rather than faith that will most certainly end in woe, despair, and destruction.

Upon what do I base my strong stance?

Not every one that saith unto me, Lord, Lord, shall enter into the kingdom of heaven; but he that *doeth the will of my father* which is in heaven. Many will say to me in that day, Lord, Lord, have we not prophesied [taught] in thy name? and in thy name have cast out devils? and in thy name done many wonderful works? And then will I profess unto them, I never knew you: depart from me, *ye that work iniquity*. (Matthew 7:21–23, emphasis added.)

True religion is more than a demonstration of love and acceptance. True religion results in contrition, remorse, repentance, conversion, old things passing away and all things becoming new. The old ways, the hereditary tendencies, the former habits, must be given up, for grace is not inherited. The new birth consists of having new motives, new tastes, and new tendencies. A genuine conversion changes hereditary and cultivated tendencies to wrong. (See 2 Corinthians 5:17.)

Any church that is approving of the gay lifestyle has totally lost its vision and sense of commission. We are to take this gospel of the kingdom into "all the world for a witness unto all nations; and then shall the end come" (Matthew 24:14).

What gospel? In a nutshell, "Thou shalt call His name JESUS: for He shall save his people from their sins" (Matthew 1:21).

What is sin? "Sin is the transgression of the law" (1 John 3:4).

A witness to all nations of what? Though "all have sinned and come short of the glory of God," He is "not willing that any should perish, but that all should come to repentance," because "the wages of sin is death, but the gift of God is eternal life through Jesus Christ our Lord." "For God so loved the world that He gave His only begotten Son that whosoever believeth in Him should not perish but have everlasting life" (Romans 3:23; 2 Peter 3:9; Romans 6:23; John 3:16).

Bottom line: if we are not, as a church, preaching that our God is mighty to save, the "whosoevers," from "whatsoever," even "to the uttermost," then we have lost our vision and failed in our commission. Our purpose for existence as an influence for good in the world, preparing a people to meet their God, has lapsed into being nothing more than a spiritual social club, pacifying its members, indeed, anesthetizing them in their lost condition until the coming of the Lord, at which time it will be too late to correct!

May God have mercy upon His sleeping church!

Victor

Question: How do we as a church relate to those identifying themselves as gay Christians but not living the gay lifestyle?

Reply: In short, we are to love them unconditionally; pray for them without ceasing; welcome them into our places of worship as souls needing salvation *from* sin, just like anyone else; accept them into the school of discipleship on condition of their willingness to be transformed into the image of Christ, as with all sinners (Romans 12:2). However, baptism and membership should be reserved for those who are willing to "bring forth fruits meet for repentance" (Matthew 3:8).

"Fruits meet for repentance," according to the dictionary, means, "to respond to a situation with a particular type of behavior." The Bible calls for acceptable fruit, suitable fruit, demonstrating transformation of character and lifestyle. The church and the world need to *see* a change of course in one's life before bringing that person into church membership with voting rights and eligibility to hold church office.

If a person wants to identify as a "gay Christian," then where is the evidence of discipleship, and a willingness to accept reproof, correction, and instruction from the Scriptures as found in 2 Timothy 3:16, 17? If a person identifies as a "gay Christian" not practicing the gay lifestyle, then why identify as gay?

Actually, the term "gay Christian" is an oxymoron. It makes no more sense than the adding of any other prefix or qualifier to the name Christian such as incestuous, polygamist, sex offender, pedophile, drug addict, alcoholic, smoker, kleptomaniac, liar, ad infinitum.

Another question: what is wrong with a Gay couple living together though not practicing the gay behavior, or lifestyle?

Reply: To answer a question with a question, a method often practiced by our Savior: Would the church accept into membership an unmarried heterosexual couple continuing to live together after "conversion"? Or, would the church expect them to separate until marriage …? What is the difference …?

Besides, the gay lifestyle involves much more than sexual intimacy. Gay couples do not usually have sexual intimacy openly, but privately like heterosexual couples. It is not the cessation of sexual intimacy that *demonstrates* conversion from the gay lifestyle. It is all that goes along with identifying as a couple openly: shared housing, close companionship, shared banking, a shared life, etc.

Obviously, there is much more to a marriage than sexual intimacy. In marriage, two become one in the eyes of the Lord, in the eyes of the community, and of the church. They are bonded. They share life with all its ups and downs, ins and outs, finances, and possessions. They commit to loving and cherishing each other through good times and bad, in sickness and in health, till death do them part. In Bible terms, they "cleave one to another." Sexual intimacy is only a very small factor in the bonding together of two souls. Many married couples, due to a multitude of factors, end up forgoing sexual intimacy within their marriage. That does not necessarily break their bond, their oneness, their commitment to one another for life.

If two want to identify as "still gay," this means that they want to continue identifying with their bondage, with their sin, rather than to take on the identity afforded them through Jesus Christ as "free indeed" (John 8:36), a new creature, with old things passing away and all things new. Again, "The new birth consists of new motives, new tastes, and new tendencies" And "A genuine conversion changes both hereditary and cultivated tendencies to wrong." (2 Corinthians 5:17, and *Seventh-day Adventist Bible Commentary*, vol. 6, 1101)

Having come out of the gay lifestyle myself 20 years ago, these are issues that I, too, had to wrestle with. I wanted my Christian experience to be genuine and not an exercise in futility. I wanted salvation *from* my life and lifestyle of sin, for I was sin-sick with a hatred for my life of sin. (See Genesis 3:15.) I had to acknowledge that homosexuality is a sin issue, and therefore turn away from it, never more to identify with it. God says in Jeremiah 3, "Only acknowledge thine iniquity… and I will heal your backsliding" (Jeremiah 3:13, 22). Identifying as a "gay Christian" reminds me of Lot's wife looking back upon all that she had to leave behind. She was still attached.

I hope and pray that these thoughts are helpful to you as you are faced with this challenge in your churches. Remember, we are, in a loving and caring way, to call sin by its right name, and also to "Cry aloud, spare not, lift up [our] voice[s] like a trumpet, and show my people [says God] their transgression, and the house of Jacob their sins" (Isaiah 58:1).

This is all a part of the redemption process.

Christian Homosexuality: Perverting the Gospel of Christ

Question: Are the "pro-gay gospel" and the "Christian gospel" one and the same?

Reply: I recently received a surprising letter from someone representing a well-known Christian music ministry challenging my understanding of the gospel. Several members of this group are openly practicing homosexuals. The letter was very revealing regarding what I see as an unfortunate interpretation and understanding of the gospel, especially as it relates to the homosexual issue. For the benefit of a general audience I have elected to address our differences publicly, though without revealing the identity of the person or music ministry. It is important that the Word be presented in its strength and purity in harmony with itself, rather than in contradiction with itself. After all, what is at stake is the eternal life of sinners in need of a Savior *from* their sins (see Matthew 1:21).

Excerpts from the letter (Emphasis mine as to points to be addressed):

> Ron,
> All of us in [this ministry] are fully committed to spreading **the gospel of Jesus Christ** to all who come to hear us and we have ample evidence over the past 31 years that God has used us in mighty ways... I would ask that you read John 8:3–11 and see if you don't find yourself in this scenario. **We are all sinful human beings...** [and] should be rejoicing in the fact that **God is using us in various ways to bring others to a closer walk with Him.** You have **your ministry, the premise of which I wholeheartedly disagree with (and which has been proven time and time again not to work)**, but I don't try to undermine your efforts. ...**Let us work together** to finish spreading **the Good News** to the whole world so that Jesus can come again and take His children home!
>
> Your Brother in Christ, _____

My response to the letter:

> Hello, Friend,
> You speak of spreading the *"gospel of Jesus Christ."* I would simply ask, "What is the gospel of Jesus Christ?" To me it is stated plainly and simply by the angel Gabriel himself in Matthew 1:21, "Thou shalt call his name JESUS, for he shall save his people from their sins." *From* their sins, not *in* their sins and sin being the transgression of the law. From a biblical standpoint, it is very clear to me that homosexuality is a sin issue, transgressing the seventh commandment of the law, and I don't need to share with you all the texts with which you are already familiar. In Jeremiah 3,

God says, "Only acknowledge thine iniquity ... and I will heal your back-sliding." My method of overcoming homosexuality over 20 years ago was in acknowledging that I was dealing with a sin (iniquity) issue, and then applying God's biblical remedy for sin. It works! It really works!

You referred me to John 8:3-11, the story of Mary being brought to Jesus under the accusation of committing adultery. In verse 11, Jesus says to Mary, "Neither do I condemn thee... " Apparently you wish to end the narrative at that compassionate statement. But we must be true to the story and realize that it was in even greater compassion that Jesus went on to say, "go, and sin no more." "Stop breaking the seventh commandment," Jesus was saying to Mary. And she did. She stopped committing adultery.

With Jesus' bidding was His grace, His divine, enabling, transforming power. And by faith Mary grasped it and became an overcomer. It's the same thing I teach in my ministry. I do not condemn the homosexual, but I do encourage him or her to "go, and sin no more." And, by God's grace, this is working very well for the people with whom I work. I simply point them to the power in the Word, "It is written," which is the same method Jesus used.

You went on to state that "we are all sinful human beings." I must agree with you. However, we are not expected by our Savior *from* sin to *choose* to continue living *in* sin. By so choosing, are we not denying Him the joy of setting us "free indeed?" Jesus Himself stated that "If the Son therefore shall make you free, ye shall be free indeed" (John 8:36). Your statement that "we are all sinful human beings" reminds me of the frequently used excuse and rationale that people make to justify sinful behavior when they say, "Well, after all, I'm only human." It is important for the Christian to realize that to make such a statement is to actually, though perhaps unintentionally, deny Jesus Christ!

The apostle Peter stated that we are given:

... exceeding great and precious promises: that by these ye might be *partakers of the divine nature, having escaped the corruption that is in the world through lust.* (2 Peter 1:2–4, emphasis added.)

You see, our divine Savior became a partaker of our humanity that we might be partakers of His divinity. "Forasmuch then as the children are partakers of flesh and blood, he also himself likewise took part of the same" (Hebrews 2:14). As Jesus was divine and partaking of humanity, so the Christian is to be human and partaking of divinity. The true

Christian is *not* only human, "For it is God which worketh in you both to will and to do of his good pleasure" (Philippians 2:13).

This amazing truth is stated beautifully in the book *Christ's Object Lessons,* page 333: "As the will of man co-operates with the will of God, it

[the will of man] becomes omnipotent. Whatever is to be done at His command may be accomplished in His strength. All His biddings are enablings."

You also referred to "*a closer walk with Him.*" Enoch had that closer walk with Jesus, and it led to victory over sin, overcoming sin. He stopped sinning and attained perfection of character through his close walk with Jesus. By beholding Him we, too, become changed. We become like Him. The Bible is filled with promises to the overcomer, the overcomer of self, Satan, and sin.

You disagree with "the premise of [my] ministry" and say it has been proven to not work. So I must ask, "Where's the proof?" Your statement suggests that Jesus is *impotent* rather than *omnipotent,* that His promises are not dependable, that the wages of sin is *not* death, that we cannot expect to be "new creatures" in Christ our Re-Creator, with new motives, new tastes, and new tendencies.

Several people of our same background along with me have formed a cooperative effort called "Coming Out" Ministries. We all testify to the power of God to transform the life, and I am witnessing some marvelous transformations in people with whom I am working. I've also come across a good number of people outside of my influence who have successfully overcome the gay lifestyle and are now living in harmony with biblical principles. I'm not the only ex-gay who is now happily married and parenting children. So I cannot accept your premise that my biblical approach to overcoming sin does not work! That is the false theology of the accuser of the brethren whom we are to overcome by the blood of the Lamb, and by the word of our testimony (see Revelation 12:11).

The big question in my mind is, "What is the word of my testimony?" That God is *powerless* to save me from sin? Or that He is *mighty* to save the whosoevers, from whatsoever, even to the uttermost? I truly believe that our testimony is to be one of victory over sin, even the sin of homosexuality, by the grace of God—by His divine, omnipotent, transforming power.

You asked that we work together to share the *good news.* So I must ask, "What is the good news?" Salvation *in* sin, or salvation *from* sin? Can two walk together, or work together, except they be agreed? (Amos 3:3).

Let us heed the warning of the apostle Paul found in Galatians 1:6–9,

I marvel that ye are so soon removed from him that called you into the grace of Christ unto *another gospel*: [The Greek definition for grace is "the divine influence upon the heart, and its reflection in the life," i.e., divine, omnipotent, transforming power.] Which is not another; but there be some that trouble you, and would *pervert the gospel of Christ*. But though we, or an angel from heaven, preach any other gospel unto you than that which we have preached unto you, let him be accursed. As we said before, so say I now again, If any man preach *any other gospel* unto you than that ye have received, let him be accursed.

Please, my friend, think on these things! There can be only one true gospel—resulting in salvation *from* sin.

Victor

Question: I am a bisexual Christian. What advice do you have for me?

Reply: First of all, we need to look at the true meaning of the label Christian. Attaching the word carelessly to a behavior quite often results in an oxymoron, a figure of speech that combines contradictory terms. For example, Christian adultery is a contradictory label within itself, as is Christian pornography, Christian pedophilia, Christian alcoholic, Christian druggie, ad infinitum. We might as well just endorse or sanction the term Christian sin. These oxymorons are not in common use, to my knowledge. However, many homosexuals do like to refer to themselves as gay Christians.

Is this not an oxymoron? Is such a label honest and credible, or even plausible? We should take an honest look at the definition and meaning of the word Christian: a person who adheres to the teachings and example of the life of Christ. A Christian is a disciple of Christ. A disciple is one who adheres to the discipline of "the Master." Therefore, attaching the label Christian to teachings and behavior that Jesus Christ the Master condemns results in a combination of contradictory terms, or an oxymoron.

A genuine Christian cannot be a homosexual, a bisexual, an adulterer, or practice any number of other lifestyles that blatantly contradict the life and teachings of Jesus Christ. Bisexual behavior involves homosexual behavior, which, along with adultery in general, is one of a number of sinful practices that God condemns in the Bible as abominations.

So, what advice do I have for the bisexual who wants to be a Christian? The bisexual actually has a real advantage over the homosexual in this matter, for a

STRAIT ANSWERS TO THE GAY QUESTION

person who claims to be bisexual is comfortable being sexually intimate with either gender. In a sense, that is really a positive factor.

We can look at it in this way: a heterosexual Christian has an unlimited number of possibilities in choosing a life partner, as long as the choice involves one of the opposite gender. Nevertheless, he must go through a process of elimination to come up with the "one and only." Does this person fall into the category in which God can add His blessing? Is this person also a Christian? Do they both share the same rule of faith and practice? Are they mutually attracted to one another? Do they share interests and have significant things in common? Are they socially and culturally compatible? Can they agree upon a locality in which to live? Eventually, the process of elimination results in the "one and only." And they hope to live happily ever after.

The "bisexual Christian" also has a virtually unlimited number of possibilities for choosing a lifetime companion: Does this person fall into the category in which God can add His blessing? Half of the possibilities can be eliminated based upon gender alone. But that's all right. If truly bisexual, then the opposite gender is still within play, and the process of elimination continues. Is this person also a Christian? Do they both share the same rule of faith and practice? Are they mutually attracted to one another? Do they share interests and have significant things in common? Are they socially and culturally compatible? Can they agree upon a locality in which to live? Eventually, this process of elimination also results in the "one and only." And they also hope to live happily ever after.

You see? If you are Christian and believe yourself to be bisexual, then God has a great solution for you. His gift to man is one woman, in marriage. Any sexual activity outside of this marriage is displeasing to Him and not in harmony with being a Christian. So if you are bisexual, and if God's plan allows for only one person as a life partner, then why not choose within the opposite gender of which He approves and can add His blessing? Does that not make sense? If you can go either way, or both ways, then why not choose God's way, His only way? The heterosexual Christian must choose and select down to one and only one person. So why should the bisexual person get a special allowance to choose one of each? Would that not be polygamy? But I digress.

In Isaiah 1:18, God Himself says, "Come now, and let us reason together." He is reasonable. His way makes sense. It is consistent and fair. He designed human sexuality to be a gift to the children He loves. And as the Creator and designer of this gift, it is only logical to acknowledge that His way is best. It is Satan who has perverted this gift in an effort to destroy the home and family and to bring to an end the gift of procreation that perpetuates human life itself. Satan hates humanity, because he hates Jesus the Creator of humanity. Homosexuality results in bringing to an end 6,000 years of procreation, the enlarging of the family of God.

But, one questions, what about the same-sex attractions? As a bisexual, how do I deal with that?

Regarding the same-sex attractions, God again has given the remedy. He says that "whosoever looketh on a woman [or man] to lust after her [him] hath committed adultery with her [him] already in his heart" (Matthew 5:28). In this question, the heterosexual Christian and the "bisexual Christian" have the same challenge: to not lust after anyone other than one's spouse. The straight guy has to take control of lustful thoughts toward women, and the bisexual guy has to take control of lustful thoughts toward men. Both straights and bisexuals have equal struggles in this area. So as Christians we are to put into practice the counsel of 2 Corinthians 10:5, "bringing into captivity every thought to the obedience of Christ."

Satan will place tempting thoughts into your mind, but you are to practice rejecting those thoughts and choosing better ones. "Submit [yourself daily] therefore to God. Resist the devil, and he will flee from you" (James 4:7). Avoid tempting situations such as are found in movies, magazines, online pornography, and the wrong kinds of friends and associations who would lead you down the path of homosexuality. In other words, you need to starve that side of yourself which is displeasing to the Lord and feed the Christian side of yourself. Attend church and prayer meetings, have your daily morning and evening devotions with Him, spend time in the Bible and in prayer. Surround yourself with good Christian friends and influences. Choose to hang this homosexual thing on the "forbidden tree" as in the Garden of Eden. Consider it to be forbidden fruit, no matter how pleasing to the eye, to the touch, to the taste, to the smell; realize that it is forbidden by your Creator God who truly knows what is best for you and your life. Learn to not trust your feelings and emotions—they are rarely a trustworthy guide to what is best for you.

So in conclusion, to the "bisexual Christian" I would have to say, if you truly want to be a Christian, then let Christ truly be your Lord and Master. Enter into His school of discipleship. "Let this mind be in you, which was also in Christ Jesus" (Philippians 2:5). "Present your bodies a living sacrifice, holy, acceptable unto God, which is your *reasonable* service" (Romans 12:1, emphasis added). As a Christian, be a disciple of Christ. Enter into His discipline. Trust Him, and obey Him. Your heavenly Father truly knows what is best for you, for your joy and happiness and fulfillment in this life, as well as in the life to come.

Chapter 10

THE BIBLE AND THE HOMOSEXUAL ISSUE

Question: Where does the Bible say that gay love is a sin? And what did Jesus say about it?

Reply: The Bible is very clear on this issue, so that we can choose to live within the parameters for our own well-being without any confusion.

First of all, we must establish what sin is. The definition of sin is found in 1 John 3:4, "Whosoever committeth sin transgresseth also the law: for *sin is the transgression of the law.*" Sin is simply defined as disobedience, disobedience to the law of God, the breaking of any one of His Ten Commandments.

1 John 1:9 tells us that "If we confess our sins, he is faithful and just to forgive us our sins, and to cleanse us from all unrighteousness."

The big question is this, is homosexuality sin? Is it wrong? Does the Bible say so? If it is sin, and you confess it to be your sin, then, according to the above text, you can be forgiven—and not only forgiven, but cleansed from it.

When we reclassify homosexuality, however, from the category of sin to that of an acceptable alternative lifestyle, then God Himself can do nothing for us. He sent His only begotten Son to save His people from their sins, not from something acceptable, not from some minority status, not from their sexual preferences, not from some genetic or psychological disorder, but from their sins.

Next, we must acknowledge that "All scripture is given by inspiration of God, and is profitable for doctrine, for reproof, for correction, for instruction in righteousness [right doing, right behavior]," according to 2 Timothy 3:16.

Furthermore, "If you love me," Jesus says, "keep my commandments" (John 14:15). One of those commandments is, "Thou shalt not commit adultery" (Exodus 20:14).

Adultery defined: The voluntary sexual intercourse of a married person with someone not the spouse; unfaithfulness; also, any lewd or unchaste act or thought. Scripturally (Matthew 5:27, 28), adultery also includes incest, prostitution, and fornication, which is voluntary sexual intercourse of an unmarried person with another unmarried person or married person of the opposite sex.[26]

God further commands His people on this subject, "Thou shalt not lie with mankind, as with womankind: it is abomination." "If a man also lie with mankind, as he lieth with a woman, both of them have committed an abomination" (Leviticus 18:22; 20:13).

These are the words of Jesus Himself found in the Old Testament. Adultery clearly is any sexual behavior or practice outside of marriage as God created it to

---

26 *Funk & Wagnalls Standard College Dictionary*

be. Gay love falls in this category, and to disobey the clear will and command of God is sin.

Romans 1:24–28 is a very plain text on this subject:

Wherefore God also gave them up to uncleanness through the lusts of their own hearts, to dishonour their own bodies between themselves: Who changed the truth of God into a lie ... For this cause God gave them up unto vile affections: for even their women did change the natural use [the natural sexual intercourse] into that which is against nature: And likewise also the men, leaving the natural use [or intercourse] of the woman, burned in their lust one toward another; men with men working that which is unseemly... And even as they did not like to retain God in their knowledge, God gave them over to a reprobate mind.

These are the principles of Jesus as spoken through His prophet and apostle Paul. You see, God cannot and will not interfere with the power of choice He has given each one of us. But if we choose to follow Him, even against our feelings, tendencies, and emotions, then He supplies His divine power (grace) to overcome our temptations and our sins, even the sin of homosexuality.

Jesus also says through His apostle Paul:

Know ye not that the unrighteous shall not inherit the kingdom of God? Be not deceived: neither fornicators ... nor adulterers, nor effeminate (sodomites), nor abusers of themselves with mankind (homosexuals) ... shall inherit the kingdom of God. (1 Corinthians 6:9, 10)

But, don't miss the promise that immediately follows:

And such *were* some of you: but ye *are* washed, but ye *are* sanctified, but ye *are* justified in the name of the Lord Jesus, and by the Spirit of our God." (1 Corinthians 6:11, emphasis added.)

There are so many great promises in the Bible assuring you that you can be made whole, that you can be everything God created you to be, that you can have a life of joy, peace, happiness, and fulfillment in harmony with His will. (See "A Rainbow of Promises" in the final chapter.)

Follow up questions: I've looked at these verses and none mention gay love as a sin at all, and nothing you sent me says what Jesus said on the subject.

I looked at Leviticus, for one, and it is a dead law anyway, we cannot apply Levitical law to the twenty-first century. After all, that would mean we can murder children who curse parents, or women who sleep with a man not their husband. However, I also looked up what abomination was in Hebrew and got *to'ebah,* which actually means idolatry, not abomination at all. So the sin was gay sex acts used in idol worship in Egypt and Canaan. Then I looked up 1 Corinthians 6:9–11, and effeminate, *malokos*, actually means soft, as in weak in faith, so nothing to do with gay people at all, and *arsenokoti* (abusers of themselves with mankind) is a two-part word, men or man and couch, or to lie with, as in a male temple prostitute who had gay sex. So again nothing to do with gay love here, either.

So then I checked out Romans, the biggest text on the subject and it says nothing on gay love either; in fact, it uses the phrase that they burned with lust. And all lust, be it hetero, homo, or whatever, is wrong. And it is all about heterosexuals in idolatry, as in Levitical laws, who had gay sex. If you read the text it seems clear. So what am I missing? And why are there no laws for gay women in any part of the Old Testament? And again, what did Jesus say on this? I can't find any comment.

I do believe the whole Bible is God's Word, and I believe it is all God-breathed. However, I also believe we can abuse the Word of God to make it mean what we want it to mean, so I've heard people use God's Bible to justify homophobia, sexism, abuse of animals and even racism. So what if the Bible is fine where gay people are concerned as I'm starting to see? After all, none of the texts you gave me mention gay love as a sin. Perhaps you have more texts to show me? I'd love to learn more, but so far I've not seen anything that says two men or two women in love is a sin. So what have I missed?

Reply to follow-up Questions: For 16 years I lived the gay life, up to the hilt. I used a lot of the same rationale then that you are using now in your questions and arguments for gay love and gay life, primarily because I really didn't want to change my behavior. I wanted to be free to be who and what I was in my carnal nature. But you know, I never had *assurance* of salvation. I never had *assurance* of eternal life with Jesus. I *hoped* I would be saved. I *wanted* to be saved. I *hoped* God would be merciful to me a sinner while I persisted in my life of sin. But I had no assurance of the favor and blessing of God. I was ashamed of my lifestyle, and, therefore, lived a double life. If I was so assured of the rightness of my lifestyle, then I should not have been so covert in its practice.

God and I invite you today to "Come now, and let us reason together" (Isaiah 1:18). He's not going to spell out every single "word" that you want to hear. You won't find the word "gay" referring to homosexuals in the Bible at all. The word "gay" is only used in James 2:3, referring to magnificent, gorgeous clothing. You won't find the word "homosexual" in the Bible, in the King James Bible anyway. Nor will you find the word "lesbian." So if you will not accept the Word of God on a subject unless it uses the contemporary words of today that you select, you may not be able to find clarity in the Word of God on many subjects. In order to find truth, you must use your God-given powers of intellect, logic, and reason coupled with the guidance He promises through the Holy Spirit.

Another principle that must be addressed before going any further is simply this. Are you sincerely and truly looking for truth, for the will of God? Or are you looking instead for justification, for loopholes, for excuses? I'm just asking you to first of all honestly question your own motives in asking these questions. The Lord said in Jeremiah 29:13, "Ye shall seek me, and find me, when ye shall search for me with all your heart." God wants you to treasure Him and His truth enough to search diligently with an open heart and mind, willing to be reproved, corrected, and instructed in right doing. (See 2 Timothy 3:16, 17.)

On the other hand, He tells us through Paul in 2 Thessalonians 2:10, 11 (emphasis added) that there are those who will:

Perish; because they received not the *love of the truth*, that they might be saved. And for this cause God shall send them strong delusion, that they should believe a lie: That they all might be damned who believed not the truth, but had *pleasure in unrighteousness.*

So you and I must daily face ourselves in our study of God's Word and ask ourselves in all honesty, "Am I searching for truth, or for justification?" "Am I willing to be changed, to be saved *from* my sins, or do I wish to be saved *in* my sins?" There's a big difference, because Jesus came to save His people *from* their sins, not *in* them, according to Matthew 1:21.

You stated that one can "abuse the word of God to make it mean what we want it to mean." I agree, and so does the Bible.

A very serious text to consider is 2 Peter 3:16 in which Peter acknowledges that in Scripture "are some things hard to be understood, which they that are unlearned and unstable wrest [or wrench, or pervert, or twist], as they do also the other scriptures, [speaking of the Old Testament which still is Scripture and applicable to our day], unto their own destruction."

At one point the disciples came to Jesus and asked, "Why speakest thou unto them in parables?" (Matthew 13:10). Jesus answered:

Because it is given unto you to know the *mysteries* of the kingdom of heaven, but to them it is not given.... [Why?] Because they seeing see not [or choose not to see]; and hearing they hear not [choose not to hear], neither do they understand [they choose not to understand]... For this people's heart is waxed gross, and their ears are dull of hearing, and their eyes they have closed; lest at anytime they should see with their eyes and hear with their ears, and should understand with their heart, and should be converted [changed], and I should heal them. But blessed are your eyes, for they see: and your ears, for they hear. (Matthew 13:11–16)

And I hope this is the case with you, that you choose to see and hear—that you truly have a love for truth and are willing to be changed and healed.

Jesus Himself watched with breaking heart as multitudes turned away from His message of salvation. Why? They were looking for salvation, not from sin, but from the Romans, from foreign occupation, over taxation, poverty, disease, the consequences of their own rebellion, apostasy, defiance, and sin. They did not have a love for truth. Instead, like every pagan who has ever lived, they served their "god" out of fear of punishment and hope of reward. They did not worship and obey the true God out of a responding love and gratitude for His providence, care, patience, mercy, forgiveness, cleansing, and creative power.

Again, before going on, let me refer you to this verse:

> All scripture is given by inspiration of God, and is profitable for doctrine, for reproof, for correction, for instruction in righteousness: That the man of God may be perfect, thoroughly furnished unto all good works. (2 Timothy 3:16, 17)

When we come to the Word of God with our questions, we should come looking for reproof, correction, and for instruction. In other words, we should search for life changing counsel and guidance and principles. If we have a genuine love for truth, God will make sure we understand His will for our lives.

You have correctly acknowledged that "the whole Bible is God's Word." The will of God is clearly manifest throughout this Word, and He says in Malachi 3:6, "I am the LORD, I change not."

You then asked, "What if the Bible is fine where gay people are concerned as I'm starting to see?" Can you give me a "for instance?" I have not seen anywhere in the Bible that indicates it is fine with God where gay people are concerned. For one thing, it never mentions gay people, gay love, lesbian relationships, or gay marriage.

You also stated, "none of the texts you gave me mention gay love as a sin," that you have "not seen anything that says two men or two women in love is a sin, so what have I missed?" You go on to say that none of the verses I shared with you "mention gay love as a sin at all."

Well, what is sin? Sin is the transgression of the law (1 John 3:4). What law?

The moral Law of God is given simply in 2 principles found confirmed by Jesus Christ in Luke 10:25-28, "Thou shalt love the Lord thy God with all thy heart, and with all thy soul, and with all thy strength, and with all they mind; and thy neighbour as thyself." This was a quote by a church lawyer referring to the still authoritative law of God found in Deuteronomy 6:5 and Leviticus 19:18. And Jesus said to him, "Thou hast answered right: this do, and thou shalt live." He did not take the opportunity to pronounce the law dead, and neither should we.

The law of God is confirmed again by Jesus more specifically to the rich young ruler in Luke 18:18–27. "Thou knowest the commandments, Do not commit adultery, Do not kill, Do not steal, Do not bear false witness, Honour thy father and thy mother" (v. 20). Jesus was quoting the Ten Commandments, not in their order, and before finishing them He was interrupted by the self-assured young man who said, "All these have I kept from my youth up" (v. 21). "I know this already," he says. "What else?"

You see, though thinking he was right in everything, he still did not have assurance of salvation. This is why he found himself inquiring of Jesus in the first place.

Jesus responded by referring him back to the two great principles saying, "Yet lackest thou one thing" (v. 22). He then revealed to the young man that while focusing on the letter of the law (the exact words and spelling, etc.), he had missed the great principles upon which the Ten Commandments were based: supreme love to God, and loving others equally with one's self.

The first commandment Jesus quoted to the young man, perhaps because it is the one most difficult for young men, was "Do not commit adultery." Well, how would this young man know what adultery was? He knew what was written in the law spelled out in the Old Testament, which you might like to refer to as "a dead Levitical law!" What is dead is the rights and ceremonies of the Levitical law that prophesied the birth, life, ministry, death, burial, resurrection, and priesthood of Jesus Christ, for He is the fulfillment of all those prophetic services, rituals, and ceremonies (see Colossians 2).

But there is nothing dead about His moral law of Ten Commandments (nor His health or civil laws). The time, place, and method of punishment for violation of the law of God seem to have been changed once the theocracy came to an end. But sin is still sin. God feels the same way about it today as He did in the beginning. It was so offensive to Jesus that it nearly crushed the life out of Him in Gethsemane when He was made to be sin for us, that we might be made the righteousness of God in Him (2 Corinthians 5:21). It did literally break His heart while He was upon the cross, which explains the water and blood that flowed from His side when pierced.

You stated that "abomination was, in Hebrew, *to'ebah*, which actually meant idolatry, not abomination at all. So the sin was gay sex acts used in idol worship." You seem to have taken a quantum leap here, and you almost lost me. This is not true to context and wording at all. You also are saying gay sex acts used in idol worship constitute sin. But if you are looking for the label "sin" to be attached to "gay" love, then you must notice that the labels "sin" and "gay" and "sex" are not attached anywhere in this chapter. So in all consistency, we cannot say that gay sex acts used in idol worship constitute sin, either—at least not in this context. I'm not trying to be "smart" here. I'm just suggesting that we must be honestly consistent in our use of the Scriptures.

Now, notice in Leviticus, which you refer to as a dead law, how God goes to great lengths to spell out specifically what adultery is, what violates the seventh commandment, for the likes of you and me who tend to excuse our own habitual sins. Granted, He does not use the word "adultery," but it is clear that He is saying, "Thou shalt not." Notice God's elaboration of the principle of what constitutes adultery in chapter 18: incest with father, mother, stepmother, sister, granddaughter, stepsister, aunt, uncle, daughter-in-law, sister-in-law, step-daughter, or step-granddaughter; taking another's wife; "thou shalt not lie with mankind, as with womankind: it is abomination" (v. 22); and sex with beasts. This passage is not referring to idol worship, except in the parenthetical verse 21, which refers to offering one's children as burnt offerings to the god Molech.

The word "abomination" here does come from the Hebrew "*tow ebah,*" which is defined as "something disgusting, an abhorrence: especially idolatry." In other words, especially in the case of idolatry which is especially disgusting and abhorrent.

Even if God was saying that lying with mankind as with womankind equated to idolatry (abomination), then "gay love" is doubly wrong, breaking not only the seventh commandment, but the first one as well. For idolatry is the first sin of the Ten Commandments.

Jesus said, "If ye love me, keep my commandments" (John 14:15). Does that mean that we can love Him and get away with doing something that He finds disgusting and abhorrent? That would be a real stretch, a real contradiction of logic, a real presumption on our part, don't you think?

You stated, "nothing you sent me says what Jesus said on the subject." But I think you have overlooked something. John 1:13 says:

> In the beginning was the Word, and the Word was with God, and the Word was God. The same was in the beginning with God. All things were made by him; and without him was not any thing made that was made.

Reading on down into that chapter, we see clearly that Jesus is the Word that was with God and who is God, the Creator of all things. You will see that in the New Testament He clearly sanctioned marriage between one man and one woman, but you won't see any sanction anywhere by Jesus of erotic love between two men or two women. Jesus is also the great I AM, by His own admission. It was Jesus who spoke the law from Sinai and who wrote it with His own finger. It was Jesus who spoke face to face with Moses. This is why He says, "If ye love me, keep my commandments." He is the one who both spoke them and wrote them on the two tables of stone, twice!

Back to your statement that "Leviticus for one … is a dead law anyway. We cannot apply Levitical law to the twenty-first century. After all, that means we can murder children who curse parents, or women who sleep with a man who is not their husband."

Are you suggesting that it is no longer a violation of God's moral law for children to curse their parents, or for women to sleep with men who are not their husbands? Are you suggesting that it is now okay to kill, steal, lie, worship idols, profane God's name, or disregard His Sabbath of the fourth commandment? What you are suggesting is total anarchy, isn't it?

I touched on this point earlier, but I just want to clarify a little further that it is the punishment that seems to have changed, or been delayed, since passing from a theocracy. It is not the principles of the moral law. And God "will by no means clear the guilty" (Exodus 34:7). We all face the Day of Judgment when some will be invited to enter into the joy of the Lord, while others will be cast aside to face the punishment of everlasting death (Revelation 20). As a perfectly just God, He will meet out and execute a perfectly just sentence for every unrepentant sinner. And as a perfectly merciful God, He will grant life everlasting to His repentant and changed believers, of which they are unworthy, but for which they are eternally grateful.

You referred back to the text in 1 Corinthians 6:9–11 with a partial look at the meaning of the Greek words when you stated, "*malokos* actually means soft as in weak in faith, so nothing to do with gay people at all, and *arsenokoti* is a two-part word: men or man and couch, or to lie with as in a male temple prostitute who had gay sex. So there is nothing to do with gay love here either."

I studied Greek for two years in college and aced those courses, but even today I refer to the Greek dictionary for a careful examination of words in question. So let's look again at that text:

Know ye not that the unrighteous shall not inherit the kingdom of God? Be not deceived: neither *fornicators* [Greek, *pornos*: a male prostitute, a libertine: one completely lacking in moral restraint; especially, a habitually unchaste or profligate man], nor *adulterers* [Greek, *moichos*: a male paramour: a lover, especially one who unlawfully takes the place of a husband or wife. So that refers to homosexual as well as heterosexual lovers.], nor *effeminate* [Greek, *malakos*: soft, a catamite: a boy used in sodomy, i.e., the one on the receiving end of sexual intercourse. We use the word "gay" today for homosexuals and sodomites. Perhaps they used the word "soft" back then for the same thing.], nor *abusers of themselves with mankind* [Greek, *arsenokoites*: a sodomite: one guilty of having unnatural sexual relations, especially between male persons or between a human being and an animal. *Strong's Concordance and Greek Dictionary; Funk and Wagnalls Standard College Dictionary*] shall enter the kingdom of God.

That's as plain as it gets to one who loves truth and is seeking for reproof, correction, and instruction. In today's language, there is nothing about the word "gay" that literally means "homosexual." Yet we use the two interchangeably. By observing the context today, we clearly know what is meant by "gay" and "queen" and "flaming queen" and "butch" and "dyke" and "bull dyke" and "girl" and "faggot," etc., though the literal meanings of all these words are far different from their usage.

Regarding your comment that there are "no laws for gay women in any part of the Old Testament," You seem to be asking for a literal word-for-word denouncement from the lips of Jesus on "gay love" in order for you to believe that it is wrong. You are looking for the letter of the law, not seeing the forest for the trees, yet you explain away Bible texts that are really quite clear on the denunciation of homosexuality.

Perhaps you should search for passages that clearly state God's blessing upon homosexual and lesbian behavior rather than seeking proof against it only in the words you choose to use. I'm suggesting that you be as consistent in your search for proving as you seem to be in your search for disproving.

You also refer to Romans 1 as "the biggest text on the subject," going on to say, "It says nothing on gay love either; in fact, it uses the phrase that they burned with lust. And all lust, be it hetero, homo, or whatever is wrong. And it is all about heterosexuals in idolatry as in Levitical laws, who had gay sex. If you read the text it seems clear. So what am I missing?"

First of all, you cannot call someone heterosexual who willingly participates in homosexual behavior. Sexual behavior between two people of the same gender is condemned biblically, regardless of the label we choose to put on it. We can't justify it because in some cases it is recreational, or ritual, while in other cases it is "true love."

In the Garden of Eden, it appeared that there was nothing wrong with eating of the Tree of the Knowledge of Good and Evil. In fact, there was nothing wrong with the tree and its fruit, in and of itself, but God had placed it off limits. Adam and Eve attempted in vain to justify their behavior, but, bottom line, they disobeyed their Creator, insinuating that He did not know what He was talking about. They lost their immortality and were cast out of the Garden of Eden. And now, here we are today, still questioning whether or not our Creator and Father knows what is best for His own creation!

What you are missing is the body of the passage that you are skipping over, or ignoring. Yes, the chapter talks about idolatry, but Romans 1:24 says:

Wherefore God *also* gave them up to uncleanness [*akatharsia*, impurity] through the lusts [*orexis*, excitement of mind, and longings] of their own hearts, to dishonour their own bodies between themselves. (Emphasis added.)

The Greek dictionary states the dishonoring (*atimazo*, to maltreat, shame, entreat shamefully). So they were shamefully treating their own bodies between themselves. How? Through vile affections (verse 26, *atimia* and *pathos*, disgraceful and shameful passions, affections, and lust).

For even their women did change the natural use [*chresis*, natural sexual intercourse] into that which is against nature: And likewise also the men, leaving the natural use of the woman [natural sexual intercourse], burned in their lust one toward another [*ekkaio orexis*, inflamed deeply, burned in their excitement of the mind and longing after one another]; men with men working that which is unseemly [*katergazomai* and *aschemosune*, working fully, accomplishing, finishing, performing, working out that which is an indecency and shameful], and receiving in themselves that recompence [or, equivalent] of their error which was meet [necessary, required, expected]. (Romans 1:26, 27)

Let me restate this as the Greek so clearly reveals its meaning: Wherefore God also gave them up to impurity through the excitement of mind and longings of their own hearts, to the shameful treating of their own bodies between themselves. For this reason God gave them up unto disgraceful and shameful passions, affections, and lusts. For **even their women** (lesbians) did change the natural sexual intercourse into that which is against nature: And **likewise also the men** (homosexuals, gays), leaving the natural sexual intercourse with women, were inflamed deeply, burning in their excitement of mind and longing after one another; men with men, working out fully (going all the way) and accomplishing, or finishing, or performing that which is indecent and shameful, and receiving in themselves the equivalent which was required or expected. (They traded roles. Turnabout was fair play.) And even as they did not like to retain God in their knowledge, God gave them over to a reprobate (or worthless) mind, to do those things which are not becoming. Who knowing the judgment of God, that they which commit such things are worthy of death, not only do the same, but have pleasure in them that do them (Romans 1:24–32, author's amplification with the Greek).

I have yet to find, or to be shown, any text of Scripture that remotely insinuates or implies God's acceptance of "gay love." On the other hand, in the face of these scriptures I have shared with you today, I would approach this subject of "gay love" with fear and trembling before our loving creator God. Some people can be fooled all the time; all people can be fooled some of the time. But God knows the deepest longings and secrets of the heart, and can never be fooled. It is He to whom we have to answer.

My appeal to you is that you go to Him with an honest, open heart. He loves you unconditionally, and He will not fail you if you truly seek Him in genuine love for truth.

In Mark chapter 4, Jesus gives us the parable of the sower whose seed fell by the wayside, on the stony ground, among thorns, and in the good ground. He goes on to explain how His Word falls on the ears of many kinds of listeners: those who hear it and let Satan take it away; those who hear and accept for a time but throw it away in times of test and trial and temptation; those who hear it and allow it to be choked out by the cares of this world, material gain, and lust; and finally those who hear the Word, receive it, and bring forth much fruit as they allow it to change every aspect of their lives.

I hope and pray that the Word I have tried to share with you today has fallen not by the wayside, not on stony ground, not among thorns, but upon good fertile ground where the Holy Spirit can water it and bring forth much fruit.

May God continue to bless you in accordance with your love for Him and for His truth.

Victor

Question: Does the Bible really *not* call homosexuality sin and wrong as people are telling me? I am a Christian struggling with my sexual identity. I want to do what is right, but I'm confused.

Reply: I know that it must be tough to express your feelings of frustration as you have. I commend you for your courage. Now I need to ask you a few thought questions to help you sort this thing out.

Is it your Christian background that makes you feel uncomfortable with the thought of being gay? If so, is it because you want to be a Christian yourself? And if you do, do you think that Jesus would be unhappy with you being homosexual?

It seems today that society doesn't care whether you are straight or gay. So I propose that if you are struggling with the idea, it is because the Holy Spirit is attempting to reach your heart and save you from making a shipwreck of your life, as I did of my own for so many years.

You have mentioned the Bible and questioned whether the Bible says homosexuality is wrong, so I want to respond to you from a biblical perspective.

Matthew 1:21 tells us that Jesus came to save His people from their sins. Why? Because the wages, or consequences, of sin is death—eternal death (Romans 6:23). God loves you, and He doesn't want to live eternally without you. He created you as someone to love and to cherish for all eternity. You are unique and very special to Him.

No one in all the universe can take your place in His heart. You and I and everyone have sinned, "for all have sinned and come short of the glory of God" (Romans 3:23), but Jesus has provided a way for us to escape the punishment of our sins if we are willing to forsake them. He has also provided for you the gift of eternal life if you are willing to accept it.

"If we [you] confess our [your] sins, he is faithful and just to forgive us [you] our [your] sins, and to cleanse us [you from all unrighteousness" (1 John 1:9).

The big question is this, "Is homosexuality sin? Is it wrong? Does the Bible say so?" If it is sin, and you confess it to be your sin, then, according to the above text, you can be forgiven; and not only forgiven, but cleansed from it as well.

When we reclassify, however, from the category of sin to that of an acceptable alternative lifestyle, then God Himself can do nothing for us, for He sent His only begotten Son to save His people from their sins, not from something acceptable, not from some minority status, not from their sexual preferences, not from some genetic or psychological disorder, but from their sins.

Contrary to what people are telling you, here's what the Bible does say about homosexuality: "Thou shalt not commit adultery" (Exodus 20:14). Adultery is defined as any sexual behavior or practice outside of marriage as God created it to be.

"Thou shalt not lie with mankind, as with womankind: it is abomination" (Leviticus 18:22). "If a man also lie with mankind, as he lieth with a woman, both of them have committed an abomination" (Leviticus 20:13).

> Wherefore God also gave them up to uncleanness through the lusts of their own hearts, to dishonour their own bodies between themselves: Who changed the truth of God into a lie ... For this cause God gave them up unto vile affections: for even their women did change the natural use [the natural sexual intercourse] into that which is against nature: And likewise also the men, leaving the natural use [or intercourse] of the woman, burned in their lust one toward another; men with men working that which is unseemly ... And even as they did not like to retain God in their knowledge, God gave them over to a reprobate mind. (Romans 1:24–28)

You see, God cannot and will not interfere with the power of choice that He has given each one of us, but if we choose to follow Him, even against our feelings, tendencies, and emotions, then He supplies His divine power (grace) to overcome our temptations and our sins.

> Know ye not that the unrighteous shall not inherit the kingdom of God? Be not deceived: neither fornicators ... nor adulterers, nor effeminate, nor abusers of themselves with mankind ... shall inherit the kingdom of God. (1 Corinthians 6:9, 10).

But don't miss the promise that immediately follows: "And such *were* some of you: but ye are washed, but ye are sanctified, but ye are justified in the name of the Lord Jesus, and by the Spirit of our God" (v. 11).

There are so many great promises in the Bible assuring you that you can be made whole, that you can be everything God created you to be, that you can have a life of joy, peace, happiness, and fulfillment. If you will go through my website carefully you will find a lot of material that will answer many, if not most, of your questions. In this reply, I'm simply trying to steer you in the right direction and give you hope and courage to make the right choices. I wish you would read my story, for I am sure that you would see many parallels with your own life, your confusion and frustration. God does have the answers for you, and He can give you freedom and peace. Higher than the highest human thought can reach is God's ideal for you.

I would suggest that you go to the other Questions of the Week, starting at the bottom of the list and work up. In the Featured Article section, I have posted an article called "A Rainbow of Promises," (it is also the closing chapter of this book). Please check it out. I am sure you will find there some very encouraging and strengthening material. Let me know how it goes.

God be with you, and I will be praying for you!

Victor

Question: I am often asked, "Where in the Bible does it say that being gay is a *greater* sin than any others?" Can you provide scriptures?

Reply: The Bible does not say that being gay is a greater sin than any others. In fact, a careful study of the Word will reveal that there are three sins especially offensive to God: pride, selfishness, and covetousness; homosexuality is not included! These are the three sins that made a devil out of God's beloved Lucifer, breaking His heart, and wreaking havoc in heaven and later here on earth.

However, homosexuality *is* referred to as an abomination in the Bible, but as one of many abominations. Elsewhere in my books and website is presented the list of abominations I have compiled from the Scriptures. You might find it a good exercise for yourself as well. By making this list, I came to realize that my sin was just as reachable by the plan of salvation as anyone else's sin. This listing was not done to make me feel better about my personal abomination, but rather to make me feel better about the possibility of overcoming.

The apostle Paul encourages us with these words:

> There hath no temptation taken you but such as is common to man: but God is faithful, who will not suffer you to be tempted above that ye are able; but will with the temptation also make a way to escape, that ye may be able to bear it. (1 Corinthians 10:13)

You, too, need to understand that the wages of your sin is no greater nor less than the wages of the sins of others who may have a particular disdain for your particular habitual sin. For the wages of *any* sin is death. Yes, the Bible does call homosexuality abomination. The Bible seems to call *all* sin abomination.

It should especially be noticed, however, in this lineup of abominations that adultery of *any kind* is included. The heterosexual sinner need not look down his nose with condescension upon the homosexual sinner, for *any* sexual behavior outside the marriage institution as designed and created by God is sin—abomination. In short, we all need a Savior from sin, from abomination of one kind or another.

Keep looking up!

Victor

Follow-up Question: If homosexuality is no greater sin than the others, why are gays told by the church that they are "automatically" going to hell (case closed)? I have not seen that in the Bible.

At some time in our lives, we all backslide in some way because we are not perfect. If at that moment, we as born-again Christians die, surely we are still going to heaven. Why is the common view among Christians that the gay person (for argument's sake: married, monogamous gay person) will go to hell?

Reply: People in the church say all kinds of things that are based upon tradition, assumption, misunderstanding of God's Word, or their own unregenerate hearts. What the Bible teaches is that "the wages of sin is death" (Romans 6:23). "Sin is the transgression of the law" (1 John 3:4). "Thou shalt not commit adultery" (Exodus 20:14) is a commandment of God's law. And the Bible very clearly condemns homosexual behavior, as stated in my former response, along with many other defiant behaviors. (See 1 Corinthians 6:9, 10; 2 Timothy 3:1–5; Revelation 21:8; 22:15)

The problem with so many homosexuals is that they want to be Christians without going through a transformation of character and behavior, when the word Christian means following the discipline of Christ—Christ, who was tempted in all points like as the homosexual is, yet without sin. He did not give in to feelings, emotions, or tendencies that were not in harmony with the will of His Father.

As Christians, we do not believe that the pedophile will go to heaven without first being transformed, neither the sex addict who is heterosexual, the prostitute, the masturbator, nor the pornography addict. Why is it so difficult to use the same standard for the homosexual?

Homosexuality generally involves all forms of perverse behavior: pornography, masturbation, sodomy, oral sex with the same gender, and not considering sexual behavior in light of its original purpose—procreation. Homosexual behavior generally is centered in self-gratification rather than the selfless love and pleasuring of a lifetime partner. Yes, there are some exceptions, but the general practice, if you were to visualize it, is just a gross perversion of God's original plan.

History shows that homosexuality has only become a tolerable, then acceptable, then celebrated, then promoted alternative lifestyle in a declining, or dying society. Homosexuality is now a global issue, indicating that we are a declining global society unprepared to meet our God. "As it was in the days of Lot … even thus shall it be when the Son of man is revealed" (Luke 17:28, 30).

You made reference to the married, monogamous gay person. I must make comment here. Marriage was instituted by God. Can there really be such a thing as a gay marriage with the blessing of God who designed marriage to be between one man and one woman? It seems to me to be a mockery to God.

And then there is the idea of the monogamous gay person. Have you ever met a gay person who has reserved himself sexually for the one and only person to be with forever in marriage? Homosexual behavior begins with experimentation, perhaps with masturbation, then playing around with someone, and usually dating around sexually with many partners before settling on just one. And then those long-term unions quite often invite others into their sexual relationship, or indulge in pornography, or have tricks outside the union.

I have found the monogamous gay person to be a very rare creature, if he even exists at all. Monogamy means one and only one. That is so out of character for homosexuality, I cannot say that I have ever met such a person. But should that person exist, we can still not escape the simple fact that homosexual behavior is a violation of the expressed will of God, found clearly in His Word. And Father knows best!

God be with you,

Victor

Question: Are same gender sexual attractions sinful? If so, then what do I do about my same gender sexual attractions?

Reply: It is a fine line between thoughts of temptation and sinful thoughts. Satan knows where he has in the past been successful with his tailor-made temptations for each one of us. We should expect that he will be relentless in his attempts at continual success in the area of homosexual attractions.

But, let us not forget, *temptation does not define who* **we** *are*. Temptation defines who Satan is! Our choices, thoughts, feelings, and emotions define our characters, or who we are. It is not our temptations, but what we choose to dwell upon, what we choose to think about, how we choose to feel and act that determines whether we are guilty of sin or not.

So to answer the question of same gender sexual attractions being sinful, we should follow the counsel of the apostle Paul in 2 Corinthians 10:5, "Casting down imaginations, and every high thing that exalteth itself against the knowledge of God, and bringing into captivity every thought to the obedience of Christ."

Here Paul is telling us how to deal with temptation thoughts without falling into sinful thinking. In other words, we should not allow these sexual attractions to find root in our minds.

Well, how do we not allow ourselves to have these homosexual attractions? What do we do about them? Here is a key: "Let this mind be in you, which was also in Christ Jesus" (Philippians 2:5). Allow it to be so in you. Stop resisting the working of the Lord by insisting, "I was born this way. There's nothing I can do about my attractions." The text tells you to let God work in you to will and to do of His good pleasure (See Philippians 2:13).

What's the point?

The point is that we should look at other people as Jesus did, not through "sex-tinted glasses." We should see in them a people for whom Jesus gave His life on the cross that they, too, might have everlasting life. Love, godly love, self-*less* love is the agency which God uses to expel sinful thoughts from the human soul. By this selfless love for another person with his or her eternal well-being in mind, God changes our pride into humility and what would be selfish lust into a genuine interest in that person's relationship with his Creator.

Acknowledging that there is an *appropriate* attraction process that draws people together for the purpose of union in marriage that meets with God's approval and blessing, we are dealing here with those attractions that do not meet with such approval and blessing. Let's face it, *inappropriate* sexual attractions of any kind find root in a heart that is selfish, self-centered, seeking self-gratification and self-fulfillment. And we all have to deal with the issue of "self."

However, Paul tells us to: Mortify (subdue, put to death) therefore your unrestrained and improper affection, evil concupiscence (sexual desires), and covetousness (desiring the "forbidden fruit"); to put off the old man with his deeds; and put on the new man, which is renewed in knowledge after the image of Him who created him. (See Colossians 3:5–10).

When a person truly gives his heart to Jesus and is baptized, he professes to be dead and declares that his life has changed—hid with Christ in God. He claims to be dead to sin and cleansed from his hereditary and cultivated traits of evil. In going forward in the rite of baptism, he pledges himself before God to remain dead to sin.

The truth must sanctify the whole man—his mind, his thoughts, his heart, and his strength. His vital powers will not be consumed upon his own lustful practices. These must be overcome, or they will overcome him. (See 2 Peter 2:19–22).

How many understand the full meaning of sanctification?

The mind is befogged by sensual malaria. The thoughts need purifying …

The true Christian obtains an experience which brings holiness. He is without a spot of guilt upon the conscience, or a taint of corruption upon the soul. The spirituality of the law of God, with its limiting principles, is brought into his life. The light of truth irradiates his understanding. A glow of perfect love for the Redeemer clears away the miasma which has interposed between his soul and God. The will of God has become his will, pure, elevated, refined, and sanctified. His countenance reveals the light of heaven. His body is a fit temple for the Holy Spirit. Holiness adorns his character. God can commune with him; for soul and body are in harmony with God. (7BC 909)

It seems to me that if we are truly attracted to Jesus and focus upon Him that all inappropriate attractions should be eclipsed by our attraction to Christ. Let us keep our focus, for by beholding Him we become changed; we become like Him who "was in all points tempted like as we are, yet without sin" (Hebrews 4:15). "Let this mind be in you, which was also in Christ Jesus" (Philippians 2:5).

Chapter 11

THE PASTOR AND THE HOMOSEXUAL ISSUE

In light of current events in the world of politics, society, and religion, we as clergy are faced with a question we can no longer afford to avoid. What is the role of the pastor when faced with the issue of homosexuality—through his ministry, within his church, within his own family, or even within himself?

I was 42 years old the year I turned my back on the homosexual lifestyle. Sixteen years I had been in total bondage, living a life of self-destruction and degradation, blaming God the entire time for "creating me this way." There were others I blamed as well for the roles they had played in channeling me down the broad, gay road that leads to destruction.

"You would do well to divorce him and get on with your life," my wife was counseled by prominent pastors and psychiatrists alike. "There's nothing we can do for him. That kind can never change!"

Granted, those were my same sentiments. But coming from these spiritual authorities, they left me feeling totally helpless and hopeless—utterly outside the reach of the Savior. To me, God appeared to be selective in His plan of salvation, to say the least, if not downright impotent rather than omnipotent. Fresh out of college, having graduated with honors and a degree in theology, I did not have a saving knowledge or understanding of God.

"How is it that He is able to change murderers, thieves, liars, atheists, heathens, devil worshipers, and other adulterers but is not able to change the homosexual?" I reasoned. "Christianity must be a farce. It certainly is not just and merciful."

Sixteen years later I came to the realization that I could blame God and others for everything wrong in my life and continue justifying my lifestyle of perversion until Jesus returned in the clouds of glory; I was still a lost man! It really did not matter how I ended up being gay. The past was the past and could not be altered. Surely there was something about God and His plan of salvation that I just did not yet understand. The responsibility, in all honesty, really did lay at my own feet. There must be a way for my life and anyone else's to be changed.

And so it was that I began my search for God's truth on this subject through intense study of His Word. Step by step I came to a saving knowledge of God's will and way for me.

1) **Realizing God's love.** I discovered that I was intensely and unconditionally loved, not condemned, even in my fallen state, by God and by His true children as well (1 John 4:8, John 17).

2) **Facing myself.** I determined to honestly face myself, and my condition, for God had invited me, "Come now, and let us reason together" (Isaiah 1:18).

3) **Acknowledging my sin.** Continuing in honesty, I came to acknowledge my lifestyle to be a sin issue, according to the law of God and many specific texts of Scripture (Jeremiah 3).

4) **Realizing salvation is for me, too.** Considering all the abominations in the Bible, I came to realize that my sin was just as reachable by the plan of salvation as anyone else's sin. This listing was not done to make me feel better about my personal abomination, but rather to make me feel better about the possibility of overcoming.

There hath no temptation taken you but such as is common to man: but God is faithful, who will not suffer you to be tempted above that ye are able; but will with the temptation also make a way to escape, that ye may be able to bear it. (1 Corinthians 10:13)

5) **Understanding the cause of homosexuality to be irrelevant.** Another important realization was that it really didn't matter how I had become homosexual: born gay, conditioned by environment, my own bad choices, etc. The simple fact was that I, too, needed a Savior from sin, and One had been lovingly provided for even the likes of me. I learned that Jesus could and would save me personally from my sin. Eventually, I obeyed His call and came out from the world (Matthew 1:21; Titus 2:12–14).

6) **Learning to forgive.** To be made whole, I learned that I had to be forgiven, pardoned, and justified. To be forgiven, I had to learn to forgive those who had wronged me, even as I wanted God to forgive me for wronging Him. All resentments, bitterness, vindictiveness, and anger had to be let go. What blessed relief to do so! (Matthew 6:12).

7) **Exercising the power of choice.** It also became evident that God created every one of us with the power of choice. He must have my permission and cooperation in order to cleanse me of my sins and to create a clean heart within me. Even if I were born gay, upon Jesus' invitation to be born-again I am now faced with a choice. Overcoming homosexuality truly is a matter of choice (Joshua 24:15; Philippians 2:5; 1 Corinthians 6:9–11).

8) **Walking with God.** I came to realize that it was vital to develop and maintain a relationship with God through daily prayer and Bible study.

He is the "power source" for one's victorious life. Plugging in is essential (1 Thessalonians 5:17; 2 Timothy 2:15).

9) **Protecting my environment.** Removing myself from the path of temptation and guarding well the avenues to my soul was a very important step for me to reach. I determined to be very careful regarding what I watched, read, touched, and heard. I began separating myself from every unclean thought and unholy practice (Philippians 4:8).

10) **Personalizing Scripture.** A very helpful tool for me was to insert myself into the context of Scripture, especially into the exceeding great and precious promises of God's Word (Isaiah 53; 2 Corinthians 5:17, 18).

11) **Acting upon God's Word.** When Jesus told the woman caught in adultery, "Neither do I condemn thee: go, and sin no more," she was empowered by faith in His Word (John 8:11). I developed faith in His Word, faith to act upon His promises. After all, it has been wisely observed by one author that "all [God's] biddings are enablings" (*Christ's Object Lessons*, 333).

12) **Being grateful.** In His infinite wisdom and love for the well-being of humanity, God gave us the gift of marriage. It is not a sin to live without that gift. But all sexual relationships—whether heterosexual or homosexual—outside of this biblical union are simply sin. I made a decided choice to accept with gratitude that which God has offered, to not press against the fence for the green grass on the other side. I chose to be content living within the parameters our loving God has established for my life, liberty, and pursuit of true happiness. That meant avoiding all sexual relations, behavior, and activity outside of the biblical union between a husband and a wife.

13) **Realizing temptation is not sin!** A very significant understanding came to me through beholding the life of Christ. Temptation is not sin. Otherwise, would not Jesus have been the chiefest of sinners rather than Paul? After all, He "was in all points tempted like as we are, yet without sin" (Hebrews 4:15). He actually "suffered being tempted" (Hebrews 2:18). And He "resisted unto blood, striving against sin" (Hebrews 12:4).

No, temptation is not sin; neither is orientation determined by temptation, by someone else's, Satan's, intentions upon one's life and destiny. Orientation is the direction one is heading, the direction one chooses for himself and then pursues. To suggest otherwise is to justify sin and to denigrate the gift of God in the power of choice.

14) Learning the secret to overcoming: The secret to overcoming sin is in helping someone else to overcome sin. "And they overcame him [the accuser, Satan] by the blood of the Lamb, and by the word of their testimony" (Revelation 12:11). Also, Jesus told the cleansed demoniac, "Go home to thy friends, and tell them how great things the Lord hath done for thee, and hath had compassion on thee" (Mark 5:19). He has enjoined me to do the same, and I do. Through sharing my own personal testimony, I live from day to day with positive reinforcement. There truly is victory in Jesus.

The bottom line from my research: I found my answers, accepted Jesus Christ as my Savior from my sin of homosexuality, turned my back on my perverted lifestyle, and began my new life in Christ Jesus. The process was not a quick and easy one, but it was a successful one. The words of the apostle Paul to the Corinthians are true, "Therefore if any man be in Christ, he is a new creature: old things are passed away; behold, all things are become new" (2 Corinthians 5:17). He has lovingly sustained me all these years since 1992, giving me second chances and double portions in life, ministry, and family.

In another epistle, the apostle Paul spoke of those "having a form of godliness, but denying the power thereof" advising young Timothy, "from such turn away" (2 Timothy 3:5). It is absolutely vital for us pastors to have faith in the *power* of the God whom we serve and represent while standing in the pulpits before our congregations from week to week. Nothing is impossible with our God, for He "is mighty to save," the "whosoevers," from "whatsoever," even "to the uttermost."

We must acknowledge, however, that salvation is not to be found *in* sin, for Jesus came to "save His people from their sins" the wages of which is death (Matthew 1:21, Romans 6:23). And sin is defined in 1 John 3:4 as "transgression of the law." In other words, disobedience, the breaking of any one of God's Ten Commandments, is defined as sin.

Here is where we pastors face a dilemma with the issue of homosexuality. This moral issue has been hijacked by political correctness and conventional thinking. Activist homosexuals have been very successful in having homosexuality reclassified from its biblically established category of sin to that of a genetic issue, a social issue, a political issue, an acceptable alternative lifestyle, and on to the advantaged and privileged minority status.

Many pastors and churches have followed the tradition of not getting involved in social and political issues, thus shying away from the social and political issue of homosexuality, overlooking the biblical fact that it is really a sin issue. This passive stance on our part has actually worked to encourage homosexuality to transcend the status of perversion, becoming first tolerated, then accepted, then protected, and now promoted, flaunted, celebrated, and specially privileged. Homosexuality seems to be running rampant throughout every echelon of our society within our present generation: government, politics, education, social services, media, entertainment, sports, and, yes, even throughout the church and clergy.

So in light of political correctness in our culture today, what is the role of the pastor when faced with the issue of homosexuality?

First of all, we must remember that the church is like a hospital. It is filled with people comprising the full spectrum of spirituality, from the terminally or chronically ill on the one hand, to the healthy on the other. It is the spiritually healthy who ideally should be in administration. In other words, we do not deny the right of worship to anyone. But church offices and church membership should be reserved for those who are not living in defense of open sin—those who have a healthy understanding and acceptance of salvation issues.

Second, in the spirit of Christ's love and acceptance, we must not shy away from honestly diagnosing homosexuality as a sin issue. What good is the physician who will not honestly diagnose his patient? What good is the mechanic who will not honestly diagnose the car problem?

The pastor must be courageous and honest enough to call sin by its right name. "Cry aloud, spare not, lift up thy voice like a trumpet, and show my people their transgression, and the house of Jacob their sins" (Isaiah 58:1). Otherwise, he gives the sheep of his flock a false security and a false hope of life everlasting in the face of eternal destruction.

This does not mean that the pastor is to publicly expose the homosexual and denounce from the pulpit such a one in the congregation. It does mean, however, that the congregation needs to know clearly where the pastor and the church stand on this "headline current events" issue. Discretion is to be used in dealing with the individual in a non-threatening environment and manner. And the pastor is not expected by God to shirk his duty of ministering to the needs of such a one within the congregation.

Paul told young Timothy in 2 Timothy 4:2–4 to:

Preach the word… reprove, rebuke, exhort with all longsuffering and doctrine. For the time will come when they will not endure sound doctrine; but after their own lusts shall they heap to themselves teachers, having itching ears; And they shall turn away their ears from the truth, and shall be turned unto fables.

Jeremiah pleads, "Only acknowledge thine *iniquity*, that thou hast transgressed against the LORD thy God… And I will give you pastors according to mine heart, which shall feed you with knowledge and understanding… and I will heal your backslidings." (Jeremiah 3:13, 15, 22). This is not hate speech, fellow pastors, but rather loving exhortation in the interest of one's eternal life.

The apostle John counsels, "If we confess our sins, he is faithful and just to forgive us our sins, and to cleanse us from all unrighteousness. If we say that we have not sinned, we make him a liar, and his word is not in us" (1 John 1:9, 10).

In other words, if we allow the issue of homosexuality to escape the biblical classification of sin, then we pastors make God out to be a liar, and His Word is not spoken nor preached through us. Jesus did not come to save His people from some acceptable alternative lifestyle. He came to save His people from their sins, from transgressing the law of God, from breaking His Ten Commandments, from disobedience. And "...as many as received him, to them gave he power to become the sons of God, even to them that believe on his name" (John 1:12). Furthermore, God promises, "He that overcometh shall inherit all things; and I will be his God, and he shall be my son" (Revelation 21:7).

Third, the pastor needs to be prepared for a hostile reception of his efforts to minister to the homosexual. Indeed, this is to be expected initially. However, the pastor is counseled to "not be weary in well doing: for in due season we shall reap, if we faint not" (Galatians 6:9).

Should the loving, interested, caring, and patient efforts of the pastor fail to bring about remorse and repentance in the homosexual, then the pastor and the church have a duty to follow through with church discipline just as with any other sin. The church should not tolerate the open sin of heterosexual adultery in its midst. Neither should it allow the open sin of homosexuality to be nurtured in its midst by membership and church office.

The apostle Paul is very clear on this in Titus 3, "A man that is an heretic after the first and second admonition reject; Knowing that he that is such is subverted, and sinneth, being condemned of himself" (verses 10, 11).

Fourth, the pastor need not be afraid to reach out beyond himself and his limitations. There are resources available to help in time of need. (See below.)

Finally, let us endeavor by God's grace to be those pastors of whom Jeremiah speaks, pastors according to God's own heart who shall feed our congregations with knowledge and understanding, that they may find healing from their backslidings, healing for their souls, victory in Jesus, and life everlasting.

"Victor J. Adamson"—Author of "*That Kind Can Never Change! Can They...?*", Ex-Gay since 1992, now husband and father, pastor, radio evangelist, and international speaker. Web address: www.victorjadamson.com

––––––––––––

Question from a Pastor: "How do I help a former gay who feels and thinks he is going back to his old lifestyle?"

Reply: First of all, I will be praying for you, for you are facing a real challenge going after a wandering sheep that may want to wander still. As a pastor myself, I, too, deal with such people, for we don't want them to be lost. It is vital for us, and them, to maintain a daily connection with Christ. The apostle Paul realized that even he had to be diligent in maintaining his daily walk with Jesus in order to not end up a castaway, "But I keep under my body, and bring it into subjection:

lest that by any means, when I have preached to others, I myself should be a cast-away" (1 Corinthians 9:27).

You are dealing with a very serious situation with one who is slipping back into his old lifestyle.

> While they promise them liberty, they themselves are the servants of corruption: for of whom a man is overcome, of the same is he brought in bondage. For if after they have escaped the pollutions of the world through the knowledge of the Lord and Saviour Jesus Christ, they are again entangled therein, and overcome, the latter end is worse with them than the beginning. For it had been better for them not to have known the way of righteousness, than, after they have known it, to turn from the holy commandment delivered unto them. But it is happened unto them according to the true proverb, ["As a dog returneth to his vomit, so a fool returneth to his folly." Proverbs 26:11], The dog is turned to his own vomit again; and the sow that was washed to her wallowing in the mire. (2 Peter 2:19–22)

I prayed about your question, and this is what I believe the Lord has laid on my heart. Jesus taught the teachers and the searchers for truth by asking direct, to-the-point questions. I would suggest that you ask your friend, "Just exactly what do you want out of life and out of eternity? I ask this because Jesus loves you and will allow you to have what you choose for yourself. Of course, every choice brings with it rewards or consequences, though Jesus loves you still, unconditionally."

Jesus speaks of two roads one can take in life when He says:

> Enter ye in at the strait gate: for wide is the gate, and broad is the way, that leadeth to destruction ["the wages of sin is death," Romans 6:23], and many there be which go in thereat. Because strait is the gate, and narrow is the way, which leadeth unto life ["the gift of God is eternal life through Jesus Christ our Lord" Romans 6:23], and few there be that find it. (Matthew 7:13, 14)

If he answers, "Freedom, liberty," share with him the texts, or reason with him from the principle of the texts, James 1:25: "But whoso looketh into the perfect law of liberty, and continueth therein, he being not a forgetful hearer, but a doer of the work, this man shall be blessed in his deed." And James 2:10–12:

> For whosoever shall keep the whole law, and yet offend in one point, he is guilty of all. For he that said, Do not commit adultery, said also, Do not kill. Now if thou commit no adultery, yet if thou kill, thou art become a transgressor of the law. So speak ye, and so do, as they that shall be judged by the law of liberty.

If he answers, "Peace," share with him the text, "Great peace have they which love thy law: and nothing shall offend them" (Psalms 119:165).

If he answers, "All that life has to offer," share with him the words of Jesus, "I am come that they might have life, and that they might have it more abundantly" (John 10:10).

If he answers, "Joy, happiness, success, or self-gratification," you might share this bit of counsel with him.

> God does not require us to give up anything that it is for our best inter-est to retain. In all that He does, He has the well-being of His children in view. Would that all who have not chosen Christ might realize that He has something vastly better to offer them than they are seeking for themselves. Man is doing the greatest injury and injustice to his own soul when he thinks and acts contrary to the will of God. No real joy can be found in the path forbidden by Him who knows what is best, and who plans for the good of His creatures. The path of transgression is the path of misery and destruction. (*Steps to Christ*, 46)

I sum it all up in this way, "Father knows best!"

I hope this little epistle will be helpful to you in shepherding your flock. Also, I would encourage you to read through my website thoroughly, especially the featured article, "A Rainbow of Promises." (Found also in the closing chapter of this book)

The Theology of Love and Acceptance

It seems to me that a very dangerous theological trend has developed among Christians of late, and that is this idea that we are to just love and accept every-body where they are and as they are and incorporate them into church fellowship without making them feel guilty for their lives of open sin. But I believe that if we are not careful, we will be loving people to death (along the broad way) and ac-cepting them in their lost condition without offering them the deliverance from bondage that Jesus so wants them to have. Indeed, He lived and ministered and died to save His people *from* their sins, not *in* them.

I truly believe that we must not only love and accept the sinner where he is, but we must go beyond that to introduce him to the transforming power of God who is mighty to save, the whosoevers, from whatsoever, even to the uttermost.

On the subject of transformation, the Scriptures speak of two very different forms. In 2 Corinthians 11:13–15 we read:

> For such are false apostles, deceitful workers, transforming them-selves into the apostles of Christ. And no marvel; for Satan himself is

transformed into an angel of light. Therefore it is no great thing if his ministers also be transformed as the ministers of righteousness; whose end shall be according to their works.

Here we are warned of false apostles, deceitful workers, transforming themselves into apostles of Christ. Let us not forget the words of Jesus, "Not everyone that saith unto me, Lord, Lord, shall enter into the kingdom of heaven" (Matthew 7:21).

We are told here that even Satan himself is transformed into an angel of light. Light represents truth, but Satan presents a spurious message, a fatal sophistry.

As one commentator wrote:

We do not realize how untiring are Satan's efforts to sap our spirituality. He is working mightily that the people of God may be only half converted. Then self will swell to large proportions, and there will be no revelation to the world of the transforming power of God. If this power does not rest upon God's people and move them to sanctified action, they cannot do the work in the earth that has been shown us must be done. Without this power, they will not realize their responsibility as his representatives in a world of unbelief. (*The Review and Herald*, June 19, 1913)

This text speaks of Satan's ministers, transforming themselves as ministers of righteousness. These representatives, or workers, or messengers, present themselves as bearing glad tidings of great joy, messages of salvation by grace (cheap grace), not by works; license to continue in sin, for you are loved and accepted just as you are; sin and live, for the wages of sin is *not* death, because the gift of God is eternal life if you just ask for it; you will "not surely die" (Genesis 3:4).

Such messages present a "form of godliness, but denying the power thereof" (2 Timothy 3:5). They actually have their origin with the deception of Satan in the Garden of Eden. And of these messengers it is stated in 2 Corinthians 11:15, "whose end shall be according to their works."

To such who love not the truth of the transforming power of God, we are told that God Himself will send strong delusion (2 Thessalonians 2:8–12). He gives to every man in accordance with the desires of his heart. If he loves not truth, he is free to receive delusion. But with every choice man makes comes consequences or rewards.

Within the church today are efforts encouraging a change of position regarding open sin, rather than encouraging a change of behavior by the sinner. We increasingly hear the plea to reach out with love and understanding to those involved in behavior explicitly condemned in the Bible. We are urged, as caring Christians, to make special efforts to include them as warmly loved and appreciated "members" of the church family, even though they are living in open sin and to surround them with loving support and acceptance, demonstrating patience and tolerance for them in their open disregard of the Word of God.

True, the church is to open its doors to anyone who wants to worship. It should present a warm, inviting atmosphere for those seeking relief from this troublous world. The key word, however, in the above scenario is "members." With membership comes the right to participate in the decision making process of the church, to assume church office, and even church leadership.

The teaching of love and acceptance is actually good doctrine, as long as it is taught from the true biblical perspective, and is not cheap love and cheap acceptance which only leads one into the trap of the dangerous doctrine of cheap grace.

A demonstration of love and unconditional acceptance toward someone can very easily lapse into indulgence. If our love and acceptance leaves one feeling complacent in his sin, then our love is not really love at all, but rather a placating of sin. God's love, if accepted, generates a responding love. That true love in return results in obedience, for Jesus said, "If ye love me, keep my commandments" (John 14:15).

Our responsibility as Christians is to take the lead in demonstrating unconditional love and compassion, not condemning someone for unwanted orientation or tendencies. However, we must be careful not to encourage someone to accept that which is less than God's will for his life. We are to support such a person with prayer and understanding as he seeks to follow God's plan for his life, through his seeking of God's grace, his divine transforming power.

Let us explore the biblical concept of love and acceptance as opposed to the cheap love and cheap acceptance that is being urged upon the church today.

At a world church conference in St. Louis a "Christian" pamphlet was left with me proclaiming, "Gay Christians are wholly loved and accepted by God," using Matthew 11:28 as the reference for this conclusion.

In unconditional love, Jesus says,

Come unto me, all ye that labour and are heavy laden, and I will give you rest. Take my yoke upon you, and learn of me; for I am meek and lowly in heart: and ye shall find rest unto your souls. For my yoke is easy, and my burden is light. (Matthew 11:28–30)

Now, we know of God's unconditional love for the sinner from such passages as:

But God commendeth his love toward us, in that, while we were yet sinners, Christ died for us ... For if, when we were enemies, we were reconciled to God by the death of his Son, much more, being reconciled, we shall be saved by his life. (Romans 5:8–10)

However, note in the following references from one of my favorite Bible scholars and commentators that acceptance with God is not unconditional, but rather conditional:

The promise is, "Come unto me ... and I will give you rest." [The question is,] Have you come to him, renouncing all your make-shifts, all your unbelief, all your self-righteousness? Come just as you are, weak, helpless, and ready to die. What is the "rest" promised?—It is the consciousness that God is true, that he never disappoints the one who comes to him. His pardon is full and free, and his acceptance means rest to the soul, rest in his love. (*The Review and Herald*, April 25, 1899)

Let not anything rob your soul of peace, of restfulness, of the assurance that you are accepted just now. Claim every promise; all are yours *if* you will comply with the prescribed terms...

The abiding rest—who has it? That rest is found when all self-justification, all reasoning from a selfish standpoint, is put away. Entire self-surrender, an acceptance of His ways, is the secret of perfect rest in His love. We must learn His meekness and lowliness before we experience the fulfillment of the promise "Ye shall find rest unto your souls" [Matthew 11:29]. It is by learning the habits of Christ that self becomes transformed,—by taking His yoke, and then submitting to learn.

Giving up the life to Christ means much more than many suppose. God calls for an entire surrender. We cannot receive the Holy Spirit until we break every yoke that binds us to our objectionable traits of character. These are the great hindrances to wearing Christ's yoke and learning of him. There is no one who has not much to learn. All must be trained by Christ." (*The Review and Herald*, April 25, 1899)

In the case of Abel, he:

Came with the blood that pointed to the Lamb of God. He came as a sinner, confessing himself lost; his only hope was the unmerited love of God. The sense of need, the recognition of our poverty and sin, is the very first condition of acceptance with God. (*Christ's Object Lessons*, 152)

It was "to the *penitent* thief [that] came the perfect peace of acceptance with God" (*Conflict and Courage*, 326)

There is hope for the penitent ... in Jesus every one who longs for help and acceptance may find deliverance and peace. (*Gospel Workers*, 213)

The religion of Christ means more than the forgiveness of sin; it means *taking away* our sins, and filling the vacuum with the graces of the Holy Spirit … It means a heart emptied of self, and blessed with the abiding presence of Christ. When Christ reigns in the soul, there is purity, freedom *from* sin. (*Lift Him Up*, 292, emphasis added.)

Why do not these words make men afraid to sin against God? There are many today who, though professing Christians, are not one with Christ. They are drifting hither and thither. May God pity them. Unless help from above reaches them, they will be lost, eternally lost.
The members of our churches need to be converted, that they may understand what the love of Jesus means,—the love that He revealed in His life of meekness and lowliness. *Profession without practice is of no value…* Fruit-bearing… is the condition of discipleship. What is the fruit that is to be borne?—Purity of character, unselfish deeds, Christlike words. Those who do not bear this fruit, those whose lives do not reveal the tenderness of Christ, are not accepted as representatives of God." (*Australasian Union Conference Record*, November 15, 1903)

Many have no assurance of acceptance with [God]. They have forfeited, and are continuing to forfeit, the conditions upon which acceptance is based. When weighed in the balances of the sanctuary, they are found wanting; for they love self; Christian principle is away down in the scale, and their profession of knowing Christ is a deception. (*The Southern Watchman*, June 4, 1903)

Let none complain that they have not the assurance of the love of God, that they cannot obtain the evidence of their acceptance with him. Let them diligently search the Scriptures, and see if they are following the example of their Lord … We need to practice close self-examination, to see what we are cherishing in ourselves that will grieve the Spirit of God …

The easy position so pleasing to the carnal heart is, that Christ has done all, that personal striving is unnecessary, and would be an evidence of unbelief. But the Bible tells us to work out our own salvation with fear and trembling. Self-complacency will never save us. Those who imagine that because Christ has done all that is necessary in the way of merit, there remains nothing for them to do in the way of complying with the conditions, are deceiving their own souls. (*The Review and Herald*, December 22, 1885)

"Come out from among them, and be ye separate, saith the Lord, and touch not the unclean thing; and I will receive you, and will be a father unto you, and ye shall be my sons and daughters, saith the Lord Almighty."

Here is a promise to us on condition of obedience. If we will come out from the world, and be separate, and touch not the unclean he will receive us. Here are the conditions of our acceptance with God. We have something to do ourselves. Here is a work for us. We are to show our separation from the world. The friendship of the world is enmity with God. It is impossible for us to be friends of the world and yet be in union with Christ. But what does this mean: to be friends of the world? It is to unite hands with them, to enjoy what they enjoy, to love that which they love, to seek for pleasure, to seek for gratification, to follow our own inclinations. We do not in following inclination have our affections upon God; we are loving and serving ourselves. But here is a grand promise: "Come out from among them and be ye separate." Separate from what? The inclinations of the world, their tastes, their habits; the fashions, the pride, and the customs of the world… In making this move, in showing that we are not in harmony with the world, the promise of God is ours. He does not say *perhaps* I will receive you; but, "I *will* receive you." It is a positive promise. You have a surety that you will be accepted of God. Then in separating from the world you connect yourself with God; you become a member of the royal family; you become sons and daughters of the Lord Almighty; you are children of the heavenly King; adopted into his family, and have a hold from above; united with the infinite God whose arm moves the world. What an exalted privilege is this to be thus favored, thus honored of God; to be called sons and daughters of the Lord Almighty." (*Signs of the Times*, January 31, 1878, emphasis original)

In our next segment I want to elaborate on what it means to be adopted as sons and daughters of the Lord Almighty. Suffice it to say for now that the love of God toward the sinner is truly unconditional. However, acceptance with Him is not. It is conditional, conditional upon an entire surrender of the will to His transforming power. If we love God and hate sin, this is not bad news, and we should not be ashamed to share it.

And how does this relate to us as church members, as pastors? We, too, are to show unconditional love to those living in open sin. But accepting them into church membership must be conditional upon *penitence*, and a willingness to be cleansed, transformed, into the image of Christ. As John the Baptist put it, "Bring forth therefore fruits meet for repentance" (Matthew 3:8).

Be Ye Transformed

> I beseech you therefore, brethren, by the mercies of God, that ye present your bodies a living sacrifice, holy, acceptable unto God, which is your reasonable service. And be not conformed to this world: but be ye transformed by the renewing of your mind, that ye may prove what is that good, and acceptable, and perfect, will of God. (Romans 12:1, 2)

The apostle Paul is here pleading with us that we not allow our natural tendencies and human natures to rule over our minds and dictate our behavior. He is calling us to come out from the world and to separate ourselves from every unclean thought and unholy practice, patterning our lives after all that is good, acceptable, and in perfect harmony with the will of God. God calls for restraint in His children, control over our passions, and a higher standard than that of the world.

Paul calls this our "reasonable service," and surely this is consistent with our reasonable God who Himself invites us, "Come now, and let us reason together" (Isaiah 1:18).

And John advises, "For this is the love of God, that we keep his commandments: and his commandments are not grievous" (1 John 5:3).

What does it mean, *"be ye transformed"*?

It means to be born again. Jesus said, "Except a man be born again, he cannot see the kingdom of God" (John 3:3).

Now notice these profound words of counsel from 2 Corinthians 5:17 along with its commentary, "Therefore if any man be in Christ, he is a new creature: old things are passed away; behold, all things are become new."

> The old ways, the hereditary tendencies, the former habits, must be given up… The new birth consists in having *new motives, new tastes, new tendencies*… When men who claim to be Christians retain all their natural defects of character and disposition… They have not been born again. (*The Review and Herald*, April 12, 1892)

> God makes no compromise with sin. *A genuine conversion changes hereditary and cultivated tendencies to wrong.* (*Seventh-day Adventist Bible Commentary* Vol. 6, 1101)

> The patchwork religion is not of the least value with God. He requires the whole heart. No part of it is to be reserved for the development of hereditary or cultivated tendencies to evil. (*Seventh-day Adventist Bible Commentary* Vol. 6, 1101)

I have to tell you, friends, that I get excited when I read such plain counsel. There is no guesswork here. We either accept it and run with it, or we reject it and attempt to explain it all away.

"Be ye transformed." How?

1) By the renewing of your mind:

> Let this mind be in you, which was also in Christ Jesus. (Philippians 2:5)

> God does not force any man into his service. Every soul must decide for himself whether or not he will fall on the Rock and be broken. Heaven has been amazed to see the spiritual stupidity that has prevailed. You need individually to open your proud hearts to the Spirit of God. You need to have your intellectual ability sanctified to the service of God. The *transforming power of God* must be upon you, *that your minds may be renewed by the Holy Spirit, that you may have the mind that was in Christ."* (*The Review and Herald*, December 24, 1889, emphasis added)

2) By loving truth. Many perish:

> ...because they received not the love of the truth, that they might be saved. And for this cause God shall send them strong delusion, that they should believe a lie: That they all might be damned who believed not the truth, but had pleasure in unrighteousness. (2 Thessalonians 2:10–12)

> *Truth* as it is in Jesus exercises *a transforming influence* upon the minds of its receivers... Those who have a living connection with God know that divinity works through humanity. (*The Review and Herald*, January 21, 1896 emphasis added)

3) There is power in the Word:

> By the word of the LORD were the heavens made; and all the host of them by the breath of his mouth... For he spake, and it was done; he commanded, and it stood fast. (Psalm 33:6, 9)

So study God's Word.

> All scripture is given by inspiration of God, and is profitable for doctrine, for reproof, for correction, for instruction in righteousness: That the man of God may be perfect, throughly furnished unto all good works. (2 Timothy 3:16, 17)

Wherewithal shall a young man cleanse his way? By taking heed thereto according to thy word... Thy word have I hid in mine heart, that I might not sin against thee. (Psalm 119:9, 11; see also verses 12–18)

4) Receive Him, Truth:

But as many as received him, to them gave he *power* to become the sons of God, even to them that believe on his name." (John 1:12)

Why do we need "power" to become the sons of God? Christians the world over acknowledge this answer in song:

Would you be free from your burden of sin?

There's power in the blood, power in the blood

Would you o'er evil a victory win?

There's wonderful power in the blood

There is power, power, wonder-working power

In the precious blood of the Lamb.

Also,

I was sinking deep in sin, far from the peaceful shore

Very deeply stained within, sinking to rise no more

But the Master of the Sea, heard my despairing cry

From the waters (of sin) lifted me, now safe am I

...When nothing else could help, love lifted me.

In John 3:16, we read, "For God so loved the world, that He gave His only begotten Son."

Yes, He loved the entire populated world, and gave his only begotten Son to redeem the entire populated world, to save the entire populated world, to save them *from* their sins. *He provided salvation to all, which means that He also accepted all* to be saved *from* their sins.

Then how can any be lost? Condemned? Resurrected to damnation? Cast into the lake of fire prepared for the devil and his angels?

Dare I say it? *God's love is not enough. God's love and acceptance is not enough.* Therefore, love and acceptance on the part of His people toward those in bondage to sin also is insufficient to save the lost. But I must quickly add, it is a very necessary ingredient.

Love and acceptance toward the downtrodden and the outcast are absolutely imperative in the redemption process. But *without the teaching of the transforming power of God, love and acceptance only leads one to a false sense of security in Jesus,* an empty gospel that is not really good news at all to one who has Genesis 3:15 in his heart. The sin-sick soul who has been led by the Holy Spirit to have enmity in his heart toward his besetting sin will be turned away from God in despair and hopelessness if he is only loved and accepted as he is.

An allegory: suppose you are homeless, and someone from the local church finds you out on the street in the middle of winter. He befriends you and spends time with you every Saturday, perhaps about two and one-half hours, and perhaps an hour here and there on a Wednesday evening. He tells you that he loves you and accepts you, and even brings you lunch, and maybe even a blanket. As your relationship grows, he tells you that he wants to adopt you into his family. He goes so far as to even take legal action to do so, bringing you all the legal papers one Saturday. For two and one-half hours you sit down and go over the documents and even celebrate the adoption with a special lunch and a bottle of sparkling apple cider.

At the end of the two and one-half hours, like right at 12:00 noon, he looks at his watch as if noticing that his time is up. He has a quick prayer with you, then shakes your hand and retreats to his late model SUV and drives away to his plush home in the suburbs. "I'll see you next Saturday, same time, same place," he calls back.

And so it is. You have been loved and accepted. Yes, right where you are. You have been loved and accepted and left where you were found. Do you feel adopted? Do you feel truly loved and accepted? Is your relationship with the one who has adopted you a meaningful one that you will cherish?

Why, of course not! You feel mocked, frustrated, and more helpless and hopeless than ever! Why? Because if this is a demonstration of love and acceptance, then who needs it? The whole purpose of adoption is for one to be given a new life! A second chance! To, spiritually speaking, be born again!

One can be loved and accepted into a complacency that leads to destruction.

Biblically, adoption seems to suggest a newness of life—transformation. Notice the following:

> And if ye be Christ's, then are ye Abraham's seed, and heirs according to the promise. (Galatians 3:29)

> If any man be in Christ, he is a new creature. (2 Corinthians 5:17)

> For as many as are led by the Spirit of God, they are the sons of God. For ye have not received the spirit of bondage again to fear; but ye have received the Spirit of adoption, whereby we cry, Abba, Father. The Spirit itself beareth witness with our spirit, that we are the children of God. And if children, then heirs; heirs of God, and joint-heirs with Christ;

if so be that we suffer with him, that we may be also glorified together. (Romans 8:14–17) (Similar to Galatians 4:4–9)

Ephesians 1:3–9 uses these terms:

> … adoption … accepted in the beloved … redemption … forgiveness … Having made known unto us the mystery of his will, according to his good pleasure which he hath purposed in himself.

> For it is God which worketh in you both to will and to do of his good pleasure. (Philippians 2:13)

> I thank my God upon every remembrance of you… Being confident of this very thing, that he which hath begun a good work in you will perform it until the day of Jesus Christ. (Philippians 1:3, 6)

> He that overcometh shall inherit all things; and I will be his God, and he shall be my son." (Revelation 21:7)

Overcometh what?

> For whatsoever is born of God overcometh the world: and this is the victory that overcometh the world, even our faith. Who is he that overcometh the world, but he that believeth that Jesus is the Son of God? (1 John 5:4, 5)

> I write unto you, young men, because ye have overcome the wicked one. (1 John 2:13)

> Ye are of God, little children, and have overcome them: because greater is he that is in you, than he that is in the world. (1 John 4:4)

> As you confess before men and women your confidence in the Lord, additional strength is imparted to you. (*Seventh-day Adventist Bible Commentary* Vol. 3, 1143) (Just as we are told in Revelation 12:11.)

I remember once in the years BC (Before Christ) being invited by friends to a church service in California. The sermon was by a woman professor from the local university, and her topic was about the love of God for gays. My heart was really stirred, and I was moved to tears hearing that God loved me, even as the degenerate I was.

I did not feel set free from the penalty of sin, though, nor from sin itself. I had no assurance of salvation. It felt good to hear that I was loved, but it also made me feel even deeper the pain of knowing that I was living a life that hurt the One who loved me so much. I appreciated being loved while in my bondage, and that realization did stir tender thoughts in my heart toward Jesus, actually giving me a longing in my heart for Him, but I still felt separated from Him because of my addictive life of sin.

You see, friends, all the love in the world did not free me from having to face the "mirror" of the law of God if I wanted to be accepted by Him, if I wanted to feel comfortable in His presence.

So much is being said these days about how the church does not make homosexuals, and other types of sinners, feel welcomed, loved, and accepted. In other words, we are not to draw anyone's attention to the "mirror" of God's law, for "that leaves him or her feeling guilty, unworthy, in need of change of heart and behavior. That is unkind, unloving, unaccepting, condemning, and judgmental."

But any church that believes in the law of God will teach and preach man's accountability to that law of God, and will be bringing every sinner's attention to the fact that we all must face the "mirror" of God's law. That is a true message of true love.

Jesus died on the cross because the law of God could not be ignored or done away with. One cannot possibly truly "behold the Lamb of God which taketh away the sin of the world" (John 1:29) and not acknowledge that it was man's behavior of transgressing the law of God that put Jesus on that cross.

When I felt truly loved and accepted by Jesus, and by Christians, I found myself wanting freedom from my guilt and shame, freedom from my bondage to sin, power to become a son of God, power to become like Jesus in thought, in word, and in behavior.

I truly believe that the best way we Christians can show open sinners godly love and acceptance (including homosexuals and those living together outside of matrimony), is the same way that Jesus did. In love and compassion, but without compromise, we show the homosexual and the adulterer his need of a Savior from his lifestyle of sin.

We show him how to "let this mind be in you, which was also in Christ Jesus" (Philippians 2:5). We teach him how to "[bring] into captivity every thought" (2 Corinthians 10:5). We lead him to realize that there is power in the Word, redeeming power, *transforming* power. We introduce him to the creator God who has that power, for "by the word of the Lord were the heavens made, and all the host of them by the breath of his mouth, for He spake and it was done; he commanded and it stood fast" (Psalm 33:6, 9). We lead him to "being confident of this very thing, that he which hath begun a good work in you will perform it until the day of Jesus Christ" (Philippians 1:6).

Another thought about being loved: being loved should generate reciprocal love. The One loving us rightfully desires and expects reciprocal love. And Jesus says, "If ye love me, keep my commandments" (John 14:15). Jesus Himself uses the measure of our adherence to the law of God as a litmus test of our love to Him.

Another thought about being accepted: acceptance expects or requires performance. To be accepted into a club, a school, the armed services, employment, etc., requires performance. To be accepted into the church of God likewise requires performance, lives of service, and lives of obedience to the Man in charge. We have a job description. It is spelled out in God's Word, and in His law.

"Eye hath not seen, nor ear heard, neither have entered into the heart of man, the things which God hath prepared for them that love him" (1 Corinthians 2:9). In other words, "Higher than the highest thought can reach is God's ideal for His children. Godliness—godlikeness—is the goal to be reached" (*Education*, 18, 19).

Genuine faith is followed by love,—love that is manifested in the home, in society, and in all the relations of life... And love will be followed by obedience. All the powers and the *passions* of the converted man are brought under the control of Christ. His Spirit is a *renewing power, transforming* to the divine image all who will receive it.

To become a disciple of Christ is to deny self, and follow Jesus through evil as well as through good report...

Jesus is a pattern for humanity, complete, perfect. He proposes to make us like himself,—true in every purpose, feeling, and thought,—true in heart, soul, and life. (*Signs of the Times*, July 14, 1887 emphasis added)

It is the specified work of the Comforter to transform us. At times it is hard for us to submit to the purifying, refining process. But this we must do if we would be saved at last. (*Seventh-day Adventist Bible Commentary* Vol 3, 1154)

I beseech you therefore, brethren, by the mercies of God, that ye present your bodies a living sacrifice, holy, acceptable unto God, which is your reasonable service. And be not conformed to this world: but be ye transformed by the renewing of your mind, that ye may prove what is that good, and acceptable, and perfect, will of God. (Romans 12:1, 2)

It is my prayer that we as God's children and ambassadors and pastors not fail the sin-sick souls who come into our midst. Let us truly love and accept them, but go the distance by also leading them to a saving knowledge of the all-sufficient *transforming* power (grace) of our Redeemer, Jesus Christ.

Amen!

Chapter 12

THE CHURCH AND HOMOSEXUALITY

Question: What is the Church's role in the issue of homosexuality?

Reply: From the Bible, we are given clear counsel on the church's role in dealing with homosexuality.

1) The church must believe and teach the good news (the gospel) that, according to Matthew 1:21, Jesus can and will save His people, personally, *from* their sins (homosexuality included), not *in* their sins. Otherwise, the church has developed "a form of godliness, but denying the power thereof" (2 Timothy 3:5).

2) The church must accept the Bible definition of sin, or it will become ineffective in battling the enemy it has failed to define, or identify. "Sin is the transgression of the law [disobedience]" (1 John 3:4). And homosexuality is a violation of the seventh commandment of God's moral law, the Ten Commandments.

3) Having accepted this definition, the church must not be silent, but must take a stand, calling sin by its right name. The church must call sin "sin." "Cry aloud, spare not, lift up thy voice like a trumpet, and shew my people their transgression, and the house of Jacob their sins" (Isaiah 58:1). If we allow the reclassification of the sin of homosexuality to that of an acceptable alternative lifestyle, then we become impotent in dealing with the issue. Jesus came to save his people from their sins, not from some acceptable alternative lifestyle. If the church refuses to call homosexuality sin, it will soon find itself accepting homosexuality into membership, into leadership, and eventually into the clergy.

4) The church must believe that there is power in the Word. When Jesus told Mary to "go, and sin no more," Mary found grace, divine strength, in His admonition. Mary became an overcomer. As one writer puts it, "All God's biddings are enablings" (*Christ's Object Lessons*, 333). In the love of Jesus Christ, the church can successfully reach out to the sin-sick homosexual and introduce him to the Way, the Truth, and the Life.

Question: Why is it important for the church to be educated about homosexuality?

Reply: The church is embroiled in a war with Satan and sin. It can be victorious in the battle only as it successfully defines and understands the enemy. For the homosexual to trust the church in guidance and counseling, he must find there not condemnation, but rather unconditional love, compassion, and understanding. The church must reflect the sympathy of our Savior.

> For we have not an high priest which cannot be touched with the feeling of our infirmities; but was in all points tempted like as we are, yet without sin. Let us therefore come boldly unto the throne of grace, that we may obtain mercy, and find grace to help in time of need. (Hebrews 4:15, 16)

Question: What are the limitations the church faces currently in ministering to struggling people?

Reply: The church today is limited in its effectiveness in that it tends to either condemn the homosexual, thus turning him away, or else it embraces the practicing homosexual, not believing that he can be restored, reconditioned, and re-created into the image of God. Unconditional love does not result in indulgence of sin. Unconditional love accepts the sinner without condoning the sin.

The following two texts of Scripture tell the church that sinners can be given power to become the sons of God. And through that power, they can be overcomers. Homosexuality can be overcome.

> But as many as received him, to them gave he power to become the sons of God, even to them that believe on his name. (John 1:12)

> He that overcometh shall inherit all things; and I will be his God, and he shall be my son. (Revelation 21:7)

Question: You are also a man who has come out of homosexuality. How did the church function in your own experience? Did you see a therapist? If so, how did the church and the therapist work together?

Reply: Unfortunately, the ill-equipped local churches at that time unknowingly worked to undermine my efforts to come out of homosexuality. They were teaching that we will be sinning until Jesus comes again, which meant I was doomed to remain homosexual. These churches did not teach me that victory was possible; they allowed openly practicing homosexuals to have church membership and leadership, and it was stated of me personally, "*That* kind can never change!" Had I not studied out the issue for myself from the Word of God, I would have given up in hopeless despair. I knew of no therapists, and therefore threw myself at the feet of Jesus where I found solace, compassion, understanding, hope, and salvation *from* my sin of homosexuality.

Question: What is the importance of a church, therapist, and support group working together in a person's life to assist in overcoming homosexuality?

Reply: The more positive reinforcement the struggling homosexual can get, the more positive an outlook for overcoming homosexuality. It is of utmost importance that these three entities be on the same page in their understanding of the homosexual issue, or they will counteract each other's influence, causing even more confusion and anxiety to the sin-sick soul.

Question: How can the church, therapist, and support group work together? How should they inform one another?

Reply: According to Revelation 12:11, we overcome Satan and sin by the blood of the Lamb, and the word of our testimony. The secret to overcoming sin is in helping others to overcome sin. The church can provide clear biblical doctrine on this issue, teaching the unconditional love of Jesus and His power to save, not compromising the Word to the detriment of the sin-sick soul. The Christian therapist can use professional counseling skills coupled with accurate scientific and biblical information from his Christian perspective to lead the homosexual step by step to victory. The support group should be found in the congregation itself. It does not have to be restricted to recovering homosexuals. "For all have sinned, and come short of the glory of God" (Romans 3:23). And the word of our own testimony, our own experience with overcoming sin of whatever nature, will be constant positive reinforcement for the struggling homosexual. After all, he, too, is simply battling against sin—his sin.

Response to "ASolemnAppeal.org"

Noteworthy: In the following "Solemn Appeal," no Scripture is cited by the authors as a basis for the conclusions drawn! It is my belief, however, that the Bible should be our only rule of faith and practice, for:

> All scripture is given by inspiration of God, and is profitable for doctrine, for reproof, for correction, for instruction in righteousness: That the man of God may be perfect, throughly furnished unto all good works. (2 Timothy 3:16, 17)

The statements below which are in *italics* are those of the article "A Solemn Appeal." My responses are in regular type.

Article: *Dear Brothers and Sisters in Christ,*
We, the undersigned, address this letter to our fellow believers in the _____
Church. We humbly share our vision of God's purposes of redemption. For
too long we have listened to the cries of hurt and despair from those in our
churches who are lesbian and gay. We can no longer remain silent, but are
compelled to speak the words of present truth we believe God has given
us. It is not our desire to be divisive or stir up controversy; we see our role
as redemptive and calling each of us to a higher level of compassion and
understanding.

We are a people of faith, concerned about each one who responds to the call
of God's Spirit and seeks to follow its promptings. We tremble before God as
we see the rejection and exclusion of our… lesbian sisters and gay brothers
by many of our churches, recalling the painful experiences of other minority
groups in our denominational history. This exclusion falls far short of the
love and inclusion our Savior demonstrated to all.

Response:

1) Present truth is not something one can conjure up on his own, but rather must be based upon a plain "Thus saith the Lord," "To the law and to the testimony" (Isaiah 8:20), and seems to be well summed up in the words of Amos: "Prepare to meet thy God, O Israel" (Amos 4:12), in the three angels' messages of Revelation 14, and in the message of the angel of Revelation 18.

2) The higher level of compassion and understanding expressed in this appeal equates to license rather than a truly redemptive love which inspires contrition, confession, repentance, and submission to the transforming power of God.

3) Classifying homosexuals as a minority group is to dismiss the biblical status of homosexuality as a sin issue. The Bible condemns no person for being Black, White, Hispanic, female, male, or for having disabilities. The Bible is very explicit, however, about homosexuality being an abomination. As Christians, we do homosexuals no favor by labeling them as a minority and, therefore, privileged class. Homosexuals are sinners in need of their Savior just like any other sinner and anyone else struggling with abomination issues as listed in the Bible: adultery, lying, pride, cross-dressing, etc.

4) Our Savior never included in His circle of disciples open sinners who justified, or rationalized their sinful behavior. The very term "disciple" means one who enters into a life of discipline, following after the lifestyle

of a master. In the case of the Christian, that means submitting to the transforming power of that Master who declares His grace to be sufficient for you and me, and that would include the homosexual as well. Grace is defined as "the divine influence working upon the heart and reflecting in the life" (Strong's Concordance and the Greek Dictionary).

Article: *We believe that God is calling our church in North America to a thorough study of all the issues related to homosexuality, including current scientific research; better and more redemptive ways of reading, in the light of the Gospel's "good news," those few biblical texts that refer to same-sex behavior; and a sincere effort to walk in the shoes of those of our neighbors and our fellow Christians who live with a homosexual orientation.*

Response: It is written, "Cry aloud, spare not, lift up thy voice like a trumpet, and shew my people their transgression, and the house of Jacob their sins" (Isaiah 58:1). We are counseled to "Call sin by its right name" (*Seventh-day Adventist Bible Commentary* Vol. 2, 996). That is a very redemptive way to deal with the homosexual issue. The Bible gives the remedy for sin, but not for some acceptable alternative lifestyle, genetic disorder, etc. And the Bible is very explicit about how God thinks and feels about homosexuality. We must be careful lest we end up wresting the Scriptures to our own destruction (see 2 Peter 3:16).

Article: *We affirm that those who disagree with us have experienced the love of God and seek to take their faith seriously. However, we, too, take our faith seriously and have experienced God's love. We believe that our church needs to engage in dialog with our lesbian sisters and gay brothers; too often the gay and lesbian community has been excluded from discussions relating to homosexual orientation. Furthermore, we believe that as God's Spirit enlightens us, we will be led to welcome in our congregations every person seeking God, and rejoice in the gifts each person brings to His service, regardless of their sexual orientation, gender identity, and racial or cultural origin.*

Response:

1) Here again, equating perversion with racial and cultural origins is like comparing apples and oranges. There are many gifts that can be brought into church fellowship by people of different races and members of all ethnic groups. But what does homosexuality (a perversion of God's creation of sexuality) have to offer the church? Homosexuality is not a gift. Sinners who are holding on to their sins can only bring sin into the church. Sin not repented of can offer no good thing to the church communion. It is true that homosexuals may be very gifted, talented,

friendly, loving, cheerful, and happy, but Satan can use all that to bring corruption into the church and to compromise its effectiveness in ministry to the world.

2) If we allow people to bring their "gifts" to God's service, *regardless of their sexual orientation* or *gender identity*, then where do we draw the line? What about people who have been involved in pedophilia, polygamy, and those involved in incest? If we endorse one perversion of sexuality, then why not others?

Article: We trust you, our [church] family, to listen faithfully as we share our journey and our resulting convictions with you:

Current scientific evidence supports our conviction that, just as with heterosexuals, a homosexual orientation is determined before birth and/or very soon after, by a complex mix of biological and environmental factors over which a person has no control. To describe people who find themselves attracted to the same sex as sinful contradicts not only science but the scriptural principles of truth, justice, and compassion taught and demonstrated by Jesus.

Response:

1) Only some scientific evidence supports this conviction, and that evidence appears to be biased. There is much scientific evidence that does not support this conviction.

2) Even if this statement were true about current scientific evidence, all are born with sinful tendencies that must be overcome. Why should the homosexual be the only one who can cling to his tendencies when the entire message of the gospel is about transformation, being born again to new motives, new tastes, and new tendencies (2 Corinthians 5:17)?

Article: While so-called "change" programs may be able to help a few homosexual individuals learn to repress their innate attractions to those of the same sex, we do not believe that a denial of reality is a healthy or honest way to live. There is no evidence that one's sexual orientation can be changed, outside of a miracle, and thousands have prayed for this miracle over many years without ever receiving it. Therefore, we believe homosexuals should be accepted and loved in our congregations just as they are: sinners saved by grace, like all of us.

Response:

1) It is written, "If any man will come after me, let him deny himself, and take up his cross, and follow me" (Matthew 16:24).

2) The work of redemption and salvation *from* sin *is* a miraculous work. "For it is God which worketh in you both to will and to do of his good pleasure." And we can be "confident of this very thing, that he which hath begun a good work in you will perform it until the day of Jesus Christ" (Philippians 2:13; 1:6).

3) "Sinners saved" from what? From sin, transgression of the law, and disobedience (see Matthew 1:21; 1 John 3:4).

4) "By grace." And grace is divine, omnipotent, transforming power, "the divine influence working upon the heart and reflecting in the life" (Strong's Concordance and Greek Dictionary).

5) Are we to accept into our congregations and membership those who openly transgress the law of God in regards to all the other commandments? Or just the seventh one? What about people with sexual addictions, people who have committed adultery, unmarried heterosexual lovers, people involved in pedophilia, polygamy, or other perversions of sexual behavior? Again, where do we redraw the line when once we alter it? And based upon what authority?

Article: Along with our [church] family, we do take seriously the guidance God has given us through the Bible. However, we have carefully studied those biblical texts that are traditionally interpreted as forbidding same-sex activity, and join with those scholars who have found that they do not address homosexuality, as we understand it today. We respect those who, in good faith, hold different conclusions, and we trust that they, in turn, will respect the integrity with which we have journeyed to reach our understanding.

Response:

1) And who are those scholars? Upon what biblical grounds do they deviate from the traditional interpretation and understanding?

2) As we who understand homosexuality today? The Bible is very explicit: "Thou shalt not lie with mankind as with womankind: it is abomination" (Leviticus 18:22). What is so nebulous about this text? "If a man also lie with mankind as he lieth with a woman, both of them have committed an abomination" (Leviticus 20:13). The text goes on to show how

strongly God feels about this issue when He, as head of a theocracy, declared, "they shall surely be put to death." In light of Malachi 3:6, "For I am the LORD, I change not," by what authority does one understand this issue any differently than the Bible, our rule of faith and practice?

3) Integrity is defined as uprightness of character; honesty, the condition or quality of being unimpaired or sound. These arguments do not reflect sound reasoning, but rather a desire to rationalize away that with which one disagrees or dislikes, in this case a plain "thus saith the Lord."

Article: We believe that in the matter of sexual orientation, where there is so much disagreement and misunderstanding, our congregations and the gospel of Jesus Christ will be well served by refraining from judgment, while showing love and acceptance to everyone who desires to worship with us, allowing all to use their God-given talents to bring glory to God. Our spiritual community can then give God's Holy Spirit free reign to change lives as He sees fit.

Response:

1) Yes, God's love is, and ours should be, unconditional. Acceptance with God, however, is *not* unconditional, but rather *conditional* upon an entire surrender of the will. As with acceptance into employment, an educational institution, a club, a sports team, the military, etc., acceptance with Christ into His school of discipleship is likewise conditional upon one's submission to the expected process of transformation, discipline, and re-creation. God asked Cain, "If thou doest well, shalt thou not be accepted?" (Genesis 4:7).

I beseech you therefore, brethren, by the mercies of God, that ye present your bodies a living sacrifice, holy, acceptable unto God, which is your reasonable service. And be not conformed to this world: but be ye transformed by the renewing of your mind, that ye may prove what is that good, and acceptable, and perfect, will of God. (Romans 12:1, 2)

For he that in these things serveth Christ is acceptable to God. (Romans 14:18)

2) Yes, our church should have an open door policy for worship. Church is like a hospital with room for those who bring healing as well as for those who need healing, but membership should be reserved for those who, through contrition and repentance, are willing to enter Christ's school of discipleship, the school of transformation *from* sinful behavior,

as defined in Scripture, to lives which are willing to "cease to do evil" (Isaiah 1:16). The church is not to be the habitation of those "having eyes full of adultery, and that cannot cease from sin" referred to as "unrighteousness," "spots they are and blemishes" (2 Peter 2:13, 14).

3) "Give the Holy Spirit free reign to change lives as He sees fit"? In other words, credit the Holy Spirit with the failure of one to have a *genuine* conversion, which would change hereditary and cultivated tendencies to wrong? Credit the Holy Spirit with the new birth which does *not* consist of having new motives, new tastes, and new tendencies? I contend that it is the Holy Spirit's purpose and desire to bring all to repentance, for it is written, "The Lord is… not willing that any should perish, but that all should come to repentance" (2 Peter 3:9).

Article: *We believe the same Jesus who said, "The Sabbath was made for man, and not man for the Sabbath," might say today in regard to this issue, "Marriage was made for humans, not humans for marriage." We believe God wants homosexuals, as well as heterosexuals, to enjoy the many blessings of a monogamous, committed relationship—companionship, support of each other, a greater understanding of God's love, and emotional and sexual intimacy—needs with which He created all of us.*

Response:

1) "We believe… " Based upon what biblical principle or grounds?

2) "Jesus… might say… " This is pure conjecture. We would do well to realize that it is not [God's] plan that His people shall present something which they have to suppose, which is not taught in the Word… "What shall I do to inherit eternal life?"This is the all-important question, and it has been clearly answered [for us by Jesus Himself who asked] "What is written in the law? how readest thou?" (*Seventh-day Adventist Bible Commentary* Vol. 7, 978, and Luke 10:26).

3) "Marriage was made for humans… " There is no scriptural basis whatsoever for this preposterous conclusion.

Wherefore, beloved, seeing that ye look for such things, be diligent that ye may be found of him in peace, without spot, and blameless. And account that the longsuffering of our Lord is salvation [from sin]; … [in the Scriptures] are some things hard to be understood, which they that are unlearned and unstable wrest, as they do also the other scriptures, unto their own destruction. (2 Peter 3:14–16)

As professed followers of Christ, calling Him Lord and Master, it is only logical and reasonable that we allow Him to actually be Lord and Master, accepting His Word on any and every issue as the final authority. "God is love," according to 1 John 4:8. We can, therefore, accept His expressed will as not only authoritative, but also for the good and well-being of all His creation.

Chapter 13
THE CHRISTIAN REACTION TO HOMOSEXUALITY

Question: Should we allow a gay partner of our son to stay in our home? Our family is struggling over this issue. Thank you.

Reply: This is a very difficult and sensitive question to deal with. In their unconditional love for me and for my partners, I believe my parents erred in allowing us to stay (together) in their home. They did so many things right, but I do believe they compromised in this area.

What is the biblical principle in this matter? I think we can find it in the fourth commandment. God said regarding the Sabbath, "In it thou shalt not do any work, thou, nor thy son, nor thy daughter, thy manservant, nor thy maidservant, nor thy cattle, nor thy stranger that is within thy gates" (Exodus 20:10).

The principle here is that our homes are Christian homes with Christian standards. We don't allow porno movies, smoking, drinking, drugs, orgies, or wild rock music. We have standards to uphold within our domicile, over which we are appointed by God to be priests, heads of family, kings and queens, and so forth.

When homosexual relatives are visiting, I think God expects us to just lovingly and politely lay it on the line with something such as, "We love you and we accept you, but God's standards are honored and upheld within these walls. We welcome you into our home, but we must ask that you refrain from sleeping together within these premises. We do not condemn you, but only ask that you respect the standards of our home while you are visiting in our home. Again, we love you and welcome you."

I hope you find this to be reasonable and helpful counsel.

Victor

Question: We just took in a Christian young man who later confessed to being a practicing bisexual along with other issues—drugs, Free Masonry, and past witchcraft. He said he is not willing to give up the person he is; therefore, he is willing to surrender his membership with the church. My question is, would you put him out of your home knowing all this, and, if so, why?

Reply: If the young man is repentant and seeking help, then I would be in God's will to assist him. However, if he is not repentant and not truly seeking my help and that of the Lord to be changed, then the situation is entirely different.

I believe I understand you correctly in that the young man does not want to surrender who he is, that he does not want to submit to the will of God in these matters, and is even willing to give up his church membership rather than give up his sinful lifestyle. Therefore, he is bringing this spirit of rebellion and defiance into your Christian home.

God does not expect us to enable the sinner in his sins. You can demonstrate unconditional Christian love for this young man without enabling him in his sinful lifestyle with room and board. It is called "tough love," but really, the right thing to do is to give him a choice. Tell him that yours is a Christian home with Christian standards. He is welcome to stay with you as long as he is willing and wanting to accept biblical reproof, correction, and instruction (2 Timothy 3:16), is willing to learn to conform to the will of God, and as long as he will honor and respect the standards of your home and family. However, if he is just looking for a place to hang out, to be taken care of and provided for while remaining in open sin and rebellion, your home is not that place. Then, if he leaves your home, he has chosen to do so. You have not put him out.

If you provide an environment that supports the sinner in his lifestyle of sin, then, in essence, you become an accomplice in that sin—an enabler. God does not expect that of you, nor will he bless your home under those conditions. This young man, if unrepentant, will bring in a bad spirit that can cause much harm to your home environment and family.

Follow-up Question: Some say the church should just stand back and let this young man come to the point of turning from all this on his own. Is this good or should there be a proactive approach? At what point do we apply Matthew 18:15–20? I believe steps one and two of Matthew 18 have already been taken, but the young man's father is upset about confronting him regarding these issues. Help me, please! I'm confused and don't want to back this young man into a corner like a caged animal. However, since he wants to continue in his old ways, I believe I have to say, "Not in my home." Is this a wrong thought?

Reply: I don't think it is biblical for us to stand back and just wait for a church member to turn from a life of open sin. Yes, there should be a proactive approach according to Matthew 18, as you have already stated.

Paul told young Timothy in 2 Timothy 4 to:

Preach the word ... reprove, rebuke, exhort with all longsuffering and doctrine. For the time will come when they will not endure sound doctrine; but after their own lusts shall they heap to themselves teachers, having itching ears; And they shall turn away their ears from the truth, and shall be turned unto fables. (verses 2–4)

Isaiah 58 is rather bold in stating, "Cry aloud, spare not, lift up thy voice like a trumpet, and shew my people their transgression, and the house of Jacob their sins" (Isaiah 58:1).

If someone is professing to be a Christian and maintaining membership within the church, yet choosing to live in open sin, then we, as loving and caring brothers and sisters, have a duty, an obligation, to lovingly reprove, rebuke, exhort—to work with them to bring them to repentance and submission to the will of God. Our responsibility is to work with these people for their salvation *from* sin, not *in* sin.

The longer this young man goes without being confronted, the more deeply rooted he will become in his lifestyle of sin. In love, compassion, and mercy, he needs to be confronted by those who care so much about him and his eternal well-being.

> But ye, beloved, building up yourselves on your most holy faith, praying in the Holy Ghost, Keep yourselves in the love of God, looking for the mercy of our Lord Jesus Christ unto eternal life. And of some have compassion, making a difference: And others save with fear, pulling them out of the fire; hating even the garment spotted by the flesh. (Jude 1:20–23)

Be of good courage!
Victor

The tight rope demonstration of loving the sinner while hating the sin.

Question: It has been my experience that most Christians either go overboard with hating the sin (ranting and condemning) or loving the sinner (unquestioningly accepting everything) when dealing with homosexuality. What are some ways that Christians can clearly demonstrate that they both love the sinner and hate the sin? In other words, how can Christians reach out to homosexuals, accepting them without condoning their sin?

Reply: In contemplating an answer to this question, I put myself back in the place I was before choosing to accept Jesus as Savior from my own lifestyle of sin as a homosexual. The kind of unconditional love demonstrated by my own parents toward me and toward my friends made a definite impression upon me, making it easier to respect their opinions and to eventually listen to their counsel. Therefore, I suggest the following:

1. Be both a loving and a loveable Christian yourself. Practice the method that Jesus Himself used to reach the sinner. He accepted their invitations to visit in their homes, to eat with them, to socialize with them, but without participating in any sinful behavior Himself. In fact, His presence was in itself a deterrent to sin because His life was consistent with His profession and attracted the sinner to its purity and holiness.

2. If the gay person is in your family, treat him or her as family. Don't exclude him or her from your own family social events.

3. Be willing to listen with sympathy and empathy. I think most gays carry a tremendous burden of guilt, pain, and shame. You don't have to condone the sin in order to show mercy and sympathy toward the sinner.

4. Don't preach and lecture—it does no good unless invited. Watch for appropriate times to slip in a word of counsel only when you are sure that it is welcome, or receivable.

5. When asked about how you feel toward their lifestyle, don't show or express revulsion. Be gentle, stating matter-of-factly that though you care very much for the person, you do not find their alternative lifestyle to be acceptable in accordance with your understanding of God's Word, that you could not recommend it, and so on. Be kind and considerate with the words you choose.

For example, while visiting a high school friend dying of AIDS in an Amsterdam hospital a few years ago, at his prompting I shared my own testimony of victory over the sin of homosexuality. He was amazed at my story, but then somberly asked, "So you are telling me that you believe homosexuality to be sin?"

"Yes," I replied.

He struggled with my answer for a while. Then we changed the subject and talked about high school and mutual friends and acquaintances before drawing our visit to a friendly close. A few days later, before leaving Holland to come back home to America, I called him, asking if I could come back for a good-bye visit.

"Do you really believe that homosexuality is a sin?" he asked.

"Yes, I do," I replied. "Otherwise, I would not have studied and prayed and struggled my way out of it."

"I really don't think you'd better come back," he said. "I don't want you to force that view on me."

I then reminded him that I had not brought up the subject. I had merely answered his questions regarding my own experience and beliefs. My purpose in visiting him was simply to renew our acquaintance and to try to encourage him in some way during this crisis in his short life. In the end, we parted cordially on the phone. I did not get back to see him again before he passed away. Nevertheless, as a representative of Christ, I had been there to show love to the sinner, but I could not deny my faith in my Savior and His ability to save me, or him, from sin. The difference between us was that I had come to love truth, the truth that sets one free, while my friend chose to believe a lie and die in sin, rejecting God altogether.

There is no guarantee, friend, that while showing love to the sinner he will respond positively. He retains the power of choice until the day he dies. We can only hope and pray that he chooses the right before it is too late.

6. Let them know in word and action that you love them and that God loves them, too, no matter how you feel about their choices in life. Romans 5:8 tells us, "But God commendeth his love toward us, in that, while we were yet sinners, Christ died for us."

7. As a Christian, though you may invite them to attend church, it would not be appropriate to invite them into church membership or to vote for their acceptance into church membership. Membership allows for decisive voting on church policy, vocalizing of one's viewpoints in church board and business meetings, and holding offices of leadership. Membership should be reserved for those who have renounced the world, sin, and Satan—those who bring forth fruit meet for repentance, as John the Baptist says. Otherwise the standards of the church might be compromised.

These are just a few tips to help those of you endeavoring to bring healing to the sin-sick soul. Your hatred for sin should work in you to labor the more earnestly in love for the sinner, to save him from that very thing you know to be so destructive in this life as well as to have eternal consequences. The wages of sin is death, eternal death, but the gift of our loving God who hates sin is eternal life to those who will accept Jesus Christ who came to save His people from their sins—even the sin of homosexuality (see Romans 6:23; Matthew 1:21).

Question: Why can't Christians just love and accept homosexuals as they are?

Response: Two texts of Scripture immediately come to mind when faced with this question:

And this gospel of the kingdom shall be preached in all the world for a witness unto all nations; and then shall the end come. (Matthew 24:14)

And I saw another angel fly in the midst of heaven, having the everlasting gospel to preach unto them that dwell on the earth, and to every nation, and kindred, and tongue, and people. (Revelation 14:6)

"What's the point?" you may ask. The point is that Jesus cannot come again until every "people" have at least been presented with the message that there is a way out of their personal lifestyle of habitual sin. This way out is the good news, the gospel. "For God so loved the world, that he gave his only begotten Son, that whosoever believeth in him should not perish, but have everlasting life" (John 3:16). And Jesus, in infinite, unconditional love for and acceptance of the sinner, then came to save his people from their sins, of whatever nature (Matthew 1:21).

The true Christian will love the homosexual sinner as he is—unconditionally, but his acceptance of the homosexual will be with the endeavor to lead him to the Way, the Truth, and the Life. The homosexual sinner, like all other sinners, then must decide either to accept or to reject the salvation from sin that Jesus came to offer. To reject Christ's efforts to change the life is, in essence, to rebel against His unconditional love, acceptance, and infinite sacrificial effort that the homosexual also might be set free at last.

For the Christian, true love is too pure to cover an unconfessed sin or to not address the issue of a lifestyle of sin that will lead to perdition. While we are to love the souls for whom Christ died, we are to make no compromise with evil. We are not to unite with the rebellious and call this love. God requires His people in this age to stand for the right as unflinchingly as did the apostles of old in opposition to soul-destroying errors, heresies, and lifestyles that receive the wages of sin—eternal death.

> Whosoever committeth sin transgresseth also the law: for sin is the transgression of the law. And ye know that he was manifested to take away our sins [to deliver us from sinful practices] ... Whosoever abideth in him sinneth not [forsakes his sinful lifestyle]: whosoever sinneth [chooses to continue in his sinful lifestyle] hath not seen him, neither known him. (1 John 3:4–6)

Why can't Christians just love and accept homosexuals as they are? Because true love will not leave the victims of Satan's deception, vice, and cunning to suffer eternal loss without making every effort to rescue them. To do otherwise is the utmost cruelty and even deception. Acceptance without leading to reform is the easy way out for the Christian steward. It is shirking the gospel commission, a betrayal of our trust, a breach of our allegiance and obedience toward our God, and it is giving in to the enemy, Satan, who is constantly seeking to deceive the followers of Christ with his fatal sophistry that it is impossible for them to overcome. In short, it is treason against the kingdom of God and the utmost cruelty toward the homosexual who is in need of his Savior.

True Christian love and acceptance will not compromise with evil, but will kindly show the Way to victory, tell truth about sin and the life free from besetting sin.

Chapter 14

INTERCESSION FOR THE HOMOSEXUAL

Question: My oldest son is nearly 17. He was convicted of child molestation at the age of 14 for teaching his stepbrother to masturbate. Now, because of the sex offender treatment program and therapy, he is beginning to believe he is bisexual or homosexual. Because of the rejection from our church, he does not believe or trust Christians any longer. I need suggestions and help. Thank you.

Reply: As wrong as your son was in teaching his stepbrother to masturbate, he needs to know that it was not necessarily an act of homosexuality. Unfortunately, many young people experiment with masturbation. It does have its consequences because it is sin, and it must be overcome by the Christian. The stigma your son has is that of being registered as a sex offender, which is unfortunate because he, too, was but a child when this occurred. What he needed was counsel, not stigma. Jesus told Mary, who was an adult guilty of breaking the same commandment, "Neither do I condemn thee: go, and sin no more" (John 8:11).

I am also disappointed that the church would give your son a sense of rejection. The church should be a place for reproof, correction, and instruction, (1 Timothy 3:16, 17), a place to feed on the Word. It should be like a hospital—a place of nurturing and healing for the spiritually ill. Your son should be able to find within the church people who show him love and compassion, for that is what being Christ-like is all about.

If your son would like to communicate with someone regarding his troubles, I would be happy to point him in the right direction. He is old enough to read my book, *That Kind Can Never Change! Can They…?* and to visit my website, www.victorjadamson.com, which he can do privately without any embarrassment or intimidation. He will find there much to which he can relate. You see, as a young person, I, too, was introduced to improper sexual behavior, and it almost ruined my life. In fact, it did for many years. I write about this in my book, which I really think he ought to read. There he will find someone with whom he can relate, someone who went through what he has gone through, to some extent, and has been able to rise above it all and go on with life as a healthy, happy, joyful Christian.

Your son, too, can be made whole! He can grow to be a blessing to society, having peace within.

Victor

Question: I have been married for 14 years and have two beautiful boys. My husband came out of a homosexual background. He became a born-again Christian, left that life behind, and married me. I ignorantly believed that because he was a Christian he was completely healed of all homosexual feelings. I was very wrong. Throughout our marriage he has had to continually fight those feelings. He has been unfaithful to me more than once in our marriage, but each time I have forgiven him and taken him back, believing that divorce was never an option. Every time I took him back I believed that our marriage became stronger as I felt we had to work harder than most to keep our love alive.

However, I have now recently discovered that he has been living a double life for a year. He has now filed for divorce, as he believes that he is gay and cannot continue living a lie. I still love him dearly and am heartbroken to think that he is not only walking away from me and from his boys, but, ultimately, he is walking away from God.

I am really struggling to come to terms with the fact that I know that he is saved; yet he is not able to walk in victory in this area. I am still prepared to forgive him and to take him back as I love him and have seen the potential in him to be used by the Lord.

I have so enjoyed your testimony and wisdom on the subject of homosexuality as it has given me new hope. I almost came to a place of doubting that a person could ever overcome this. I would like to know what I as a wife or even friend to my husband can do in order to help him.

Reply: My heart aches for you in this situation. My! What a patient, loving, and lovable Christian you must have been to hang in there for so long, knowing your husband's past and present double life.

I must first inquire regarding your statement of "the fact that I know that he is saved, yet he is not able to walk in victory in this area." From what, in fact, is your husband saved? Jesus came to save His people from their sins (Matthew 1:21). Homosexuality is a sin issue, is it not? Unless your husband has overcome his homosexual lust and behavior, by God's grace, he has not been saved from sin. Does that make sense?

Is there yet hope for him to be saved from his sins? Yes, of course! An emphatic "yes"!

The theme of my ministry is that nothing is impossible with God, for He is mighty to save, the whosoevers, from whatsoever, even to the uttermost. The problem, however, is this: God says in Jeremiah 3, "Only acknowledge thine iniquity … and I will heal your backsliding" (verses 14, 22).

Before the Lord can help him overcome, your husband must come to the place where he can acknowledge that what he is dealing with is a sin issue—not an acceptable, alternative lifestyle, not a genetic inheritance of gay tendencies, but a sin issue. He must then come to believe that Jesus can and will save him personally from this sin issue, then he will be one of the elect and chosen of God, His peculiar treasure. He will come out from the world, by God's grace, and separate himself from every unclean thought and unholy practice.

Grace, by the way, is that divine influence working upon the heart and then reflecting in the life, according to the Greek dictionary. In other words, grace is divine, omnipotent strength to overcome any and all temptation. Jesus promised that "My grace is sufficient for thee: for my strength is made perfect in weakness" (2 Corinthians 12:9).

It is not enough for you to want victory for your husband. Your husband must himself want this victory, and want it badly enough to "seek… first the kingdom of God, and his righteousness" (Matthew 6:33). Perhaps you can convince him that temptation is not sin, that his orientation is determined by the direction he chooses for his life, not the direction that Satan, through temptation, chooses for him. Perhaps he would be encouraged by the text of Scripture where Paul advises us to bring into captivity every thought to the obedience of Christ (2 Corinthians 10:5).

You see, so many gay people have been conditioned to believe that if they are ever tempted homosexually that they are homosexual, and that there is no hope of ever changing. But Jesus was tempted in all points like as your husband, yet without sin (Hebrews 4:15). Who would dare say Jesus was homosexual? Jesus *suffered* being tempted (Hebrews 2:18). Jesus resisted unto blood being tempted, striving against sin (Hebrews 12:4). Yet, He chose to lay down His life rather than yield to that temptation. So the nature of one's temptation does not define who he is as a person; his choice of direction makes that definition.

Joseph, in Potiphar's house, resisted that almost overwhelming temptation of Potiphar's wife by responding, "How can I do this great wickedness, and sin against God?" (Genesis 39:9). He put the thoughts and feelings of God ahead of his own powerful urges, tendencies, and temptations, then he fled from the scene of the temptation. Joseph submitted himself to God, resisted the devil, and then fled from the scene in accordance with our counsel in James 4:7. This has been my own practice in the face of homosexual temptation. And it works!

If your husband is open to your communication, you might want to share this with him. Try to encourage him also to go through my website before he dives headlong into this world of self-destruction and degradation. I do know whereof I speak as I lived in this same world for 16 years.

My heart goes out to you and your family. Love your husband unconditionally, and pray without ceasing that the Lord will give him no rest, day or night, until he makes an entire surrender of his will to Jesus. Pray that the Lord will do whatever it takes to bring him to the foot of the cross. But also remember that your husband has the freedom of choice, which God Himself will not violate.

———————

Question: What would be the best way to share your information with a gay friend? Quite frankly, I don't know if he wants to change. One thing I know for sure is that God does not create people as homosexuals or lesbians. Please give me your input.

Reply: True, God does not create homosexuals or lesbians. If so, the Bible would be condemning the works of God Himself. If your friend is content with his lifestyle and does not want to change or to investigate available help, then God Himself has to wait. A person must recognize His need and acknowledge that need before God can be of assistance. "Only acknowledge thine iniquity... and I will heal your backsliding" He says in Jeremiah 3:13–22. In other words, "Acknowledge that your homosexuality is a sin issue, and then I can heal you."

You, however, can pray that God will do whatever it takes to get your friend's attention, to help him recognize and acknowledge his need. Continue also to maintain your friendship with him, loving him unconditionally that he may see Jesus in you and be drawn toward Him through you.

As you are able to read my book and other information for yourself, you are more credible in introducing your friend to it as well. If you can get your friend to read my book and/or visit my website, I think he will find much interesting material there to consider.

Question: As a Christian, what can I do to help a lesbian friend? Can your book help and how can we encourage her to read it?

Reply: A couple things I tell people to do for their loved ones who are leading sinful lives and who are not open to counsel:

1) Pray. Pray without ceasing in intercession for them that the Lord will do whatever it takes to get their attention. He cannot force the will, but rather respects the power of choice He has given to each one of His children. But He can bring circumstances around to where the loved one must face eternal realities.

   Pray that He will lead someone across their path to whom they will be able to relate and listen.

   Pray that He will give you wisdom, discernment, and understanding so that you yourself may be more effective in influencing them for good.

2) Love them unconditionally, both in word and in action. I truly believe that homosexuals are people who are looking for love in all the wrong places. They need to know that they are loved, even in their sins. Jesus

loves the sinner with an infinite love, but He hates the sin. We, too, can demonstrate godly, unconditional love without condoning the sinful lifestyle. "The strongest argument in favor of the gospel is a loving and lovable Christian" (*Signs of the Times*, August 12, 1908).

3) Perhaps I can throw in a third point. You must also, in your own life, demonstrate joyful Christianity. You may be the only Bible someone else may ever read. What are they reading in you? We Christians should be the happiest, most joyful, most content people in the world. The Bible tells us "in every thing give thanks" (1 Thessalonians 5:18), to "Rejoice in the Lord alway[s]: and again I say, Rejoice" (Philippians 4:4).

Our loved ones, steeped in lives of self-destruction and degradation, need to see in us something they don't have that they would really de-sire—the fruits of the Spirit: love, joy, peace, longsuffering (patience), gentleness, goodness, faith, meekness, and temperance. They need to see in us an assurance, stability, a "Rock of Gibraltar," an unwavering loyalty to Christ and moral principles. This they cannot help but respect and admire. Perhaps someday they will desire to have the same in their own lives.

4) Now you've got me going, and I'm on a roll here. Trust in the Lord. God loves your loved ones even more than you do. After all, He gave His only begotten Son for a ransom to "purchase" that loved one back for Himself. In the face of that infinite love, we need to place our trust in Him and place our loved ones into His hands.

5) Regarding my first book, the last chapter is titled, "You, Too, Can Be Made Whole!" (It is also posted on the website: www.victorjadamson.com, under Featured Articles) This chapter is a step-by-step process I believe the Lord led me through in order to give me victory at last and to sustain me in that victory. I enumerated these steps and expounded upon them, because the Lord was successful in using them with me.

Yes, I do believe the book could be very helpful in reaching your friend. That's why I wrote it. To successfully share it, you should first read it yourself. Then you will know what you are offering her, and you will be able to introduce it better having read it yourself. If it is a blessing to you, introduce it that way. "I have come across the most amazing book! I started reading this man's story and couldn't put it down! You've just got to check this out!" (Actually, this is the feedback I get from some people. So that's not too far-fetched of a suggestion.)

All power to you as you continue to reach out to the wayward.

Victor

Question: How do I reach out to a very angry loved one who is resistant to Christianity and to help in overcoming his life of self-destruction and degradation?

Reply: This is really a tough situation of which you speak. But there is nothing too tough for God. Through your unconditional love and persistent intercessory prayer He can do marvelous things to get the attention of your loved ones. In short, my counsel to you would be to just be yourself—consistently a loving and lovable Christian, for it has been rightly stated that "The strongest argument in favor of the gospel is a loving and lovable Christian." (*Signs of the Times,* August 12, 1908)

Never forget that "The Christian is the world's light, and the only Bible that many read. Through Christians men see God. How careful, then, should those be who have taken the name of Christian." (*Signs of the Times,* July 10, 1901)

Question: I have two gay siblings who have decided they can no longer be around my sister and me because, as Christians, we believe homosexuality to be a sin. We've loved our siblings for years and have never condemned them and have always embraced them and their partners. Now they will have nothing to do with us. Should we simply stay silent and respect their wishes?

Reply: I'm sorry this is happening to you and your family. But let's take a look at what is really happening here.

In the beginning, when Adam and Eve sinned against God, what did they end up doing? They hid from Him. They were afraid to be around Him. They were riddled with guilt. Sin cannot stand in the presence of a holy God, for He is a consuming fire wherever impurity (sin) exists. God loved Adam and Eve no less after their sin than before their sin. He, knowing what had happened, walked in the garden to be with them. Of course, He had to shield them from His presence in order to protect them now that they were "unclean." God was grieved at the loss of His intimate relationship with His children. But we see in this story the sober fact that sin separates. "But your iniquities have separated between you and your God, and your sins have hid his face from you, that he will not hear" (Isaiah 59:2).

Like God, you and your sister are now grieved because the sin of homosexuality has come between the two of you and your two gay siblings. Most likely you have done nothing to offend them. They just no longer feel comfortable around "holiness." I say "holiness," not to judge you as being perfect, but to make the point that as you are growing in grace day by day as Christians, becoming more and more like Jesus (and I hope this is so for by beholding Him daily we become changed into His likeness), the guilt of your siblings makes it very difficult for them to be around you.

You say that you have never condemned them and have always embraced them and their partners, so the fault is not in yourselves. What you are experiencing is what Jesus is experiencing every moment of every day. People He loves so dearly that He was willing to give His life so they might not receive the wages of their sins (John 3:16), are throwing all that love and sacrifice back into His face, not wanting it, nor caring about it. Oh! How He must continue to suffer because of the sins of His children!

Your question is, "Should we simply stay silent and respect their wishes?"

I'm sorry, but you can only get as close to them as they will let you. Yes, it is the right thing for you to do. Respect their wishes. However, never stop taking every opportunity that they do allow to show them unconditional love and acceptance. And never stop interceding for them in your prayers. Talk to the Lord about their lifestyle of sin, not to them. Commit them daily to His keeping. After all, He loves them more than you do, right?

Try to never miss an opportunity to send them greeting cards: birthdays, holidays, thinking of you notes, and thank you cards, etc. Like with anyone and everyone else you keep in touch with, don't mention their sins. Mention your love and fond thoughts and interest in their activities and work that are not related to their life of sin. There's much to mention in these types of greeting cards.

Another thing I believe to be very important is to make sure that they always see Jesus in you, in your life, in your behavior, in your words. "Let this mind be in you, which was also in Christ Jesus" (Philippians 2:5). Be consistent in your own lifestyle, so that they have no room to see hypocrisy in you. You may be the only Bible they ever read. So make sure that what they do read in you and see in you is the character of Jesus Christ.

Please don't be too hard on yourselves. You must stop and realize that even Jesus, even God the Father, cannot save someone against his/her will. Look what happened to Lucifer in heaven. However, you can pray that the Lord will do whatever it takes to get their attention—whatever it takes to make them face eternal realities. He cannot force the will, the power of choice, but He can get their attention and bring circumstances around so they have to face eternal realities. This you can pray for, and then rest your minds at ease.

God be with you, dear ones. Be of good courage! Jesus will step in where you reach your limitations.

Victor

Question: As a Christian, how do I befriend someone of the same sex knowing she is interested in being more than friends with me?

I'm a female Christian who was just approached by a female, stating she has had a crush on me for a long time and desires to get to know me better with hopes of beginning a relationship. I shared with her that dating females is not my preference, and as far as building a relationship, I will only be interested in that of a friendship.

I have had other females in the past who have been attracted to me and have boldly expressed that to me. Their homosexual spirit has been so strong as to try to come upon me, although I know and truly recognize that this is an abomination unto the Lord.

What is your insight into this? Thank you in advance, and I pray that God will bless you a hundredfold for sowing seeds of righteousness. Your website is an inspiration. I have read many of the comments listed, and I appreciate how you answer everyone with the heart of God, which is His Word.

Reply: I know your situation is not an uncommon one. And it should be addressed to help others as well as yourself.

As a Christian, it is important that you always show yourself to be friendly, loving, and loveable. However, in this case your friendliness needs to be with wisdom and caution. You cannot afford to become close friends with someone who has designs upon you for a homosexual relationship. The Bible tells us "not to company with fornicators" (1 Corinthians 5:9, 11), but you can be friendly.

We are also counseled that if anyone obeys not the Word of God, "note that man, and have no company with him, that he may be ashamed. Yet count him not as an enemy, but admonish him as a brother" (2 Thessalonians 3:14, 15).

I would suggest that you only associate with someone like this within a group setting. In this way, you are free to be friendly without it being misinterpreted as a mutual attraction. Also, in this way this lady will not need to feel shunned, slighted, or left out, and can be the beneficiary of godly love, friendship, and counsel, even though her ways and persuasion may not presently be righteous.

From you and others in your circle of friends she needs to experience unconditional love and acceptance toward herself without being led to believe that her behavior is loved and accepted. Does that make sense? Work along with others toward her redemption.

Jesus loved Mary and said to her, "Neither do I condemn thee: go, and sin no more" (John 8:11). He obviously loved and accepted her but not her sin. He maintained a wholesome and godly relationship with Mary that never led her to believe that He condoned her previous lifestyle of adultery. We also have no record of Him ever socializing with her alone, but rather always in a group setting.

Pray for wisdom that you may be a blessing to this lady without encouraging her in the direction of sin.

Victor

Question: I have a younger brother, married, with children who came out about five years ago and said that he is gay.

All of my family attended a Baptist church regularly as we were growing up. When he announced this to the family I first thought about our upbringing in the church and asked him about it. He said that people can be gay and Christian and gave me a book to read by Mel White called *Stranger at the Gate*. I started to read it but didn't finish it because I disagree with Mr. White's opinion and interpretation of the homosexual issue—especially when he wanted to justify it with Scripture.

My question is: can anything be done to rescue my brother from this life-style in which he really seems to be entrenched? Even though my family attended church regularly growing up, I am labeled as being judgmental when I voice my opinion that I love my brother but cannot condone or accept this lifestyle. Every-one one in my family thinks that what he is doing is okay, that he was born this way, and that I will eventually have to come to accept it.

Reply: First of all, rest assured that you are not being judgmental toward your brother. You seem to have compassion without compromise, which is God's way. From what you have shared with me, I believe that you have a level head about this issue.

My counsel is found in the Word of God, for there is truly power in the Word. One has to recognize his need before that help can be given and received though. Of course, you are right in your understanding of this situation, because you are basing your position on the Word of God. My suggestion is that you:

1) Continue loving unconditionally in thought, word, and action toward your brother.

2) Pray without ceasing that the Lord will do whatever it takes to get his attention and help him to recognize his need.

3) Don't push, but always be ready to share a word of counsel from the Word of God should the occasion arise.

4) Pray for wisdom to be able to say and do the right thing at the right time for your brother.

5) Be at peace yourself, knowing that the Lord loves your brother more than you do and desires his salvation more than you. He is in safe hands with Him, though He Himself cannot and will not work against your brother's will.

6) Be a loving, lovable, and cheerful Christian. Attract your brother to Jesus' way through your happiness in Him.

7) Look for an opportunity to share resources with your brother such as my book and website information. He may be more likely to seek help in privacy that he would not want anyone to know about initially. So informing him of these resources might be very helpful.

I know that when I was in your brother's position, I was not only considered to be "unchangeable" but "unreachable" as well. I would not listen to anything or anyone, talk to anyone, watch anything, read anything, or go anywhere that had anything to do with religion or that might help me out of my situation. Pride is a great factor in the homosexual situation.

My parents quietly left behind many helpful resources whenever they visited. I knew them to be tokens of love and would, therefore, not discard them. Looking back on it, I refer to that collection as my "left behind series," all of which was purely biblical. When the time was right, the Lord led me to go to these very resources for assistance in my desire to be set free. And there in the Word of God alone I found all the answers I needed.

I hope these tips will be helpful to you in your effort to save your brother from his lifestyle of sin.

Be of good courage!

Victor

Chapter 15

HOMOSEXUALITY AND RACISM

Question: Many argue that opposition to same-sex marriage is similar to the opposition that was against interracial marriage. Do you agree or disagree?

Reply: Great question! I've never had this one before, but I totally disagree with this argument. Here's why: the Bible says, "Be ye not unequally yoked together with unbelievers" (2 Corinthians 6:14). That says nothing about interracial marriage, but rather speaks to unions made between the righteous and the unrighteous, and light with darkness. Though there may be many cultural obstacles to deal with in an interracial marriage making it, therefore, unwise for some, I have not seen anything in the Bible that condemns it or even advises against it. This is not a sin issue, in other words.

On the other hand, same-sex relationships are plainly condemned in the Bible. This is very clearly a sin issue. (Romans 1; Leviticus 18:22; Leviticus 20:13; 1 Corinthians 6:9–11.) It was God who created and established the parameters for marriage to be between one man and one woman, and to ask God to bless the union of one man and one man is to mock Him and His authority in this area. Having been gay myself and involved in long-term gay relationships that we deemed the same as marriage, I always knew that I was living outside the expressed will of God and would never have asked God's blessing on my sinful union. I just couldn't! The only way I could have peace in my relationships was to leave God out of them entirely. Whenever I began thinking about God, or wishing Him back into my life, I would realize my guilt for living out of harmony with His expressed will for me.

In short, the argument against same-sex marriage is based upon a plain "thus saith the Lord." It is not an argument initiated by supposed bigoted, narrow-minded, prejudiced Christians. It is an argument initiated by God Himself and accepted by loving and lovable Christians who only want to follow Jesus and allow Him to be Lord and Master in every area of their lives. Yes, of course there are those intolerant types of "Christians" as well, who argue against same-sex marriage out of hatred and prejudice, with the wrong spirit and attitude. But the argument is Bible-based and should be made in love and compassion, offering help and hope to those who will receive it.

Blessings!

Victor

Chapter 16

DESPERATION AND THE SUICIDE OPTION

Question: I am plagued by this curse since the age of eight. I am so tired of it and have even thought suicide to be the way out, though I have never attempted it. Nevertheless, I need help!

Reply: It intrigues me that you have been plagued by "this curse" since you were eight years old. I myself was plagued with it since the age of four! But then I have to ask, why would a 4-year-old, or an 8-year-old, be sexually interested at all? In a normal and healthy environment, children are not sexual human beings until they reach puberty. Children are not really equipped to deal with sexual issues physically, mentally, or emotionally.

My theory is that for a child to be mentally, emotionally, and/or physically sexual, he must have been introduced to it in some way. This could be done through any number of possibilities such as through media, the power of suggestion, conversation, observation, or deliberate physical or sexual molestation and abuse. Such was the case with me. I was robbed of my innocence by a farm hand at the tender age of four. And from that age onward my mind was obsessed with sexual fantasies about men, for that was how it was introduced to me. I had no knowledge of or interest in sexual behavior with a girl, for I had not been introduced to that. By the time I was in puberty, homosexual fantasies had taken control of my mental and emotional sexuality, and heterosexuality was at a great disadvantage.

Do you see where I'm going with this? My first question to you would be regarding any possible introduction to sexual ideas or behavior at or about the time you were eight years old. Unfortunately, this is much more common than we would like to think. So many people I know were sexually abused or taken advantage of in their childhood, and this worked to derail them emotionally and sexually in later life.

I hope you won't mind opening up a little to me on this so I can be better able to help you. In the meantime, please do not consider suicide anymore. It is so final. There's no way to reverse that once you go through with it. As a friend of mine once told me, "Put suicide off until tomorrow, it can always be a last option. Don't rush into it, because you can't take it back." Instead, I want to invite you to go through my website at: www.victorjadamson.com. There is much information there that I know would be helpful to you. Please take everything I have written there as being written to you personally, because I did write it for you. Yes, my answers may have been generated by someone else's questions, but after sending them to those people I posted them on the website, for you.

STRAIT ANSWERS TO THE GAY QUESTION

Be of good courage. God loves you, just as you are. Of course, in His love for you He wants to not only forgive you for your sins, but also to cleanse you from all unrighteousness. He wants to recreate you in His own image. He's a loving Father who takes pride in you, His son, wanting to reprove, correct, and instruct you in all the ways that will make you a noble, respectable, loving, and lovable person, just as He is.

Keep looking up, my friend!

Victor

Question: Why me?! It seems so unfair! Why was I selected to have this gay problem, and how do I get out of it?

I am a teenage Christian and a homosexual, and I have been feeling for a long time like a hypocrite because of the nature of my temptations and unwanted feelings. I want to get out of this addiction, or curse. I want to change. What should I do?

I know that God did not make me like this, but He could have prevented certain events in my life that lead up to my homosexual addiction. Why do I have to have these feelings? Why doesn't God just take them away already? What is He waiting for?

Why do I have to strive to become something I am not when other people don't have to? By nature they will not commit that sin. Straight people, by their nature, are avoiding a very dangerous sin (homosexuality) and many of them don't realize or care that they are so blessed to not be imprisoned by this curse. They don't know of all the sacrifices people like me have to make in order to become like them while they have to do nothing. It feels so unfair, doesn't it?"

Reply: Thank you, young man, for your letter. It takes a lot of courage for a young person like yourself to really reach out and talk about personal homosexual feelings, temptations, tendencies, and behavior. But talking about it in the right arena, getting it out, dealing with it, can all be very therapeutic and productive. So keep on searching your own heart, motives, tastes, and tendencies along with the Word of God on this subject. If you love truth and truly love Jesus, He has promised to lead you into all truth.

One thing I want to say right up front in response to some of your comments above is this: *temptation is not sin!* Jesus himself "was tempted in all points like as we are, yet without sin" (Hebrews 4:15). Do not let your temptation define who you are. Rather realize that your choices define who you really are. You can choose to be whomever and whatever you really want to be. Jesus promises that His grace, His divine power, is sufficient for you to give you victory and to sustain you in that victory.

Even in your victory you will be tempted to feel like a failure if you ever have another temptation. Temptation defines Satan's plan for your life. Temptation exposes *his* thoughts and feelings and motives for you. So please do not be discouraged because of the nature of temptations he throws your way. "Submit [yourself] therefore to God. Resist the devil, and he will flee from you. Draw nigh to God, and he will draw nigh to you" (James 4:7, 8).

You stated that you know God could have prevented certain events in your life, and then you asked why God doesn't just take away your feelings. My young friend, God must allow Satan to play his hand, to reveal his character and the character of his government, to be exposed as the destructive force in the universe that he is, in order for sin and misery and death to never rise up again throughout eternity.

It is a privilege for you and me to be able to stand before the world and before Satan and his mischievous masses as brands plucked from the burning, as captives set free, demonstrating to the universe the power of God to save the likes of you and me from our unique and seemingly unchangeable lifestyle of sin and degradation. When you and I stand to give our testimonies of deliverance from the hand of Satan, people are in awe and wonder at the love and power of God to work out His saving grace in such a powerful way through us.

I see this all the time. People have come to me, after hearing my story, with wonder and amazement, saying, "Pastor Ron (that's my real name), if God can save you, then ... why ... He can save anybody!" Some of these same people have then asked me, *me*—the once self-destructive and degraded homosexual—to baptize them once again now that they see and understand the amazing power of God to deliver His people *from* their sins.

God does not leave you to battle this issue alone. He does not leave you fighting these temptations and having this struggle for no good reason. Through you and your struggle, through the cross that you bear, you share in the sufferings of Jesus and should have a better understanding of His struggle against Satan and temptation. After all, He was tempted in all points like as we are, yet without sin (Hebrews 4:15). He suffered being tempted (Hebrews 2:18). And He resisted unto blood, striving against sin, against temptation (Hebrews 12:4). He had that battle until He drew His last breath on the cross.

Jesus was never removed from temptation, just as you and I may never be, but He was victorious nonetheless! He did not give in to it. Through you, and through me, Jesus' victory continues to be played out to the watching world, and watching universe.

Count your afflictions as a blessing. They can be to the glory of God if you will focus upon the vindication of His character and not your own struggle. Does that make sense? It's almost 1:00 a.m., so I may be just rambling here. But I do think the Lord is giving me fresh insights at this wee hour of the morning as I write to you—new insights that are helpful to myself as well!

You inquire about straight people not having this same struggle that you and I may have to deal with, but let me help you with this concept. Homosexuality is a violation of the seventh commandment. So is pre-marital sex, extra-marital sex, bisexuality, masturbation, pedophilia, pornography, lust of the heart. Do you get my point? These are all variations of a violation of the seventh commandment. They are all the same sin, just with different people, or methods. Homosexuality is not the unpardonable sin, or any worse than any of those just mentioned above. Be thankful that you are not dealing with *their* difficult tastes and tendencies!

You mentioned that homosexuality is an addiction, and that is a very good observation. But we can take it a little further and acknowledge that sin itself is addictive. That's why the Bible alludes to the bondage of corruption and sin. It is addictive and must be dealt with very seriously, like putting something to death.

Be of good courage, my young friend. Jesus loves you immensely, even with the struggle you are in. He wants to spend eternity with you by His side, as His peculiar treasure. He can and will save you personally *from* your sin, if you will but believe and trust in Him to do so. Focus upon His great and loving sacrifice for you that you might have eternal life with Him, and this will give you direction in your life that will lead you up the narrow way which leads to eternal life.

Do not be discouraged by temptation. Always remember in such circumstances that you are in good company. Jesus knows what you are going through, and He will be there to see you through, to assist you, if you will but call out to Him.

> For we have not an high priest [Jesus] which cannot be touched with the feeling of our infirmities; but was in all points tempted like as we are, yet without sin. Let us [my friend] therefore come boldly unto the throne of grace [where we receive divine power to resist and to overcome], that we may obtain mercy, and find grace to help in time of need. (Hebrews 4:15, 16)

Victor

Question: God placed me in the home where He knew I would be abused. He knew what was going to happen. Why then does He leave me with homosexual feelings to overcome?

Reply: My friend, you and I must have had the same childhood, for I, too, had the very same question for most of my life. When I finally got to the place where I stopped blaming Him, I was able to hear His answer, which was there all along.

God's Word to you, as it was to me, through Jeremiah 1:5 says, "Before I formed thee in the belly I knew thee; and before thou camest forth out of the womb I sanctified thee, and I ordained thee."

God did not *place* you in the home where He knew you would be abused, though He did know what was going to happen. He *allowed* you to be born in spite of the parents who conceived you, loving you, and being hurt along with you as Satan and sin played its hand against you. He allowed you to be born, not because of the bad that He foresaw, but for the good person He knew you could become if you would turn to Him as your Savior.

Should you accept Jesus Christ as your personal Savior from sin, through you the testimony can be given of God's unconditional love toward every one of His children, despite circumstances, genetics, environment, conditioning, and even their own poor judgment and bad choices resulting in sin and degradation. God not only loves you still, but He can and will save you personally from your life of sin and degradation. He is the Creator and the Re-Creator.

Those who are forgiven much, love much. People like you and I have the opportunity to reveal this love and power of God in a profound way that can make a serious impact on others who likewise feel hopeless and helpless.

You ask why God leaves you with homosexual feelings to overcome. Every child ever born is the product of generations of sinful parents, of inherited and created and cultivated tendencies to evil. Due to environmental circumstances beyond our own control, you and I were left with homosexual feelings to overcome, while someone else has other tendencies and feelings to overcome which are just as evil and just as overwhelming. But through the power of choice, which is yours, and the free gift of divine power known as grace, through Jesus Christ old things may pass away, and all things can become new, according to 2 Corinthians 5:17.

He will work within you to give you the desire and the ability to overcome (Philippians 2:13). And to you, the overcomer (for I know you, too, can be made whole), He has made some beautiful promises:

To him that overcometh will I give to eat of the tree of life, which is in the midst of the paradise of God. (Revelation 2:7)

He that overcometh shall not be hurt of the second death [eternal death]. (Revelation 2:11)

In other words, you are promised eternal life, together with Him.

He that overcometh, the same shall be clothed in white raiment; and I will not blot out his name out of the book of life, but I will confess his name before my Father, and before his angels. (Revelation 3:5)

In the judgment, He will proudly claim you as His beloved child to God the Father in the presence of the entire heavenly host. Amazing!

To him that overcometh will I grant to sit with me in my throne, even as I also overcame, and am set down with my Father in his throne. (Revelation 3:21)

Jesus, likewise, had to overcome inherited tendencies to evil, for He "was in all points tempted like as [you] are, yet without sin" (Hebrews 4:15).

He that overcometh shall inherit all things; and I will be his God, and he shall be my son. (Revelation 21:7)

You are very dear to Him, and He wants you to be as His son through all eternity. That is a very special and dear relationship.

If you are still looking for "Mr. Right," I give you Jesus.

Chapter 17

PORNOGRAPHY AND SELF ABUSE

Q uestion: I am a married woman and watch porn behind my husband's back. I am not a lesbian, but sadly, lust over women being with other women. I want to stop, but it is so hard. I always seem to fall. Please help me with advice. I do not want to lose my salvation and do not want to commit this adultery any longer, for I love my husband. Please write back. God bless.

Reply: Thank you for your inquiry. I know that God has victory in store for you. Be of good courage, for you are in good company. Jesus Himself "was in all points tempted like as [you] are, yet without sin" (Hebrews 4:15). So by this we know that temptation is not sin. We go on to read that Jesus "suffered being tempted" (Hebrews 2:18). Therefore, we know that the battle can be fierce and painful, yet victory can be won. Further on, in Hebrews 12:4 we discover that Jesus resisted unto blood, striving against sin. Yet, by His Father's grace, He did not yield. Grace is the divine influence working upon the heart and reflecting in the life, according to the Greek dictionary, and Jesus promises that His grace is sufficient for you.

You have a great start on this problem, for you already despise the sin and want victory. Jesus promised in Genesis 3:15 that He would create in the hearts of His children a hatred for sin and Satan. With that hatred for sin, you can go to Him acknowledging that you are dealing with a sin issue We are coming dangerously close to passage of the Gay Bill of Special Rights in Congress and the creation of *a superior class* of Americans, for He invites you to "Only acknowledge thine iniquity… and I will heal your backsliding" (Jeremiah 3:13, 22).

He came to save you *from* your sin, and He delights in doing so. "Submit yourself therefore to God. Resist the devil, and he will flee from you. Draw nigh to God, and he will draw nigh to you" (James 4:7, 8).

I like the method that Joseph used, "How then can I do this great wickedness, and sin against [my] God?" (Genesis 39:9). Then he fled the scene. Isn't that a great one?

David said, "Thy word have I hid in mine heart, that I might not sin against thee" (Psalm 119:11). So commit the exceeding great and precious promises to memory. When faced with temptation, bring "into captivity every thought" (2 Corinthians 10:5) by changing the subject, turning the page, flipping the switch, moving to a new location or activity, changing the channel, turning the dial, choosing something else to occupy your mind. There is power in the Word!

Another tip: Try mentally hanging pornography upon the "forbidden tree" and don't fall into the temptation of Eve when Satan whispered to her, "Ye shall not surely die" (Genesis 3:4). Just remind yourself that it is outside the parameters which God has established for your life and well-being. Renounce it and deny yourself access to it. This you can choose to do, and God will give you the grace, the divine strength to do so.

Remember, "Satan finds in human hearts some point where he can gain a foothold; some sinful desire is cherished, by means of which his temptations assert their power" (*Seventh-day Adventist Bible Commentary* Vol. 7, 927). However, "Not even by a thought could Christ be brought to yield to the power of temptation" (Ibid.)

Just a few tips that I hope will be helpful to you.

Victor

Question: I wanted to ask if masturbation is a sin?

Reply: Yes, I believe it is. Of course, the word "masturbation" is not used in the Bible, as is the case with many sins of contemporary nomenclature. Two texts that *hint* at this act being sin are as follows:

> And Onan knew that the seed should not be his; and it came to pass, when he went in unto his brother's wife, that he spilled it on the ground, lest that he should give seed to his brother." (Genesis 38:9)

> Know ye not that the unrighteous shall not inherit the kingdom of God? Be not deceived: neither fornicators, nor idolaters, nor adulterers, nor effeminate, nor abusers of themselves with mankind ... shall inherit the kingdom of God." (1 Corinthians 6:9, 10)

A common literary term for "masturbation" is "self abuse." The above text refers to "abusers of themselves" with mankind. Masturbation is a very prominent behavior within homosexuality and between homosexuals. I personally know this after years of living the gay lifestyle myself.

Another indicator of the sin of the behavior is the consequential feelings of guilt that follow. I never indulged in this behavior that I did not have a keen sense of guilt to follow. Guilt is the result of sin and is actually a valuable sense in convincing one of his need of a Savior.

Another test of this question is to try to imagine Jesus participating in this type of behavior. You cannot honestly picture Him compromised in this way, right? You might say, "But I can't imagine Him having sex with a woman either!" True, but we do know that not only did He sanction marriage with His very first miracle, He Himself created it in the beginning with the admonition to Adam and Eve to "Be fruitful and multiply" (Genesis 1:28).

There are those who argue that masturbation is only "normal human behavior," but we must remember that normal human behavior is sinful, fallen, and carnal. As Christians we are to rise above normal human behavior, becoming partakers of divine nature (2 Peter 1:4), allowing the mind of Christ to be in us (Philippians 2:5), cleansing "ourselves from all filthiness of the flesh and spirit, perfecting holiness in the fear of God" (2 Corinthians 7:1).

So, yes, there you have it. I do believe masturbation to be a sin issue. If we acknowledge it as such, then we can deal with it as such, for Jesus came to save His people *from* their sins (Matthew 1:21). God has said through the prophet Jeremiah, "Only acknowledge thine iniquity [sin]… and I will heal your backsliding" (Jeremiah 3:13, 22).

The Bible gives us the formula for success against sin. If we follow it, we can overcome.

Here's to your healing and success!

Victor

Chapter 18
THE PEDOPHILE ISSUE

Question: What about pedophiles? Seems like this sin is even more addicting and heinous.

Reply: I agree, somewhat. We can always find a sin more disgusting than our own. I remember shortly after my conversion in 1992 all the slander and rumors that were being circulated about me. I laughed it all off, saying, "There's nothing they can say that can be worse than the truth about my past."

Then someone informed me that among the rumors was the insinuation that I was not safe company in the presence of children! "By the way," one minister told the mother of a family I was preparing for baptism, "you'd better keep your children away from this man." I was shocked and extremely disturbed.

"Do you mean to tell me," I asked the informant, "that they believe I was a pedophile?"

"That's what they're saying," he said.

I was so disgusted and disturbed. I couldn't imagine being that way myself. It hurt me very deeply. And yet, the nature of my past lifestyle was just as evil in the sight of the Lord. Somehow I was always able to diminish my guilt by thinking, "Well, at least I'm not a pedophile! That's sick!"

Aren't we funny about our own sins? I believe that we can always find someone else's behavior to be worse than our own in our efforts to feel less guilty about our own failures and habitual sins. But sin is sin. One can miss out on heaven for lack of overcoming socially acceptable sins just as easily as he can lose out over what we label as disgusting sins.

You use an interesting expression, "addicting" when referring to these types of sins. I agree whole-heartedly that homosexuality is an addiction, just as is pedophilia. But then, is not all sin addictive? That's why the Bible speaks of being in bondage to corruption, to sin, and Satan, because sin is addictive.

But to answer your question, I truly believe that the addiction of the pedophile can be broken just as that of any other sin. Otherwise, we take the position that "*that* kind can never change!" That position exhibits one's having a form of godliness, but denying the power thereof.

I stand by the theme of my ministry that "Nothing is impossible with our God, for He is mighty to save, the whosoevers, from whatsoever, even to the uttermost"—the pedophile included.

Chapter 19
THE GENDER CHANGE ISSUE

Question: I have a friend that was born completely female, according to her, and then at three years of age somehow arrived at the conclusion that she was a boy. This conclusion led to a rough childhood and youth due to persecution, etc., resulting in introversion. After high school she went into a deep depression and then sought out a therapist who helped her. She then began a process of becoming a man via hormone replacement therapy and eventually surgery. Please comment on changing one's gender.

Reply: With so little information this is a tough question. It leads me to question what the circumstance and environment might have been for this three-year-old child to even make her aware of sexuality at such a young age. I, myself, was derailed sexually and emotionally at the tender age of four by a pedophile farm hand. My own circumstance and environment caused me to question my masculinity at that very young age and from then on until I finally chose to submit to the divine reconditioning and re-creative process of my loving heavenly Father. Surely our creator God knows and understands all the dynamics involved in this case and others like it.

It is very probable that this lady's homosexual attraction to another woman is the basis for choosing to change her gender. And this drastic medical procedure does not then justify her homosexuality, nor cleanse her from it. It only facilitates the sexual perversion that has been in her heart all along, resulting in much more confusion in her life and in the life of anyone who finds herself drawn into a relationship with her.

In the step-by-step program for understanding and overcoming homosexuality outlined in my book, step #11 is about being grateful. I believe it is very important to maintain an attitude of gratitude for the gender we were born with, or created with. Long ago a professor taught my father, who then taught me, that true happiness and joy come not from doing what one likes to do, but rather from liking what one *has* to do. Applying that principle to one's gender would mean choosing to cheerfully and gratefully live within the parameters our Creator has established for our eternal joy and fulfillment.

If marriage to one of the opposite physical sex, as designed and instituted by the Creator of sexuality, is not a viable option for someone like the friend mentioned above, then one must realize that biblically there is no other option for sexual expression, only abstinence and celibacy. We must also realize that society is filled with people who, for one reason or another, and in opposition to their hearts' desires, are unable to have sexual fulfillment. There are those who are widowed, divorced, disabled, handicapped, or mentally challenged, not to mention the myriads of heterosexuals who never find a desirable mate or who never are found to be a desirable mate by someone else.

What do we as Christians and society expect of all these? What does God expect, according to His expressed will? If a heterosexual woman who cannot find a mate for marriage indulges in sexual expression anyway, out of wedlock, we think of her as an adulteress, harlot, or whore. The same goes for the promiscuous heterosexual man, who likewise is an adulterer and whoremonger.

At the next level, if one cannot find a sex partner even out of wedlock due to being undesirable, disabled, handicapped, disfigured, or mentally challenged, and then resorts to masturbation, he or she has stooped to the practice of self-abuse. This also is unacceptable and unbiblical behavior for a Christian. Why would Christianity condone homosexuality and gender change as an exception to the biblical standard applied to every other possible situation relating to the seventh commandment, "Thou shalt not commit adultery" (Exodus 20:14)?

Jesus, our example in life, was One who lived His entire life without sexual expression and fulfillment. In this, perhaps, He has aligned Himself in a special way with those who are unable biblically or physically to participate in sexual expression. He "was in *all* points tempted like as we are, yet without sin" (Hebrews 4:15). That includes the temptations of sexual intimacy and expression.

The apostle Paul was another one who lived "without." He suggested:

But I speak this by permission, and not of commandment. For I would that all men were even as I myself [celibate]. But every man hath his proper gift of God, one after this manner, and another after that. I say therefore to the unmarried and widows, It is good for them if they abide even as I. But if they cannot contain, let them marry: for it is better to marry than to burn [to burn in lust for one another]. (1 Corinthians 7:6–9)

Jesus also gave some wise counsel, though very hard to understand:

All men cannot receive this saying, save they to whom it is given. For there are some eunuchs, which were so born from their mother's womb [destined from birth to a life without sexual expression or fulfillment]: and there are some eunuchs, which were made eunuchs of men [as when captured and made slaves, such as Daniel and his three friends in Babylonian captivity]: and there be eunuchs, which have made themselves eunuchs for the kingdom of heaven's sake. He that is able to receive it, let him receive it. (Matthew 19:11, 12)

I understand this to mean that if sexual expression in harmony with God's original plan is for some reason not an option in one's life, that he then chooses a life of abstinence and celibacy rather than to resort to self-abuse, masturbation, sex change, or perversion of any form of that beautiful gift given to mankind in the beginning designed by the Creator for the joy of procreation and intimacy, between husband and wife, man and woman.

Father truly knows best.

Victor

Chapter 20
LEGAL ISSUES AND POLITICAL CORRECTNESS

Question: Would it not be a violation of the principle of "separation of church and state" for Christians to urge a 'Yes' vote on the Federal Marriage Amendment to the Constitution? And would we be opening up the door for the last days by passing an amendment regarding religion?

Reply: Many of the laws of our great land are based upon the moral law of God, which deal with man's duty to his fellow man; in other words, the last six of the Ten Commandments. Parental rights are based upon the fifth commandment stating, "Honor thy father and thy mother" (Exodus 20:12). The sixth, eighth, and ninth commandments stating that we should not kill, steal, or bear false witness are all principles protected by the laws of our land. Protecting the institution of marriage (a seventh commandment principle) by the Federal Marriage Amendment is not a law establishing or enforcing religion. It would not be any more of a violation of the principle of separation of church and state than is the enacting of laws based upon these other moral commandments.

In fact, we Christians have a moral obligation to vote in favor of laws that uphold morality, rather than to allow immorality to run rampant. Our silence can be interpreted as consent. Our indifference can contribute to the downward trend toward anarchy in our great nation, which, by the way, was founded upon Christian principles by Christians who were fleeing religious persecution. We must remember that laws *protecting* morality are not the same as *establishing* morality or religion.

For example, the Workplace Religious Freedom Act is presently being promoted and debated in the U.S. Senate. This, too, is an effort to uphold and protect the moral rights of American citizens to live and work in harmony with their religious convictions. It is not a legislation of morality, but a protection of morality.

An amendment to the constitution is not a drastic measure without precedent. Historically, there have been 27 articles of amendment passed, the last one passing in 1992. In 1791 the very first one passed which involved the protection of the rights of religion.

Where cause for concern arises is when the state begins enacting laws dealing with our relationship to God as spelled out in the first four commandments; in other words, in passing civil laws regarding the worship of God. According to Revelation 13, that day is coming, but it will not be concerned with the issue of social morality. It will involve the passing of laws establishing and enforcing religious morality, the worship of God based upon man's tradition rather than upon the will of God as spelled out in His own moral law, namely the fourth commandment. But we will save that for another discussion.

Thanks for the great question,
Victor

––––––––––––––

Question: Is California's Proposition 8 really an attack against diversity?

"Proposition 8 and the Need for Diversity" —(from Cross Ministry website, with permission by Tim Wilkins)

WAKE FOREST, NC––Voting "yes" on Proposition 8 will define marriage by adding fourteen words to California's State Constitution: "Only marriage between a man and a woman is valid or recognized in California."

Some argue that voting for Prop 8 is an attack against diversity—i.e., a ban on same-sex marriage. Opponents of Proposition 8 argue that not recognizing same-sex marriages undermines the need for diversity.

Tim Wilkins, a speaker and writer, has an interesting take on California's current confusion.

"A defeat of Prop 8 would require the word 'married' to be qualified by either 'to a person of the opposite gender' or 'to a person of the same gender,'" says Wilkins. While at first glance such qualifiers appear to promote diversity, Wilkins says voting for the proposition will ensure just the opposite—the need for diversity. How so?

Says Wilkins, "Americans, particularly Californians, need to be reminded that 'same-sex marriage' lacks the very diversity it seeks to promote. A 'same-sex marriage' is characterized by sameness whereas a husband-wife marriage is characterized by difference or diversity."

"The prefix 'homo' means same while 'hetero' means different. Most Americans know that. What many Americans may not know is the fundamental meaning of 'diversity.'"

Definitions include "differing from one another" (Merriam Webster) and "The fact or quality of being different" (American Heritage Dictionary). Synonyms of diversity are also of interest: varied, different, distinct, unlike, dissimilar, and "noticeable heterogeneity" (online-thesaurus.net)

"Notice that last synonym 'noticeable heterogeneity,'" says Wilkins, who just returned from a 19-day speaking tour in Hong Kong where he addressed homosexuality in multiple venues. "Do you know that 'heterogeneity' comes from the same root word from which we get the word heterosexual"?

"Diversity, in its purest form, is marked by difference, which is found in the union of a husband and wife. To define diversity—or marriage—any other way is to alter its meaning."

Tim Wilkins directs www.CrossMinistry.org, an evangelical outreach to gays and lesbians. Wilkins is married; he and his wife have three daughters.

Question: What is happening in the legal world relating to homosexuality and the gay agenda? As Christians, what are we facing?

Reply: In Luke 17:28, 30, Jesus warns that "As it was in the days of Lot… thus shall it be in the day when the Son of man is revealed." In other words, the evils that were associated with the local society of Sodom and Gomorrah will be globally present just before the coming of Jesus. We know that one of the major evils was that of homosexuality. The sins of Sodom and Gomorrah included pride, idleness, haughtiness, fornication, and going after strange flesh (Ezekiel 16:49, 50; Jude 7).

In my short lifetime, the gay movement has sought and fought for the following successive issues for themselves: tolerance—to just be left alone—acceptance, equal rights, celebration (with gay pride month and parades), and promotion (through the education system and the media). And now, beyond promotion, they claim privilege with minority status (being *born* gay). In my opinion, this is affirmative action on steroids. Also, what we are witnessing and experiencing today is legislation against opposing opinions and the never-ending push for legislation to ensconce homosexuality within all echelons of society, including the church, to give themselves every freedom, advantage, and privilege available, all while silencing any expression of opposing opinion, biblical or otherwise. But beyond that, the gay movement is fast becoming a militant and persecuting power.

Militant & Persecuting Power:

Upon presenting my first manuscript for publication in the year 2,000, I was advised to use a pen name for my protection.

"Why?" I asked

"One of our recent authors broaching this subject had his house burned to the ground," I was informed, "and his speaking engagements were hounded by hecklers. We don't want that to happen to you and to your family."

In January, 2014 it was reported that an Oregon Christian bakery was facing hundreds of thousands of dollars in fines after refusing to make a wedding cake for a lesbian couple who took them to court. The business experienced a severe backlash with protests and picketing, threats to customers, death threats to their children. (Was this not hate speech?) In the end, the owners had to close their retail shop.

Just one month earlier, in December of 2013, a similar case occurred in Lakewood, Colorado with the same outcome. Those who trumpet the message of tolerance seem to have no tolerance for people who disagree with them. Any other bakeries could have been approached for the lesbian wedding cake, but Christians appear to have been targeted.

In just the past few years, a Mennonite bistro in Iowa, a Kentucky art gallery, and a New Mexico photography shop have also faced civil and legal complaints from gays who say their rights were violated when the business owners refused to serve them. They, too, were taken to court and ruled against.

Regarding the field of education:

1) In doing a search on Google of "teaching, homosexuality, kindergarten," the result was many pages of articles and video clips exposing the indoctrination and brainwashing going on in K–8 grades regarding homosexuality.

2) There are currently two bills which were introduced April 18, 2013, pending before the Senate and the House of Representatives in Washington, D.C., S. 555, now S. 1088, and H.R. 998, now H.R. 1652, both having the deceptive wording in their title, *Student Non-Discrimination Act of 2011*. These bills violate public school children in all 50 states by requiring mandatory pro-homosexual lectures to kids of all ages (including kindergarten and first grade). Schools that decline will lose government funding.

Other Legislation:

In light of the finding in 2002 by sociologists, Drs. Bearman and Brueckner, that "from 16 to 17 years old, if a person had a romantic attraction to the same sex, almost all had switched one year later," one must wonder what is behind the recent legislation in California and New Jersey:

California, SB 1172, Lieu. Sexual orientation change efforts. Approved by Governor Jerry Brown and filed with the Secretary of State September 30, 2012. This bill prohibits a mental health provider, as defined, from engaging in sexual orientation change efforts, as defined, with a patient under 18 years of age. The bill would provide that any sexual orientation change efforts attempted on a patient under 18 years of age by a mental health provider shall be considered unprofessional conduct and shall subject the provider to discipline by the provider's licensing entity.

Even if a 16- or 17-year-old *wants* counseling in this area, it is now prohibited by law. However, counseling one to embrace homosexuality is perfectly legitimate under this bill.

In the same calendar year, August 19, 2013, a similar bill was passed and signed into law in New Jersey by Governor Chris Christie, and a significant number of other states are now considering the same legislation.

The push to ban sexual-orientation "change" therapy for children is growing as lawmakers in at least eight states have introduced bills to outlaw the practice and gay-rights advocates expect at least a few to become law this year.[27]

Another bill in the works is The Employment Non-Discrimination Act of 2009 (ENDA), also referred to as the Gay Bill of Special Rights. It is legislation proposed in the United States Congress that would prohibit discrimination in hiring and employment on the basis of sexual orientation or gender identity by civilian, nonreligious employers with at least 15 employees.

Now, "In liberal cities across America, there are hundreds of lawsuits by radical homosexuals using local 'tolerance' laws to punish business owners, charities and even religious institutions. We are coming dangerously close to passage of the Gay Bill of Special Rights in Congress and the creation of *a superior class* of Americans."—Eugene Delgaudio of Public Advocate.

What is the ultimate goal of the gay agenda? The ultimate goal of the gay agenda is the eradication of marriage altogether. Notice: "*Fighting for gay marriage generally involves lying about what we're going to do with marriage when we get there.*" Those words were spoken by journalist Masha Gessen, a radical homosexual activist in an interview on March 2013, easily accessed on YouTube. "*The institution of marriage should not exist… We lie that the institution of marriage is not going to change. That is a lie. [What we want] is not compatible with the institution of marriage.*"

These and similar issues and laws are now being promoted on a global basis. Surely the warning words of the Lord are noteworthy: "As it was in the days of Lot… thus shall it be in the day when the Son of man is revealed."

Are we prepared to meet our God?

---

27   Cheryl Wetzstein, *The Washington Times*, Sunday, February 16, 2014.

Chapter 21

UNDERSTANDING AND OVERCOMING HOMOSEXUALITY

Q uestion: Is homosexuality a sexual orientation or a sexual preference?

Reply: A very popular social columnist recently suggested that we not refer to homosexuality as a sexual preference, but rather as a sexual orientation. Until this statement, I had really never given much thought to the difference between the two terms. To me they seemed synonymous, but, obviously, to the columnist there is a difference, a clear distinction between the two terms.

To her, using the term sexual orientation is to embrace the myth of once gay, always gay and to recognize homosexuality as an acceptable alternative lifestyle. Using the term sexual preference is to indicate that one could *choose* between homosexuality and heterosexuality, and, therefore, there could be no excuse for one to be gay or to remain gay. Consequently, for those espousing the theory of once gay, always gay, the term sexual preference is unacceptable, generating a little uneasiness and giving cause for the questioning of their position.

So just what is the case with homosexuality? Is it a sexual preference? Or is it a sexual orientation?

In light of the fact that one's perception is one's reality until such perception is altered, we might offer the simplistic answer, who cares? Or what difference does it make? If a person believes himself to have been born gay, then he might as well have been born gay, because as long as he perceives himself as hopeless, he is hopeless. As long as he sees no need, then there can be no assistance. As the old saying goes, "You can lead a horse to water, but you can't make him drink."

The homosexual who wants to remain gay and sees no need of being saved from homosexuality cannot be saved from it. If, in fact, someone was truly born gay, a theory I have come to doubt, then we could label his condition as purely sexual orientation. But even if he is not born gay, and instead was conditioned, or programmed, or taught to be gay through childhood molestation, abuse, or environment, his homosexuality could still be labeled as sexual orientation. That is the road he is traveling, the life he is living; that is the focus of his sexual attractions, and, yes, that is his sexual orientation.

However, once the homosexual has been shown that his lifestyle is one of sin, and that Jesus came to save His people *from* their sins, and that there is newness of life through Jesus Christ, that there is a way out, that one can be "born-again…"; then, if Jesus, who is the Way, the Truth, and the Life, is *rejected*; if His way out is *spurned*, then at that point the homosexual lifestyle becomes not only one of sexual orientation but also now one of sexual preference. He has been presented with a choice and *prefers* to remain unchanged. Instead, he may want the world around him to change their opinion, or he may want the church to change its stand and become more accepting of that which the unchangeable God of the church has condemned.

"God is love" (1 John 4:8), and in this love, Jesus came to "save his people from their sins" (Matthew 1:21)—from their orientation to sin, of whatever nature, "for all have sinned, and come short of the glory of God" (Romans 3:23). "Sin is the transgression of [God's] law" (1 John 3:4) which states clearly "Thou shalt not commit adultery" (Exodus 20:14). And "the wages of sin is death; but the gift of God is eternal life through Jesus Christ our Lord" (Romans 6:23). And He is "not willing that any should perish, but that all should come to repentance" (2 Peter 3:9), for "he is able also to save them to the uttermost that come unto God by him" (Hebrews 7:25).

So is homosexuality a "sexual orientation," or is it a "sexual preference"? Yes!

Question: How does the Lord bring about healing after someone has damaged themselves through participation in a homosexual relationship?

Reply: My experience and study is based upon such scriptures as:

"Seek ye first the kingdom of God, and his righteousness; and all these things shall be added unto you" (Matthew 6:33).

"Come unto me, all ye that labor and are heavy laden, and I will give you rest" (Matthew 11:28).

"Only acknowledge thine iniquity... and I will heal your backsliding" (Jeremiah 3:13, 22).

"But unto you that fear my name shall the Sun of righteousness arise with healing in his wings" (Malachi 4:2).

Jesus is the balm of Gilead and the heavenly Physician (Jeremiah 8:22), the Comforter who promised to send another Comforter (John 14:16). He wants to be Friend, Companion, and first Love in our lives. He wants a deep and abiding relationship with each of us. As we grasp hold of these concepts, promises, and invitations, we will have healing for our souls.

I was deeply in love with my partner with whom I had to break up when accepting Jesus. I learned through study, prayer, and contemplation to love Jesus more—more than my partner. I left the relationship with G___ physically wounded myself, for the devil took control of him, turning him to violence against me. I was emotionally damaged and scarred, and a mental wreck. My breakup with G___ was more traumatic than my divorce from my wife years earlier, but I trusted Jesus to bring sanity back to my life and healing for my badly wounded soul; and He did. Within a matter of months I was in ministry; within a year I was married. The rest is history: 22 years now in ministry (at the time of this article) and having the time of my life! I have learned firsthand the truth of the promise in *Steps to Christ*, chapter 5, that God's plan for my life far exceeds anything I could even imagine for myself.

God's way is best! As the title of the old TV program says, *Father Knows Best!* If we practice putting Him first in our lives, others second, and ourselves last, in accordance with His two great commandments, we will truly have the healing we desire and need—healing of heart, mind, and soul.

Question: How long did it take you to overcome homosexuality?

Reply: Under great conviction by the Holy Spirit, I chose to walk away from homosexuality, even with all my tendencies still in that direction. In other words, the day after I walked away, I was still just as strongly tempted as the day before. But I had chosen a new path for myself and leaned heavily upon God's grace (His divine power) to create in me a clean heart and to renew a right spirit within me. It was a process, a process of starving the old and feeding the new.

I chose to relocate myself, for I was still very much in love with the man I had lived with for a number of years. I chose to bring every thought into captivity unto the obedience of Christ, in spite of my feelings and emotions. I chose to be careful what I watched, read, listened to, and was careful about where I chose to socialize. Within one year of my baptism, I was married to a lovely young lady I had known since childhood. We now have two wonderful children together, a girl and a boy. They are the light of our lives.

I cannot say how long it would take for you or someone else. It depends upon how much effort you put into the process yourself, and how badly you want to be changed. But God's promise is sure in 2 Corinthians 5:17 that "if any man be in Christ, he is a new creature: old things are passed away; behold, all things are become new." This promise states that a genuine conversion results in new motives, new tastes, and new tendencies. When one is born-again, he is to overcome every inherited and cultivated tendency to wrong.

Does it mean that one is forever free from temptation? No! Of course not! Jesus Himself was tempted in all points like as we are, yet without sin. He suffered being tempted. He resisted unto blood being tempted, unto death, even the death of the cross (See Hebrews 2, 4, 12). Yet, He would not yield to temptation.

Temptation, my friend, does not define who you are. Temptation defines Satan's plan for your life. Please do not make the mistake that so many people make in believing that as long as they ever have homosexual temptations they are still homosexual. What matters with God is your choice of direction, your choice of thoughts, and your choice of behavior. Your orientation is determined by the direction you choose to go in life, not the direction that Satan wishes you to go.

I write much about this issue throughout my website and in my previous book. Please feel free to dig deeper in these resources.

Response from Questioner: Thank you for answering my question. I am 18 years old and have decided that I do not want to be a homosexual. You are such an inspiration to me, and when I watched the "Set Free"* episode on *It Is Written*, it gave me great encouragement. You said that you have praying parents, and I am pleased to say that I have praying parents as well. I have not ever acted on my feelings, and I thank God that I haven't.

Like you said, it is not in God's Word, so it is not right.

Thank you so much. God will bless you, and one day I intend to meet you and introduce you to my wife!

Reply: Thank you for that inspiring testimony and your encouraging words to me. I am looking forward to meeting you someday with your wife! But as you are 18, I do hope you will give the wife part a little more time, okay? You will be very wise to do so!

God bless you, too, my young friend!

Victor

* The "Set Free" episode is one of a four-part television series now available on a two-hour DVD titled *Compassion Without Compromise*.

Question: Can my homosexual tendencies actually be made to pass away?

Reply: Yes, they can be made to pass away, for the apostle Paul tells us in 2 Corinthians 5:17, "Therefore if any man be in Christ, he is a new creature: old things are passed away; behold, all things are become new." However, we must realize that this is a process that requires time and cooperative effort on the part of the one struggling against the bondage and addiction of homosexuality as with other sinful orientations.

It is important that you make a daily commitment to follow Jesus, that you daily submit to His lordship, that you daily resist the devil's temptations to homosexual thoughts and behavior. This daily conversion process brings you into a new relation with God. *Old things, your natural passions and hereditary and cultivated tendencies to wrong, to homosexuality, pass away, and you are renewed, redirected, and reconditioned.* But this work must be continual, for as long as Satan exists, he will make an effort to carry on his work.

He who strives to serve God will encounter a strong undercurrent of wrong. His heart needs to be barricaded by constant watchfulness and prayer, or else the embankment will give way; and like a millstream, the undercurrent of wrong will sweep away the safeguard. No renewed heart can be kept in a condition of sweetness without the daily application of the salt of the Word. *Divine grace must be received daily, or no man will stay converted...*

Test and trial will come to every soul that loves God. The Lord does not work a miracle to prevent this ordeal of trial, to shield His people from the temptations of the enemy... Characters are to be developed that will decide the fitness of the human family for the heavenly home—characters that will stand through the pressure of unfavorable circumstances in private and public life, and that will, under the severest temptations, through the grace of God grow brave and true, be firm as a rock to principle, and come forth from the fiery ordeal, of more value than [precious gold]. God will [claim as His own, as His elect and chosen], those who possess such characters...

The Lord accepts no halfhearted service. He demands the whole man. Religion is to be brought into every phase of life, carried into labor of every kind. The whole being is to be under God's control. We must not think that we can take supervision of our own thoughts. They must be brought into captivity to Christ. *Self cannot manage self; it is not sufficient for the work... God alone can make and keep us loyal.*

For which cause we faint not; but though our outward man perish, yet the inward man is renewed day by day. 2 Corinthians 4:16. (*Our High Calling*, 215, emphasis added)

Question: Is it possible to overcome my homosexual urges? Does anybody have a magic answer to this?

Reply: Yes, of course, it is possible to overcome your homosexual urges. I left that lifestyle behind myself 22 years ago. Now, don't expect to be relieved of the urges immediately. It is a process, a process of starving the old and feeding the new. I have written much about this on my website www.victorjadamson.com, and I invite you to please go through that website thoroughly. It will be very helpful to you.

In the meantime, rather than looking for a "magic answer" to this, I would encourage you to look in God's Word for the answer, for there is power in the Word. "By the word of the LORD were the heavens made; and all the host of them

STRAIT ANSWERS TO THE GAY QUESTION

by the breath of his mouth. For he spake and it was done; he commanded, and it stood fast" (Psalm 33:6, 9).

Second Corinthians 5:17 tells us that, "If any man be in Christ, he is a new creature: old things are passed away; behold, all things are become new." This simply and profoundly means that when a person is truly born-again, he can overcome every inherited and cultivated tendency to wrong, that a genuine conversion changes both inherited and cultivated tendencies and results in new motives, new tastes, and new tendencies. (Not necessarily overnight.) This is a marvelous concept, and it is truth in verity.

This does not mean that you will never be tempted again in this area, but remember, temptation is not sin. The nature of your temptation need not define who you are. Jesus was tempted in all points like as you are, yet He was without sin. So don't be discouraged by the nature of your temptations. Rather be encouraged by the promise of Jesus that "My grace [divine power] is sufficient for thee" (2 Corinthians 12:9). And when He promises to save you *from* your sin, you can know that "If the Son therefore shall make you free, ye shall be free indeed" (John 8:36).

Be of good courage!

Victor

———————————

Question: I've committed my life to Jesus and am a Christian. My issues lie with pornography and having impure thoughts every time I see a good-looking guy. What I'm most concerned about as a Christian is that it still turns me on. What do I do about lustful desires? Any advice would be great.

Reply: Your question addresses a very common concern among repentant gays. First of all, I think you will find some significant help in this area of my various resources, i.e., the book *That Kind Can Never Change! Can They...?*, my website featured article titled "You, Too, Can Be Made Whole!", and various "Question of the Week" articles on the website: www.victorjadamson.com.

Here are some brief pointers, however:

The Bible tells you that you can bring every thought into captivity. Temptation is not sin, for Jesus was tempted in all points like as you, yet without sin. But dwelling upon the temptation is lust, which is sin. So whenever you detect a lustful thought or idea, turn the page, flip the switch, change the channel, or look away. God will help you to do this, if you re-consecrate your life to Him each and every morning, and perhaps throughout the day as well.

David the psalmist said, "Thy word have I hid in mine heart, that I might not sin against thee" (Psalm 119:11). Commit some of those exceeding great and precious promises to memory, and draw upon them whenever tempted. Jesus beat back Satan's temptations by saying, "It is written ... "

I like the way Joseph handled his almost overwhelming temptation with Potiphar's wife. He was young, the hormones were raging, and he was confronted repeatedly by her. Putting the will of God first, and that of his friend and master Potiphar second, he ran from the scene saying, "How then can I do this great wickedness, and sin against [my] God!" (Genesis 39:9)

His feelings, emotions, desires, and urges were subjugated to those of God, and he fled in victory.

Just a few pointers; I hope they are helpful. Please go through the information on my website thoroughly, for I know there are more answers there for you.

Victor

Question: I am an ex-gay Christian struggling with lust in my heart, and I get really down about it. I keep praying that these desires will disappear, but I get the feeling this will be the thorn in my flesh, that I will have to work extra hard at getting deliverance from it. I gave up all the small stuff first, i.e., smoking, drinking, and swearing. But lust really has a hold of me.

Reply: Yours is a very common frustration, but in His Word, God has given you the answer and assurance of victory. Allow me to enumerate a few biblical suggestions:

1) Know "that the goodness of God leadeth thee to repentance" (Romans 2:4). What is repentance? The act of turning with sorrow from past course of action. You obviously have the sorrow, but you don't quite know how to turn away, right? The text says that the goodness of God will show you how to turn away.

2) "Submit [yourself] therefore to God. Resist the devil, and he will flee from you" (James 4:7). To have a complete victory you must completely submit your entire will to Him. Daily (sometimes even moment by moment) re-consecrate your life and will to Jesus, asking for His will to be worked out in your life. Then, obviously from this text, there is something for you to do: resist the temptation. All God's biddings are enablings. So if the Word says to resist, then God's grace will aid you in that resistance.

3) "But we all, with open face beholding as in a glass the glory of the Lord, are changed into the same image" (2 Corinthians 3:18). In other words, by beholding we become changed. By beholding the life and habits and sacrifice of Christ, we become like Him. Can you picture Jesus lusting after another man, or involved in self-abuse?

4) "Turn away mine eyes from beholding vanity, and quicken thou me in thy way" (Psalms 119:37). Take control of what you look at and what you watch, whether it be people, TV, movies, magazines, pictures, or billboards. You can choose where your eyes focus and linger.

5) "[Bring] into captivity every thought to the obedience of Christ" (2 Corinthians 10:5). How do you do that? Again, flip the switch, change the channel, turn the page, or divert your attention to something else, to something higher and nobler. "Thy word have I hid in mine heart, that I might not sin against thee" (Psalm 119:11). You can do this, for you have the gift of the power of choice. Jesus promises to help you.

6) "For it is God which worketh in you both to will [desire] and to do [act, behave] of his good pleasure." And you can be "confident of this very thing, that he which hath begun a good work in you will perform it until the day of Jesus Christ" (Philippians 2:13; 1:6).

7) The secret to this whole question is to act quickly, based upon knowledge rather than upon feelings, emotions, and unholy desires of the heart. Remember how Joseph dealt with his almost overwhelming temptation as a very young man with raging hormones when approached by Potiphar's wife. "How then can I do this great wickedness," he cried, "and sin against [my] God?" (Genesis 39:9).

Joseph placed the feelings, emotions, and desires of His God above those of his own self. He also considered the feelings, emotions, and desires of his master Potiphar above his own.

8) Here is a method that I came up with for myself. I picture two trees in the Garden of Eden: the Tree of Life, and the Tree of Knowledge of Good and Evil (death). You remember that one could be partaken of freely, while the other one was off-limits. I mentally hang on the Tree of Knowledge of Good and Evil (death) all things God has placed off limits to me in His love for me and desire for my well-being. Try it! If you are tempted by cigarettes, mentally hang them on the forbidden tree. If your desire is for alcohol, hang that beer (or martini) on the tree. If you find yourself lusting over someone or his body, mentally hang him on that tree. Then turn from it, and walk away.

9) "Therefore if any man be in Christ, he is a new creature: old things are passed away; behold, all things are become new" (2 Corinthians 5:17). Believe this! When one is truly born-again (it's a process) he will develop new motives, new tastes, and new tendencies. A genuine conversion will change every inherited and cultivated tendency to wrong.

"For if we confess our sins [our lust], he is faithful and just to forgive us our sins [of lust], and to cleanse us from all unrighteousness [including lust]" (1 John 1:9). "Only acknowledge thine iniquity [lust, as a sin issue] … and I will heal your backslidings" (Jeremiah 3:13, 22).

10) You have referred to your problem with lust as a possible thorn in the flesh, but for every thorn in the flesh Jesus has promised, "My grace is sufficient for thee: for my strength is made perfect in [your] weakness" (2 Corinthians 12:9). Grace is defined as the divine influence working upon the heart and reflecting in the life. Grace is none other than divine omnipotence, and it is yours for the asking. "And all things, whatsoever ye shall ask in prayer, believing, ye shall receive" (Matthew 21:22).

Victor

P.S. One more thing! In order to have assurance of sufficient grace for you to overcome in this one area, the breaking of the seventh commandment, it is important that you acknowledge God's authority as expressed in all 10 of His commandments. "If ye love me," Jesus says, "keep my commandments" (John 14:15). He doesn't say "keep nine commandments," but "keep *my* commandments." There are 10! Think on these things!

Testimonial: An interesting point of view: the link between temperance and victorious living.

I have more of a remark than a question. For a long time now, I have been struggling with the burden of unwanted sexual sins. I'd seemingly gain victories only to find myself crashing down in defeat again. Bible promises were repeated, agonized prayers were offered, but to no avail. I believed I was trusting Jesus and looking to Him for salvation, but I was ignoring a very fundamental issue that I didn't realize was standing in the way of God's help and grace. It was my diet that was rich in spicy sauces, gravies, meats, pizzas, rich cheeses, sweets, Cokes, Pepsis, and even an occasional beer. Also I liked to "stuff" myself so full that I could hardly walk! All of these pleasures were hindrances to gaining the total victory over my besetting sins. It wasn't until I started heeding the scriptural counsel offered in the book *Counsels on Diet and Foods* that I started to gain true victories in my battles. A simple diet is advised, free from those elements that harm the digestive system and the body as a whole.

I also noticed the biblical mandates offered in God's Word for living a healthful live. I would suggest every one of your readers take a long, intense inventory of their dietary lifestyle and see if it measures up to God's original plan. Fresh fruits, nuts, vegetables, grains, pure water, and a temperate intake routine has helped me take hold of the rich source of power offered by Christ in His Holy Word, now that my mind is freed from the enervating and debilitating habits of my former life.

Please examine this point of view, Pastor Ron. Of course, diet is not the sole answer to the problems we face, nor is it the one single key to victory, but possibly we ourselves are the biggest obstacles to God's plan for our lives.

Reply: Wow! You hit one nail right on the head. That is great insight on your part. You are absolutely right. As you have read in the book *Counsels on Diet and Foods*, I'm sure, there is much counsel about the influence of intemperance on behavior, how it actually brings out the animal instincts in mankind.

Thank you for your thoughts. You make a very good and important point.

Victor J. Adamson (Pastor Ron)

Question: What hope is there for the non-Christian to overcome homosexuality?

Reply: First of all, I would ask what would be the motivation for a non-Christian homosexual to overcome? From a Christian perspective, assisting such a person in this endeavor would actually *not* be the place to start. Jesus said, "Seek ye first the kingdom of God, and his righteousness; and all these things shall be added unto you" (Matthew 6:33).

As one accepts Jesus as His personal Savior from sin and then looks to Jesus as Lord and Master of his life (his thoughts, his words, and his actions), by beholding Him he will want to change, for Jesus will create in him a hatred for his life of sin. (See Genesis 3:15).

Regarding the question of overcoming as a non-Christian, I would have to answer as a Bible-believing Christian. I must take the Word of God as it reads regarding this question. So let me lay it out as simply and plainly as possible straight from the Word.

1) Salvation is possible through, and only through, Jesus Christ:

Be it known unto you all, and to all the people of Israel, that *by the name of Jesus Christ* of Nazareth, whom ye crucified, whom God raised from the dead, even by him *doth this man stand here before you whole… Neither is there salvation in any other: for there is none other name under heaven given among men, whereby we must be saved.* (Acts 4:10, 12 emphasis added)

2) Salvation is to be a saving from sin, not only from its penalty, but from its power as well:

And thou shalt call his name JESUS: for he shall save his people from their sins. (Matthew 1:21)

3) Sin is defined as the breaking of God's moral law of Ten Commandments:

Whosoever committeth sin transgresseth also the law: for sin is the transgression of the law. (1 John 3:4)

4) Disobedience in any regard, or the breaking of any one of the Ten Commandments, is defined as law breaking:

For whosoever shall keep the whole law, and yet offend in one point, he is guilty of all. For he that said, Do not commit adultery, said also, Do not kill. Now if thou commit no adultery, yet if thou kill, thou art become a transgressor of the law. (James 2:10, 11)

5) Homosexuality is the transgression of the seventh commandment of God's moral law of 10 commandments, which states, "Thou shalt not commit adultery" (Exodus 20:14). Homosexuality is therefore sin. Homosexuality is one of 17 abominations I have found listed in the Bible, and as such certainly leaves one being less than whole, needing divine intervention, divine therapy, divine reconditioning, and re-creation.

If a man also lie with mankind, as he lieth with a woman, both of them have committed an abomination. (Leviticus 20:13; see also 18:22)

6) Homosexuality is identified as vile affection, the product of a reprobate mind, and is included in a long list of wicked behaviors worthy of the punishment of death (to be carried out by God in the final judgment):

For this cause God gave them up unto vile affections: for even their women did change the natural use into that which is against nature: And likewise also the men, leaving the natural use of the woman, burned in their lust one toward another; men with men working that which is unseemly, and receiving in themselves that recompense of their error which was meet. And even as they did not like to retain God in their knowledge, God gave them over to a reprobate mind, to do those things

STRAIT ANSWERS TO THE GAY QUESTION

which are not convenient; Being filled with all unrighteousness, fornication, wickedness, covetousness, maliciousness; full of envy, murder, debate, deceit, malignity; whisperers, Backbiters, haters of God, despiteful, proud, boasters, inventors of evil things, disobedient to parents, Without understanding, covenantbreakers, without natural affection, implacable, unmerciful: *Who knowing the judgment of God, that they which commit such things are worthy of death*, not only do the same, but have pleasure in them that do them. (Romans 1:26–32 emphasis added)

7) Deliverance from homosexuality must be preceded by an acknowledgement that homosexuality is sin:

Only acknowledge thine iniquity, that thou hast transgressed against the LORD thy God, and hast scattered thy ways to the strangers under every green tree, and ye have not obeyed my voice, saith the LORD... Return, ye backsliding children, *and I will heal your backslidings*. (Jeremiah 3:13, 22 emphasis added)

8) *So if we deny the sinfulness of homosexuality and reclassify it as an acceptable alternative lifestyle, then God Himself is powerless to deliver the homosexual—powerless to change one from gay to straight. And if God cannot work, then who can?*

The blood of Jesus Christ his Son cleanseth us from all sin. If we say that we have no sin [that homosexuality is an acceptable alternative lifestyle], we deceive ourselves, and the truth is not in us. If we confess our sins [that our homosexuality is sin], he is faithful and just to forgive us our sins, and to cleanse us from all unrighteousness [even that of homosexuality]. If we say that we have not sinned [by denying the sinfulness of homosexuality], we make him a liar, and his word is not in us. (1 John 1:7–10)

"So," you ask, "are you saying that the Buddhist, the Muslim, the Hindu, the Atheist, the Agnostic, the freethinker, etc., cannot be saved from his homosexuality unless he accepts Jesus Christ? Why! That's preposterous!"

Is it, friend? It was a Christian pastor that said of me 10 years ago, "*That* kind can never change!" If we as Christians doubt that a homosexual can be changed by the omnipotent (all-powerful) creator God of the universe, why would we think that a homosexual who acknowledges no god, or a lesser god, would be able to overcome?

It is true, however, that homosexuals can, without Jesus Christ, suppress their behavior. Monasteries and convents of various religions around the world are filled with people who have taken vows of chastity, silence, and poverty. These monks and nuns suppress their natural desires and unnatural desires in things both good and bad with all the human strength they can muster, but none of this changes the heart. I fear that these poor souls are not familiar with the blessed words of Jesus, "I am come that they might have life, and that they might have it more abundantly" (John 10:10).

Having squandered my youth and the prime of my life in the sinful, self-serving pit of homosexuality, I can personally testify to the accuracy of the words of the apostle Paul: "By the name of Jesus Christ... doth this man stand here before you whole. Neither is there salvation in any other: for there is none other name under heaven given among men, whereby we must be saved" (Acts 4:10, 12).

Victor

Question: Is the battle against homosexuality within myself simply an exercise in futility?

Reply: First of all, we have to acknowledge that no one receives a spotless character as an inheritance from his parents, or as a gift from any other human being. The apostle Paul counsels, "that ye put on the new man, which after God is created in righteousness and true holiness" (Ephesians 4:24).

A noble life and character is received as the gift of God through Jesus Christ. Those who receive Jesus as their Savior from sin, including the sin of homosexuality, become sons and daughters of God. They are His spiritual children, born-again, renewed in a life of doing right according to *His* standard, not that of the increasingly degenerate world. They accept and receive the divine power, or grace, of God. In cooperation with the proposition to "Let this mind be in you, which was also in Christ Jesus" (Philippians 2:5), their minds are changed. With clearer vision they can see the evil of their homosexuality in light of eternal realities. They are adopted into God's family, and they become conformed to His likeness and changed by the working of His Spirit from victory to victory against homosexual tendencies and temptations. From cherishing supreme love for self (the root of homosexuality, as well as of all other sin), they come to cherish supreme love for God and for Christ.

Accepting Jesus Christ as a personal Savior from the sin of homosexuality, and *following* His example of self-denial in the area of sexual gratification—this is *the secret of success* in battling homosexual tendencies and temptations.

Overcoming homosexuality is not the result of depending upon one's feelings, it is the result of surrendering all to God and living by "every word that proceedeth out of the mouth of God" (Matthew 4:4). It is doing the will of our heavenly Father, trusting in God through trial and temptation, and believing in His promise in the darkness as well as in the light. A successful relationship with

Jesus results from walking by faith as well as by sight, trusting in God with all confidence, and resting in His love.

A genuine victor over homosexuality is one who is changed from within as well as in outward behavior, one who guards his thoughts as well as his actions, one who is entirely and without reserve the Lord's, not in form, but in truth. Every impurity of thought, every lustful passion, separates the soul from God, for Christ can never put His robe of righteousness upon a homosexual sinner, to hide his abnormal sexual orientation.

> There must be a progressive work of triumph over evil, of sympathy with good, of reflection of the character of Jesus. We must walk in the light [of truth], which will increase and grow brighter unto the perfect day [from day to day until complete and total victory is achieved]. This is real, substantial growth, which will finally attain to the full stature of men and women in Jesus Christ ...

> Conformity to the likeness of Christ's character, *overcoming all sin and temptation,* walking in the fear of God, setting the Lord continually before us, will bring peace and joy on earth, and ensure us pure happiness in heaven. (*Our High Calling,* 214)

Question: I no longer wish to practice homosexuality, but neither do I want to be with a woman. Can the Lord accept me as a celibate single man, as opposed to a reformed ex-homosexual married man? I believe that God is more interested in us working for Him in these last days, than with the final disposition of our sexuality. God has told us, "Be ye holy, even as I am holy" (1 Peter 3:8). Does someone like me really need to practice heterosexuality in order to demonstrate freedom from this pernicious sin? Thank you again for your wonderful ministry.

Reply: My friend, you are the first to ask me this question, and I must say that it is a very good one for which I believe the Bible gives us very clear counsel. Yes, of course the Lord can accept you as a celibate single man. God has offered a most beautiful gift to man in creating woman to be a "helpmeet" to him, an equal partner in life. However, it is not a sin for man to forgo that gift and to not marry, or for a woman to not marry.

Jesus was never married, neither were many notable Bible personalities. The apostle Paul himself was never married and had this to say about it:

> Now concerning the things whereof ye wrote unto me: It is good for a man not to touch a woman. Nevertheless, to avoid fornication, let every man have his own wife, and let every woman have her own husband. Let

the husband render unto the wife due benevolence: and likewise also the wife unto the husband. The wife hath not power of her own body, but the husband: and likewise also the husband hath not power of his own body, but the wife. Defraud ye not one the other … For I would that all men were even as I myself. But every man hath his proper gift of God, one after this manner, and another after that. I say therefore to the unmarried and widows, It is good for them if they abide even as I [single]. But if they cannot contain, let them marry: for it is better to marry than to burn [meaning, with lust]. (1 Corinthians 7:1–9)

The apostle Paul is here talking very plainly about appropriate sexual behavior: about being single, about celibacy, about not withholding sexual intimacies from one's spouse, and not seeking self-gratification through masturbation, but rather saving all sexual expression for the beloved spouse, etc.

He actually encourages those who feel called to be single and celibate to remain so. However, he cautions that if singleness and celibacy result in lust and sexual fantasies and fornication, it would be better for one to marry and avoid those sins of the flesh, to find sexual fulfillment through marriage, the only divinely approved arrangement for sexual expression.

Allow me to share with you from my own experience. When I was born-again, I was very content to spend the rest of my life in celibacy. After all, I felt unworthy of being married since I had squandered that gift in my youth and had lived a life filled with perverted sexual self-gratification for 16 years.

But then I was called into ministry. Everything was great for a while, until someone started spreading rumors when my Bible worker associate and I went somewhere together alone. He was young and attractive, and people started accusing him of being gay—led astray by me, his pastor. I was shocked and frustrated. Our relationship was more like that of a father and son, for he was from a broken home and had a very poor father image with which to relate. But I could understand how the evil surmising could get started. So I tried to be very careful to avoid any appearance of evil and to avoid any situation that would feed such rumors and consequently stigmatize my associate.

It was necessary one day for me to give one of the ladies of our church a ride to town. We were together alone in the car only a short distance, because we stopped to pick up a third person. But the gossips who saw us drive off together didn't know about the third person and started spreading rumors about this lady and me and a developing romance.

Needless to say, I became even more frustrated. "Lord!" I cried, "how can I effectively work for you in ministry? How do I follow your plan of going two by two? I cannot be seen with either a man or with a woman without feeding the minds and empowering the tongues of the evil surmisers."

Shortly after that, the Lord placed in my path the lady who is now my wife. We had known each other since childhood, and she was a good friend with both of my younger sisters. She knew my story of falling from grace, self-destruction, degradation, contrition, remorse, repentance, conversion, newness of life, and call to ministry. She believed in the power of God to change the "unchangeable," to re-create the fallen and broken creation. She trusted God, and she trusted me. This made it easier for me to relate to her and to be relaxed as a romance blossomed between us at the hand of the Lord. When I eventually proposed to her, she responded, "[Victor], I always knew you were slow. But I never thought it would take you 30 years! I've been in love with you since the eighth grade, but you always were interested in someone else."

When we were married, of course I was very nervous. So was she. But aren't all brides and grooms nervous? We didn't know whether we would be able to fulfill the expectations of one another, and we both had our own reasons. The Lord has richly blessed our marriage; we are very compatible. He has blessed us with two beautiful children, giving us both second chances and double portions in life and in ministry.

When I read in the Bible, "Eye hath not seen, nor ear heard, neither have entered into the heart of man, the things which God hath prepared for them that love him" (1 Corinthians 2:9), I truly believe that "Higher than the highest human thought can reach is God's ideal for His children" (*Education*, 18). And do you know what? I don't deal anymore with evil surmising about my still being gay, or about inappropriate relationships with women. The Lord put an end to that by placing me in a very fulfilling marriage and in giving us beloved children. Now, and no surprise here, Satan comes at us from other directions, for "all that will live godly in Christ Jesus shall suffer persecution," we are warned (2 Timothy 3:12).

My friend, when we place ourselves trustingly into the hands of God, submitting ourselves entirely to His care and keeping, we can trust that life will be more than we could ever imagine for ourselves. I encourage you to do just what you have suggested: choose to live your life as a celibate, single man. Marriage in and of itself is not a convincing demonstration of heterosexuality. After all, many homosexuals disguise their sin by marriage.

Grow strong in the Lord, in faith, in doctrine, and in spirit. Let the Lord do with you as He will. He may choose to assist you by His grace (His divine power and strength) to live a godly, pure life in single celibacy, empowering you to focus on living for Him and blessing others, even as the great, single, celibate apostle Paul.

However, He may also choose to surprise you someday down the road of life. All He wants from you right now is a willing and obedient heart. Buckle your seat belt, my friend, and enjoy the ride. You can demonstrate freedom from the pernicious sin of homosexuality by living godly in Christ Jesus, by being a loving and lovable Christian, by being a blessing wherever you go. Heterosexual marriage is not the solution to homosexuality. Jesus is!

Chapter 22

TEMPTATION AND ORIENTATION

Question: Understanding that homosexuality is not in accordance with the will of God, am I guilty of sin because of continued homosexual temptations?

Reply: In response, I would like to share with you a passage I read this morning in our family worship from a book titled *Our High Calling*, page 87:

> Blessed is the man that endureth temptation: for when he is tried, he shall receive the crown of life, which the Lord hath promised to them that love him. (James 1:12)

> It is not the order and will of God to shield His people from temptation… When truth takes possession of the heart, the Christian will be brought into conflict… There are opposing elements in his own household, even in his own heart, and nothing but the free Spirit of God can ensure for him the victory.

> The beginning of yielding to temptation is in the sin of permitting the mind to waver, to be inconsistent in your trust in God. The wicked one is ever watching for a chance to misrepresent God, and to attract the mind to that which is forbidden. If he can, he will fasten the mind upon the things of the world. He will endeavor to excite the emotions, to arouse the passions, to fasten the affections on that which is not for your good; but it is for you to hold every emotion and passion under control, in calm subjection to reason and conscience. Then Satan loses his power to control the mind. The work to which Christ calls us is to the work of progressive conquest over spiritual evil in our characters. Natural tendencies are to be overcome… Appetite and passion must be conquered, and the will must be placed wholly on the side of Christ.

> We pray to our heavenly Father, "Lead us not into temptation," and then, too often, we fail to guard our feet against leading us into temptation. We are to keep away from the temptations by which we are easily overcome. Our success is wrought out by ourselves through the grace of Christ. We are to roll out of the way the stone of stumbling that has caused us and others so much sadness.

> Temptation and trial will come to us all, but we need never be worsted by the enemy. Our Saviour has conquered in our behalf. Satan is not

invincible... Christ was tempted that He might know how to help every soul that should afterward be tempted. *Temptation is not sin; the sin lies in yielding.* To the soul who trusts in Jesus, temptation means victory and greater strength.

Victor

Question: I'm being tempted where I work. My boss has been giving me signs that he's attracted to me. I've been ignoring them and even show my displeasure. I have also been keeping a distance from him. But now I'm feeling like I'm very drawn to him, even getting jealous. So I have decided to quit my job in order to remove myself from this temptation as in Matthew 5:29, 30. My question is, should I just quit? Run from it? Or do I really need to face it? I know that I can't run forever, but I really don't want to fall into sin. Thanks.

Reply: The secret to overcoming this temptation is not in quitting your job, because Satan will follow you with more temptation at another job location. It is true that if you are leaving behind a gay lifestyle that it is helpful to relocate, if possible, to new surroundings and to create a new circle of friends—straight ones, Christian ones. However, if you are wanting to resist temptation, you need to build up strength, primarily through "bringing into captivity every thought to the obedience of Christ" (2 Corinthians 10:5). This you can do, for all Christ's biddings are enablings. If God says to do it, there is supplied grace to follow through.

He promises, "My grace is sufficient for thee: for my strength is made perfect in weakness" (2 Corinthians 12:9). Grace is defined as that divine influence working upon the heart and reflecting in the life. Grace is nothing less than omnipotent, divine power.

Another tip from King David himself is this, "Thy word have I hid in mine heart that I might not sin against Thee" (Psalms 119:11). So build up your strength and resistance to temptation by filling your mind with the exceeding great and precious promises of God, many of which you will find in the final chapter of this book as "A Rainbow of Promises." Choose what you will think about, flip the switch, change the channel, turn the page, turn your head, or change the subject. "Submit [yourself] therefore to God [day by day, and moment by moment, if necessary]. Resist the devil, and he will flee from you" (James 4:7). In your behavior and deportment, do not give your boss any "come-ons" or invitations. Give him no reason to believe that he can have his way with you.

Now, if these steps do not alleviate the problem you face, then you might consider leaving your job and seeking employment elsewhere. I do understand that as he is your boss this does create a very difficult situation. Pray that the

Lord will give you wisdom and good judgment to make the right decisions at the right times. Remember that Joseph was in a similar situation with the wife of his boss Potiphar. He did flee from his duties rather than yield to sin with her. His reaction, if implemented, will bring you great strength as well: "How can I do this great wickedness, and sin against [my] God?" (Genesis 39:9).

Grace to you, my friend!

Victor

Temptation and Orientation

Within the community of those aiding homosexuals in their struggles to come to Christ and come out of homosexuality there are divergent views on the issue of orientation and temptation and the relationship between the two. Some hold the position that one's orientation is defined by the nature of his or her temptations. I personally disagree with that position and would like to explore that subject in this study.

First of all, it is helpful to look at authentic definitions of the word *orientation:* "the act or process or orienting or of being oriented; a usually general or lasting direction of thought, inclination, or interest; a person's self-identification as heterosexual, homosexual, or bisexual."[28] Also, "the adjustment or alignment of oneself or one's ideas to surroundings or circumstances. Basic beliefs or preferences, as in sexual orientation."[29]

Sexual orientation is a pattern of emotional, romantic, and/or sexual attractions to men, women, both genders, neither gender, or another gender. According to the American Psychological Association, "sexual orientation refers to the sex of those to whom one is sexually and romantically attracted. Categories of sexual orientation typically have included attraction to members of one's own sex (gay men or lesbians), attraction to members of the other sex (heterosexuals), and attraction to members of both sexes (bisexuals)… In addition, some research indicates that sexual orientation is fluid for some people. This may be especially true for women." (Excerpt from: *The Guidelines for Psychological Practice with Lesbian, Gay, and Bisexual Clients, adopted by the APA Council of Representatives, February 18-20, 2011.* The Guidelines are available on the APA website at http://www.apa.org/pi/lgbu/resources/guidelines.aspx)

In the above definitions, it appears that adjustment, adaptation, alignment, and choice are dynamics that should not be excluded in our understanding of orientation, but should, rather, be factored in. The idea that one's sexual orientation

---

28   www.merriam-webster.com (accessed June 4, 2014).

29   www.thefreedictionary.com (accessed June 4, 2014).

is identified by the nature of his/her temptations does not allow for the broader range of definitions regarding the issue.

Second, we need to consider the definition, source and/or sources of temptation. From where does temptation come? Who is the originator of suggestive, impure, tempting thoughts? Is it not Satan?

The definition of *tempt*: "To attempt to persuade (a person) to do something evil or unwise, as by promising pleasure or gain. To be attractive to; invite. To test; prove." [30]

From where does temptation come? To answer this question, let us examine a few Bible verses.

Then was Jesus led up of the Spirit into the wilderness to be tempted of the devil... And when the tempter came to him... (Matthew 4:1, 3)

And when the devil had ended all the temptation, he departed from him [Jesus] for a season. (Luke 4:13)

A certain lawyer stood up, and tempted him. (Luke 10:25)

Let no man say when he is tempted, I am tempted of God: for God cannot be tempted with evil, neither tempteth he any man: But every man is tempted, when he is drawn away of his own lust, and enticed. Then when lust hath conceived, it bringeth forth sin: and sin, when it is finished, bringeth forth death. (James 1:13–15)

In these above texts are revealed three sources of temptation: Satan himself, other people, and the lusts of the flesh or our own tendencies and propensities and habits. Therefore, to say that our orientation is defined by the nature of our temptations is not an accurate statement. It can be correct, but temptations can also come from outside ourselves as well as from inside.

This is why I contend that temptation may be a revelation of Satan's plan for my life rather than a revelation of my own orientation. Is it necessary that we allow Satan's customized plan for our lives to define who we are and the nature of our orientation?

In years past, I was a private pilot for a while. During that time I flew in various weather conditions, sometimes fighting a head wind or a crosswind, sometimes being pushed along by a tail wind, and once (on my first solo cross-country flight) even struggling to make my way through a violent storm. But in every case, I refused to let the wind and weather conditions determine my orientation or alter my destination.

Likewise, in my walk with the Lord, I have charted a course for myself and *oriented* myself to successfully reach my spiritual destination. Satan may blow

30   Funk & Wagnalls Standard College Dictionary–Harcourt, Brace & World

at me his crosswinds, tail winds, and head winds of temptation and may even embroil me in a violent storm as he battles for my soul, but he cannot alter my orientation. He cannot force me to yield to his devices. Contrary to conventional thinking perhaps, I do not allow Satan's customized plan for my life to define who I am or define my orientation. I believe that temptation reveals Satan's orientation for my life, not my own orientation. Only if I give in to his plan can I be identified with it.

"Why is this so important?" you may be asking. "What difference does it make, anyway?"

To me it is a very important issue, as I have spent the past 18 years using the method of positive reinforcement to live victoriously in this area and to maintain that victory. Upon my conversion, I chose a new orientation for myself by God's grace and have practiced replacing old thoughts and old ways with new ones. When asked to use a pen name for my protection in the publishing of my story I chose the name Victor J. Adamson, a name with a message of positive reinforcement. I don't want to live the rest of my life wearing a label reflecting Satan's plan for my life, and I don't find a biblical basis for this opposing view of sexual orientation, as I will continue to show in this study.

Another point to consider is revealed in the text of Hebrews 4:15 which states that Jesus "was in all points tempted like as we are, yet without sin."

Therefore, if one's orientation is defined by the nature of his temptations, what would we say was Jesus' orientation? "Oh! But—", some would say, "Jesus was God. He did not have the same fallen nature that we have. He was the second Adam and had the nature of Adam before the fall."

And I believe that herein lies the crux of the whole matter. Is this true according to the Word of God? Is this a biblical point of view? Notice the following:

"God sending his own Son in the likeness of sinful flesh, and for sin, condemned sin in the flesh" (Romans 8:3).

"And [Christ Jesus] was made in the likeness of men" (Philippians 2:7).

"*Forasmuch* then as the children are partakers of flesh and blood, *he [Jesus] also himself likewise took part of the same*" (Hebrews 2:14, emphasis added). Notice the literary emphasis used in this verse to point to Jesus' human nature being like yours and mine: *forasmuch, he also himself likewise.*

Now, this definition of orientation being determined by the nature of one's temptations might be in harmony with conventional thinking, logic, reasoning, and understanding, but I'm not sure that such sources of our definitions are always in harmony with the Word of God. Especially do I think this to be true in light of so many texts of Scripture that teach us of the transforming power of our creator and re-creator God. For example:

"Let this mind be in you, which was also in Christ Jesus" (Philippians 2:5).

"Be not conformed to this world: but be ye transformed by the renewing of your mind, that ye may prove what is that good, and acceptable, and perfect, will of God" (Romans 12:2).

As we consider the subject of orientation in light of the gospel of salvation from sin, we must also consider the possibility of reorientation: "a fresh orientation; a changed set of attitudes and beliefs; a change of direction; the act of changing the direction in which something is oriented; setting or arranging in a new or different determinate position; to adjust or align something in a new or different way."[31]

Once a person goes through the reorientation process he is now able to self-identify with a new and different orientation. This fact is imbedded in the very definition of the word reorientation, is it not?

By the way, is this not what the gospel, the plan of salvation is all about? Change? Newness of life? From all walks of life to newness of life? For example: does acceptance of God's health message not require a reorientation? How about the Christian counsel on standards of dress and adornment? Does not this counsel also initiate a reorientation? Does the truth regarding the seventh-day Sabbath not initiate a reorientation in one's thinking and life practice resulting in a drastically altered lifestyle? Yes, of course, the gospel is all about reorientation.

What is the natural orientation of every man, woman, and child, anyway? Is it not an inward orientation? A self-focused, self-centered, self-pleasing orientation? Is not this true of everyone's carnal nature? And what does God's Word say about the natural man?

> But the natural man receiveth not the things of the Spirit of God: for they are foolishness unto him: neither can he know them, because they are spiritually discerned. (1 Corinthians 2:14)

> Among whom also we all had our conversation in times past in the lusts of our flesh, fulfilling the desires of the flesh and of the mind; and were by nature the children of wrath, even as others. (Ephesians 2:3)

In contrast, we read further:

> But God, who is rich in mercy, for his great love wherewith he loved us, Even when we were dead in sins, hath quickened us together with Christ, (by grace ye are saved;) And hath raised us up together, and made us sit together in heavenly places in Christ Jesus; That in the ages to come he might shew the exceeding riches of his grace in his kindness toward us through Christ Jesus. For by grace are ye saved through faith; and that not of yourselves: it is the gift of God; Not of works, lest any man should boast. For we are his workmanship, created in Christ Jesus unto good works, which God hath before ordained that we should walk in them. (Ephesians 2:4–10)

---

31   www.thefreedictionary.com (accessed June 4, 2014).

Wow! This sounds like a major reorientation process to me! A reorientation from self*fish*ness to self*less*ness, loving God supremely (totally unnatural), and loving others as our selves (also totally unnatural).

Some other texts of Scripture that support the principle of reorientation are as follows:

"Casting down imaginations, and every high thing that exalteth itself against the knowledge of God, and bringing into captivity every thought to the obedience of Christ" (2 Corinthians 10:5).

"For as he thinketh in his heart, so is he" (Proverbs 23:7).

"Out of the abundance of the heart the mouth speaketh" (Matthew 12:34).

"Whatsoever things are pure, whatsoever things are lovely… if there be any virtue… think on these things" (Philippians 4:8).

In being born-again, we are counseled that, "If any man be in Christ, he is a new creature: old things are passed away; behold, all things are become new" (2 Corinthians 5:17). According to a Bible commentary on this text, "The new birth consists in having new motives, new tastes, new tendencies," and "a genuine conversion changes hereditary and cultivated tendencies to wrong" (*Seventh-day Adventist Bible Commentary* Vol. 6, 1101).

In other words, orientation can be changed, converted, by a reorientation. To believe otherwise is to believe once gay, always gay, a myth akin to that converse presumption of once saved, always saved, both of which I believe to be easily dispelled by a proper understanding of the Word of God.

This is also why the apostle Paul could say of the Corinthian believers and converts from sins such as fornication, idolatry, adultery, homosexuality, and alcoholism: "Such **were** some of you, but ye **are** washed, but ye **are** sanctified, but ye **are** justified in the name of the Lord Jesus, and by the Spirit of our God" (1 Corinthians 6:9–11, emphasis added).

When asked by the jailor of Philippi, "What must I do to be saved?" Paul answered by saying, "Believe on the Lord Jesus Christ, and thou shalt be saved" (Acts 16:30, 31). If we insert the definitions for the words "Lord" (used so often in place of Jehovah, the great I AM, the self-existent One), and "Jesus" (Deliverer, from sin, Matthew 1:21), and "Christ" (Messiah or Anointed), we can translate Paul's statement to say "Believe on the Eternal Self-Existent One who was anointed to be your personal Savior from sin, and you shall be saved *from* your sins."

I really appreciate these encouraging words:

Through all ages and in every nation those that believe that Jesus can and will save them personally from sin, are the elect and chosen of God; they are His peculiar treasure. They obey His call, and come out of the world and separate themselves from every unclean thought and unholy practice. (*The Review and Herald*, August 1, 1893)

In conclusion: "All we like sheep have gone astray; we have turned every one to his own way" (Isaiah 53:6). "All have sinned, and come short of the glory of God" (Romans 3:23). We all, by nature, are the children of wrath, carnal, fallen human beings, but our hope is in Jesus, who took upon Himself our fallen nature and, therefore, was also tempted in all points like as we are, yet demonstrated that we, too, can reach the point of living without sin.

Temptation is not sin, and we need not be discouraged by it or allow it to define who we are. It matters not that we are of a fallen nature, but that we can be partakers of the divine nature, that we can be reoriented, with the mind of Christ, with new motives, new tastes, and new tendencies, to lives of obedience to Christ rather than rebellion against God.

As one commentator wrote:

> All true obedience comes from the heart. It was heart work with Christ. And if we consent, He will so identify Himself with our thoughts and aims, so blend our hearts and minds into conformity to His will, that when obeying Him, we will be but carrying out our own impulses." (*The Desire of Ages*, 668)

The plan of salvation is all about new beginnings, reconciliation, restoration, and reorientation. If we will receive Jesus for who and what He is, we can and shall receive power to become sons and daughters of God (see John 1:12).

Take heart:

> There hath no temptation taken you but such as is common to man: but God is faithful, who will not suffer you to be tempted above that ye are able; but will with the temptation also make a way to escape, that ye may be able to bear it. (1 Corinthians 10:13)

> Grace and peace be multiplied unto you through the knowledge of God, and of Jesus our Lord, According as his divine power hath given unto us all things that pertain unto life and godliness, through the knowledge of him that hath called us to glory and virtue: Whereby are given unto us exceeding great and precious promises: that by these ye might be partakers of the divine nature, having escaped the corruption that is in the world through lust. (2 Peter 1:2–4)

Amen!

Chapter 23

HOMOSEXUALITY AND THE FOURTH COMMANDMENT

The Sabbath/Homosexual Connection!

Question: I've been dealing with homosexuality most all my life, pleading with God to take it away as a youth, and giving up for years because it just wouldn't go away… I always knew it was wrong and against God, regardless what anyone would say. I take the Word of God very seriously and believe it to be true. Knowing what the Bible said about the issue and its consequences and believing it, I have left the gay life… I am now doing my best to live a life of obedience to God through the Word even though I am still attracted to men.

I have been scoping the web for some possible help and I came across your site… The reason why I chose to at least contact you is because when I was reading your questions section you had answered a question about the Sabbath. Are the Sabbath commandment and seventh commandment relevant to each other?

Reply: I'm impressed that you do want the Word of God to be your rule of faith and practice, regardless of how politically, religiously, or socially "incorrect" it may at times seem to be.

The Sabbath issue to me is really a no-brainer if one is allowing the Word to speak for itself and to be his infallible guide. Throughout the Bible the seventh-day Sabbath is highlighted. So to those who wish to accept another day as holy, I simply ask, "Show me from the Word of God the basis for such a change, and we will then have something to study and discuss." In other words, if it is not substantiated by God's Word, then it has no credibility with me.

The Sabbath was created as the seventh day of the week in Genesis 1 and 2. We have no reason to believe that all of the patriarchs and prophets were not Sabbath keepers. Jesus and His disciples were Sabbath keepers. Jesus declared that He was Lord of the Sabbath day. And John the Revelator, in the last book of the Bible told us how he was in the Spirit on "the Lord's day"—Sabbath. Also, the seventh-day Sabbath was observed throughout Christianity for over 300 years after Jesus' ascension, and it took a couple centuries for the pagan "Sun-day" to replace it at the hands of Roman Catholicism. Isaiah 66 tells us that we will be keeping Sabbath throughout all eternity.

When I accepted Jesus as Lord and Master of my sexual identity and the seventh commandment, I had to accept Him as Lord and Master in regards to all 10 of the commandments if I wanted assurance of His sustaining grace regarding that seventh one. Therefore, I am a seventh-day Sabbath keeper in harmony with the fourth commandment, and, by God's grace, an ex-gay in harmony with the seventh one!

There are several principles that really helped me in dealing with my same-sex attractions as a new Christian 20 years ago. (By the way, I've been married now for 21 years and have two beautiful children, ages 19 and 17, as of this writing.)

1) I learned that temptation is not sin and should not be allowed to define who I am. Why? Because Jesus was tempted in all points like as I am, yet He didn't sin (see Hebrews 4)!

2) No matter how strong the temptation, attraction, desire, or tendency, it really doesn't matter. Why? Because Jesus, too, suffered (struggled) being tempted in all points as I am.

3) In fact, even if that struggle should be relentless, it's still okay. Why? Because Jesus resisted unto blood striving against sin (see Hebrews 12). Jesus is not only our *Saviour from sin* (Matthew 1:21), He's also our *example in life*.

   The very term "Christian" means follower of Christ, a disciple of Christ, one who follows the discipline and lifestyle of Jesus Christ, one who takes up the cross of Christ in temptation and in persecution. So that means that we face temptation head on, no matter how big the struggle, even to the point of choosing to die rather than sin if necessary, even as Jesus did and as did millions of martyrs throughout the Dark Ages and beyond.

   When faced with temptation, we should say with Joseph, "How can I do this great wickedness and sin against God?" (Genesis 39:9).

4) The Bible advises us to bring every thought into captivity to the obedience of Christ (2 Corinthians 10:5). So I practice flipping the switch, turning the page, changing the channel, turning my head, or changing the subject when faced by a tempting situation.

   James advises, "Submit yourselves therefore to God. Resist the devil, and he will flee from you" (James 4:7). God does not promise to remove temptation from us. He promises that His grace is sufficient for us. Grace, by the way, is defined in the Greek dictionary as the divine influence working upon the heart and reflecting in the life. In other words, divine, omnipotent, transforming power. Isn't that great?

5) Another thing to remember is this: you may have been converted some time ago, but I can assure you that the devil has not! So? Well, he will continue doing what he has always done best, and that is to tempt, to deceive, to lure, to entice, and to destroy. Our only hope is to continue in Jesus Christ, daily submitting to His will for our lives, making an entire surrender of the will regardless of our tendencies, attractions, and

desires. In fact, the apostle Paul counsels us to "present [our] bodies a living sacrifice, holy, acceptable unto God, which is [our] reasonable service" (Romans 12:1). "His commandments are not grievous" (1 John 5:3).

Paul goes on to say in 2 Corinthians 5:17, "Therefore if any man be in Christ, he is a new creature: old things are passed away; behold, all things are become new." This simply means that the new birth consists of having (or developing) new motives, new tastes, and new tendencies, and that a genuine conversion changes both hereditary and cultivated tendencies to do wrong.

I have practiced over the past 22 years starving the old self and feeding the new, the self I want to be, the self like Jesus Christ.

I hope these thoughts will give you something to think about and much encouragement.

Victor

Question: How should we celebrate the Sabbath? There are so many different views on this, and I know it has nothing to do with being gay. But I really do want to do the Lord's will. Our church believes that we can choose any day to celebrate Sabbath, but then that day must be set aside for the Lord. What are your views on the Sabbath?

Reply: When I accepted Jesus and entrusted my life to Him, allowing Him to be Lord and Master of my life, I believed I needed to submit to Him in relation to all 10 of His commandments, not just one or two, or nine. I could not expect His promised grace (divine, transforming power) to sustain me in regard to the seventh commandment and victory over homosexuality if I did not acknowledge His authority as expressed in *all* the other nine! The fourth commandment states clearly that the Sabbath day is the seventh day of the week and then itself refers back to creation week to remind us that the Sabbath is a memorial to creation, and to Jesus as the Creator.

> For in six days the LORD made heaven and earth, the sea, and all that in them is, and rested the seventh day: wherefore the LORD blessed the sabbath day, and hallowed it. (Exodus 20:11)

You will remember from the Genesis account that on the seventh day of the week God rested from all His creative work from the previous six days, and then set aside the seventh day, blessing it, sanctifying it, making it holy, to be a day of special fellowship between the created and the Creator.

The Sabbath has nothing to do with the Jews. There were no Jews when Jesus created the Sabbath. Jesus Himself said to the Jewish leaders who had so corrupted the Sabbath with all their impossible rules, regulations, and rituals, "The sabbath was made for man [meaning mankind], and not man for the Sabbath" (Mark 2:27). Jesus also stated that He, Jesus Himself, "is Lord even of the sabbath day" (Matthew 12:8). So when John was in the spirit on the Lord's day in Revelation, he was talking about the Sabbath, not Sunday.

Elsewhere, in Ezekiel 20:12, 20, God informs us that the Sabbath was to be a sign (seal, mark) between Himself and His people, like a covenant, that He the creator God was their God and that they were truly His people, the children of the creator God. Any other holy day would indicate allegiance to another god, not the creator God who created the Sabbath in the first place to forever be a memorial to His creation and to Him as Creator, as stated above.

Christians the world over were observing the seventh-day Sabbath for 300 years after the resurrection and ascension of Jesus Christ. It was in the fourth century AD during the counsel of Laodicea that the Catholic Church attempted to change the Sabbath to Sunday. She today boasts that Sunday is her mark of authority, and virtually all Protestant denominations officially state in their literature and manuals that Saturday is the biblical Sabbath, not Sunday. This attempted change of God's law was an effort to make it easier for sun worshipping pagans to join the Christian church by negating the need for a lifestyle change. Many other biblical Christian doctrines have likewise been altered for the sole purpose of dismissing the need of lifestyle change.

But the gospel is all about lifestyle change. We are counseled, "Be ye transformed by the renewing of your mind" (Romans 12:2). "If any man be in Christ, he is a new creature: old things are passed away; behold, all things are become new" (2 Corinthians 5:17). "Except a man be born again, he cannot see the kingdom of God" (John 3:3). There are many such references in the Bible that reveal the need for Christ's children to be changed (converted), transformed, to become perfect, reflecting the very image of Christ Himself.

Volumes could be written on the Sabbath and how to properly observe the Sabbath. But suffice it to say that in no place anywhere in the Bible is another day referenced as an acceptable day of worship to God who gave us the Sabbath in the very beginning. And in Isaiah 66 we are told that we will be assembling and worshipping before God from one Sabbath to another throughout all eternity.

If the Sabbath was instituted at creation and will be observed throughout the endless ages of eternity in heaven with Jesus, then why would there be a substitute today? And why would that substitute be the day established by pagans for the worship of their god the sun (a created entity), if there was to be a change? "Come now, and let us reason together, saith the LORD" (Isaiah 1:18).

The truths of the Bible can easily be understood if we just accept the simplicity of the gospel and take the Bible as it reads. As I write this to you, it is Friday, the preparation day for the Sabbath of the Bible. I hope you have a blessed Sabbath tomorrow!

Victor

P.S. For your further study, I'll give you a teaser. The Bible refers to the Sabbath as God's sign, His seal, His mark. The Bible also refers to the mark of the beast, which no man wants in the end-time. The mark of the beast is greatly misinterpreted today to be anything from a computer system in Belgium to bar codes and microchips. But it's really a simple thing to understand, right out in the open. The sign, seal, or mark of the beast is but a counterfeit of the sign, seal, or mark of God. (You might want to chew on that one a little bit.) I would encourage you to follow the example of the Bereans of old who, "searched the scriptures daily, whether these things were so" (Acts 17:11).

Happy Day!

Question: I do appreciate your self-sacrificing testimony. But my question is, where is Jesus in all this? Your responses certainly have a lot to do with behavior of the sinner and how most people will not be saved. Why not focus on Jesus and His sacrifice and suffering rather than our law-abiding? Are you a legalist?

Reply: No, I am not a legalist. And I am wondering what the source is of your information about my beliefs. Are you referring to my interviews on television? Or have you read my book? Or are you reading on my website? Whatever the case may be, if you will take an honest and thorough look at my material, I think you will be hard pressed to miss the fact that Jesus *is* the center of my understanding, for the theme of my ministry is that our God is mighty to save, the whosoevers, from whatsoever, even to the uttermost.

Jesus came to save His people *from* their sins, not *in* their sins, sin being the transgression of the law (see Matthew 1:21; 1 John 3:4).

The wages of sin, transgression, and disobedience is death—eternal death (see Romans 6:23).

All have sinned and come short of the glory of God (Romans 3:23), and are, therefore, subject to this death, should we not accept by faith the sacrifice that Jesus has made for those willing to repent of their sins and turn from their backsliding. There are many biblical references to this point.

Jesus' grace, His divine power, is sufficient for anyone of us to transform us into His likeness. "If we confess our sins, he is faithful and just to forgive us our sins, and to cleanse us from all unrighteousness [even that of homosexuality]" (1 John 1:9).

If any man be in Christ, he is a new creature, a new creation. Old things, like homosexuality, are passed away; behold, all things are become new—new motives, new tastes, new tendencies (2 Corinthians 5:17). When one is born-again and is truly converted, he is empowered to overcome every inherited and cultivated tendency to wrong.

You question the importance of our law abiding. Jesus Himself said, "If ye love me, keep my commandments" (John 14:15). That's law abiding. James refers to the law of God as the law of liberty (James 1:25; 2:12). What kind of a society would we have if we were not subject to law? What kind of a society would God have if His creation were not subject to law? It is God's law that denounces murder, stealing, lying, dishonoring parents, idolatry, etc. So why can't we accept His commandment that forbids perverse sexual behavior? He created sexuality, and He should know what is good and what is not good in that area of life as well as in all others.

I make no apology for promoting law abiding, for I love Jesus and want to live in harmony with His will, as expressed in His Ten Commandments. Obedience to God's law is *not* a means to salvation. If Jesus came to save His people from their sins, from their disobedience, then obedience is the *result* of Jesus' influence in the life. In other words, salvation *results* in obedience, in law abiding. I don't think that is legalism. It's a biblical fact.

Again, however, let me point out that Jesus is the center of my belief system and the center of my message of victory over sin, for Jesus Himself told us in John 8:31–36 that if the Son sets you free, you are free indeed! This is the point I am trying to get across to those who are struggling with the addiction of homosexuality, to those who want to be set free from it. Homosexuality is a sin issue for which God has made provision in His plan of salvation from sin.

However, God Himself will not force His will upon anyone. If one is happy and content in his homosexual lifestyle, God will not force His will upon that person. But as one looks into the mirror of God's law and sees himself to be out of sync with God's will and then desires to be transformed to be in harmony with the will of God, then God can go to work in that person to will and to do of His good pleasure.

To the homosexual I have this to say, "You, too, can be made whole!" But you must *want* wholeness, and you must *choose* wholeness. Jesus provides all that one needs to be made whole. "My strength," He says, "is made perfect in [your] weakness" (2 Corinthians 12:9).

Be strong in the Lord!

Victor

Chapter 24
ANSWERING THE SKEPTICS AND THE CRITICS

Question: I was wondering what troubles you about gays and lesbians? Do you not think that you are hurting them?

Reply: First of all, I'm not sure why you would think that I am troubled. I am not troubled about gays and lesbians. I have friends of this persuasion around the country whom I love very much. Though I am not troubled *about* them, I am troubled *for* them. I do have a burden for their salvation from sin.

As an ex-gay myself, I know how I felt while in the gay lifestyle. And I know of many like me who have openly stated that if homosexuality were a choice they would never have chosen it for themselves. They are, and I was, convinced that we were born that way; that's just who we are; there was nothing to do but accept it and try to have a good life. Yet, I, as many others like me, was never free from guilt. In God's Word, we are informed that by his very nature man knows to a great extent the difference between right and wrong (see Romans, chapter 1).

In a love and desire for truth, I decided to search my life and the Word of God honestly, and with an open mind, to see if I could find assurance of salvation and eternal life while hanging on to my pet sin. I could find neither. Instead, I discovered a God who loved me in spite of my sinful life and offered me a way out. Bottom line, I accepted His plan for my life, accepted His grace, and His divine strength to walk away from my life of sin and to walk into newness of life with Him. He has given me a wonderful new life, with a wife and children, a loving church family, a meaningful and productive career, and hope and assurance of everlasting life.

I have peace, my friend. And I am compelled to share with others who likewise are sin-sick, who want a new direction in life, the good news that our God is mighty to save the whosoevers, from whatsoever, even to the uttermost, for nothing is impossible with God.

I am not interested in debating with those who are content with their homosexuality. I am not out to persuade others against their will. But I know for a fact that there are many homosexuals, like I was, who desperately want a way out. For them I wrote my book and set up my website: www.victorjadamson.com.

How do I know they want a way out? Not only from knowing them personally, but from the response to my website. Many are praising the Lord for finally being directed to a God who loves them enough to give them newness of life. I firmly believe that a genuine conversion results in new motives, new tastes, and new tendencies, that when a person is truly born-again, he can overcome every inherited and cultivated tendency to wrong. Otherwise, God is impotent, rather than omnipotent. Homosexuality is very clearly defined in God's Word as wrong, unnatural, sin, abomination. God loves the homosexual enough that Jesus gave His life for him, too. But Jesus came to save His people *from* their sins, not *in* their sins (see Matthew 1:21).

The more I think about it, the more I realize that, yes, there is something that troubles me about gays and lesbians: their quality of life, their short life expectancy, the pain and suffering they cause themselves as well as their families and friends through lives dedicated to self-gratification, self-advancement, self-glory, self-exaltation, and self-abuse.

Homosexuality is focused inward rather than outward. It is not focused upon being a blessing to others, but rather serving self to the detriment of others. Homosexuality is a dead-end street. It brings to an end a 6,000-year line of procreation, of passing on life to another human being. It preys upon and depends upon the children of others (heterosexuals) to perpetuate its existence, thus continuing its legacy of inflicting heartbreak, pain, and suffering upon others.

I know homosexuality well, for I was immersed in it for many years. I devastated my wife and children, parents, families, and friends. As I traded in one lover for another, over and over, I hurt others in my own mad career of pleasing myself. God's plan was for one man and one woman for life, a life of honor, trust, fidelity, dignity, and productivity.

Yes, there is much that troubles me about homosexuality. From God's Word, I know the destiny of those who fail to walk in newness of life. I am sad for them, but I respect their power of choice. And so does God. That's why He says that to those who love not truth, He Himself will send strong delusion (2 Thessalonians 2:10–12).

You asked: "Do you think that you are hurting gays and lesbians?"

No! Absolutely not! I am exercising my freedom of speech and imposing my beliefs upon no one. My website is a help site. I am not a lobbyist, an activist, or a politician. I am simply following the gospel commission, offering a better way to those who are seeking and desiring it.

Thank you for your inquiry, and may God bless you in accordance with your love and desire for truth!

Victor

Question: I was reading your website again today and became troubled by the passage below. It seems to indicate that being whole, happy, and filled with purpose are incompatible with being gay. I don't find the two being mutually exclusive. The message that you can't be whole and gay, or gay and fully Christian troubles me. I fear that it fosters internal homophobia.

The quote in question: Today, after a determined struggle to understand and to overcome his homosexuality, Victor J. Adamson lives a totally new life filled with purpose, genuine love, joy, and peace. No longer walking in confusion, frustration, and despair, he lives a full and productive life as a husband and father.

It is his desire to draw from his own life and experience to show others how they, too, can be made whole.

Reply: I don't quite see in my statements what you see. I do stand by what I wrote and believe it wholeheartedly, and I'm not homophobic in the least. Homophobia means fear of homosexuality. In my ministry to homosexuals, I have coined the phrase "homo-agapic." I am ministering to those within the homosexual community who do not wish to be homosexual, who know that it is a sin issue, who want freedom from their bondage to this sin just as others want freedom from their particular habitual sins, and who want to walk in harmony with the will of God for their lives. All these desires for change I once had for myself when I was in bondage to the sin of homosexuality. So I know what I'm talking about, and I know many people who are in harmony with these same desires.

I do not minister out of fear of homosexuals or fear of homosexuality. Rather, I minister out of love, compassion, and concern. It puzzles me that anytime anyone speaks out against the sin of homosexuality he is thought of as being homophobic. I don't think Jesus was homophobic. I don't think he was adultery-phobic when He told Mary to "go, and sin no more" (John 8:11). I don't think He was phobic when He told the paralytic to "sin no more, lest a worse thing come unto thee" (John 5:14). I don't think God was homophobic when He denounced homosexuality as an abomination or when He destroyed Sodom and Gomorrah. He simply wants His creation to act in accordance with His original plan, design, and purpose for their creation.

I am not convinced that the apostle Paul was homophobic, afraid of homosexuals and homosexuality, when he said in Romans 1 that God gave them up (those who refused His grace, His power to give them victory) to uncleanness, unto vile affections, and over to a reprobate mind (verse 26). Nor do I believe God Himself was homophobic in eventually giving them up to their lusts as Paul stated. When artists, composers, or inventors are not satisfied with how their product turns out or works, they generally destroy their work and start over, because that work is not in harmony with what they have in mind.

In light of all that the Bible says about homosexuality, I do not see how anyone can possibly truly believe that the gay lifestyle offers wholeness, and that it can possibly be in harmony with true Christianity. The term Christian denotes discipleship, discipline, one who follows after the example of Christ. Homosexuality in no way complies with His life and example, nor with His expressed will and counsel.

Of course, there are those who say, "Well, neither does marriage and heterosexual behavior. Jesus never married, and I can't picture Him having sex with a woman." I would have to take issue with that rationalization also, because although Jesus was never married, He certainly put His stamp of approval upon marriage during His ministry on earth, in His parables, and in the fact that He created marriage in the first place, saying, "Be fruitful and multiply" (Genesis 1:28). Homosexuality cannot be fruitful and multiply. It is a perversion of that which God created to be beautiful, enjoyable, and to be a blessing to others in procreating and in perpetuating the human race. The homosexual act never results in procreation, neither does it contribute to the perpetuation of the human race. It is based upon self-gratification and is a dead-end street.

Actually, this raises an interesting question in my mind. How can homosexuality be genetic, passed on, or inherited if homosexual behavior is not an act of procreation? No homosexual is the child, grandchild, or great-grandchild of a homosexual encounter. So how can he inherit his homosexuality? In all honesty, we must recognize and acknowledge homosexuality to simply be a perversion of God's gift of sexuality.

You speak of internal homophobia. I'm not sure what that means, but there certainly is nothing wrong with hating sin. Jesus hated sin, but He loved the sinner. God told us in Genesis 3:15 that He Himself would create a hatred in the hearts of His people for sin and Satan when He said, "I will put enmity between thee [Satan] and the woman, between thy seed and her seed."

My friend, so many people of your persuasion tell me how they feel about homosexuality, that they believe it is okay, that they feel loved and accepted by God as they are, and that God does not expect or desire them to change. My question, or challenge, or respectful request is simply this: show me from the Word of God my error. Show me a plain "thus saith the Lord" that justifies, condones, blesses, rewards, or excuses homosexuality in any way, shape, or form. I will then be silenced forever and cease to instill in others an internal homophobia.

In Christian love and acceptance, but believing in and experiencing the transforming power of God,

Victor

Question: Are you not giving people false hope? I feel that it is very wrong for you to give people false hope. Not everyone can change, and maybe they are happy with their lives. Let things be, and let people live their lives.

Reply: I agree that those who are happy with their homosexuality may be beyond change. To those who are proud of being gay, my message of hope may not be well received. After all, God Himself was unable to arrest Lucifer in his mad career, because he felt no need. He was proud of who and what he was.

However, through the intercession of believing parents, God intervened on my behalf, taking drastic measures to get my attention, helping me to eventually realize my need. Then came hope, blessed hope, and salvation from my life of sin as a homosexual.

The whole point of the gospel can be summed up in the words of the angel of the Lord to Joseph in Matthew 1:21, "and thou shalt call his name JESUS: for he shall save his people from their sins." Jesus' perfect life of obedience, discipline, and self-control was a demonstration of what our lives are to become through the gift of divine strength, otherwise known as grace. Through faith in His death, burial, and resurrection we can be forgiven, cleansed, and can begin new lives as new creatures in Christ. "Therefore if any man be in Christ, he is a new creature: old things are passed away; behold, all things are become new" (2 Corinthians 5:17).

However, for some reason, many Christians and non-Christians alike look at homosexuality as something unique, something out of the reach of God Himself to correct. In essence, they are worshiping an *impotent* God rather than the *omnipotent* God, demonstrating "a *form* of godliness, but denying the *power* thereof" (2 Timothy 3:5, emphasis added). From such weak doctrine we are told to turn away.

Such Christians hesitate to include homosexuality in the category of sin, and herein lies the confusion. We must accept the definition of sin found in God's Word in order to be able to believe in victory over homosexuality. "Sin is the transgression of the law" (1 John 3:4). The seventh commandment of God's law says, "Thou shalt not commit adultery." Any sexual behavior outside of the institution of marriage as God designed it to be is a transgression of this commandment, and therefore is sin.

Now, I believe all God's biddings to be enablings. In other words, anything God asks us to do, He gives us the grace (divine strength) to accomplish. Otherwise His commandments are nothing but mockery to mankind, and He in turn can be accused of being unfair, unjust, unreasonable, tyrannical, and unmerciful.

Once we accept the simple fact that homosexuality is sin, then we can claim all the promises in the Bible that assure us of victory over sin in our efforts to overcome homosexuality. To see it any other way is to blame God instead of Satan for that which He Himself condemns as an abomination. A merciful and just God will not condemn that which is unchangeable, or irreversible, in one of His children.

Yet, in no uncertain terms He does condemn homosexuality, and this very fact proves that it can be overcome. "Thou shalt not lie with mankind, as with womankind: it is abomination" (Leviticus 18:22). "If a man also lie with mankind, as he lieth with a woman, both of them have committed an abomination" (Leviticus 20:13). "Know ye not that the unrighteous [those who persist in sin] shall not inherit the kingdom of God? Be not deceived: neither fornicators... nor adulterers, nor effeminate, nor *abusers of themselves with mankind*... shall inherit the kingdom of God" (1 Corinthians 6:9, 10). Or "them that defile themselves with mankind" (1 Timothy 1:10; see also Romans 1:24–28).

The Word of God is full of wonderful promises of victory over sin, including the sin of homosexuality: "And such *were* some of you: but ye *are* washed, but ye *are* sanctified, but ye *are* justified in the name of the Lord Jesus, and by the Spirit of our God" (1 Corinthians 6:11, emphasis added). Please see "A Rainbow of Promises" at the end of this book. These promises should give every Christian hope. Salvation from the sin of homosexuality should not be looked upon as an exercise in futility, but rather as the marvelous working of God in the life of the believer. Grace is defined in the Greek dictionary as the divine influence working upon the heart and being reflected in the life.

Becoming a Christian, a child of God, a disciple of Christ, requires conversion which is defined as: 1. The act of being converted in substance, condition, form, function, etc., 2. A change in which one comes to adopt and uphold new opinions and beliefs; especially, in matters of religion, a spiritual turning to righteousness (obedience) and faith. (*Funk & Wagnalls Standard College Dictionary,* Harcourt, Brace, and World, 1966)

Philippians 2:13 informs us that "it is God which worketh in you both to will and to do of his good pleasure." And we are also assured in Philippians 1:6 that we can be "confident of this very thing, that he which hath begun a good work in you will perform it until the day of Jesus Christ."

Genuine hope can be yours, dear friends: "That they might set their hope in God, and not forget the works of God, but keep his commandments" (Psalm 78:7).

Thou art my hiding place and my shield: I hope in thy word. Depart from me, ye evildoers: for I will keep the commandments of my God. Uphold me according unto thy word, that I may live: and let me not be ashamed of my hope." (Psalm 119:114–116)

Happy is he that hath the God of Jacob for his help, whose hope is in the LORD his God: Which made heaven, and earth, the sea, and all that therein is: which keepeth truth for ever... The LORD openeth the eyes of the blind. (Psalm 146:5, 6, 8)

And Jesus came and spake unto them, saying, All power is given unto me in heaven and in earth. Go ye therefore, and teach all nations, baptizing them in the name of the Father, and of the Son, and of the Holy Ghost: Teaching them to observe all things whatsoever I have commanded you: and, lo, I am with you alway, even unto the end of the world. Amen. (Matthew 28:18–20)

Question: How exclusive were your homosexual attractions formerly and are your heterosexual attractions now? I am skeptical that total re-orientation is readily available for anyone. Tell me a little more about yourself and what I would find in your book.

Reply: This line of questioning is uncomfortably personal. However, I believe it to be sincere. So I'll give it a shot. My former attractions were exclusively homosexual. I found nothing interesting about a woman sexually once I gave in to my lifelong homosexual orientation and began living an active homosexual life. The very idea of sexual intimacy with a woman I found to be repulsive.

Many people are skeptical about my new heterosexual life, but I can only testify to what it truly is. I am now attracted only to my wife with whom I find complete and joyful fulfillment. We have known each other since childhood. Being close friends with my sisters, she knew much more about me than I ever wanted her to know, but that made me more relaxed with her as I became interested in her. She truly believes in victory over sin, that Jesus came to save His people *from* their sins, and, therefore, from the beginning she has trusted me and loved me and made me feel very comfortable in my role as husband and lover, and now father of two beautiful children whom I would not trade for anything.

Should anything ever happen to her, should I lose her by some tragedy, I know that I could possibly sooner or later find myself exclusively attracted to another woman, should the Lord bring another one into my life, but my wife would be hard to beat. We not only have a good intimate life, but we are best friends as well. The point I am trying to make is that I am not attracted sexually to women. I am attracted sexually and exclusively to my wife. I practice taking every thought captive and guarding well the avenues to my soul so that I don't have eyes for other women, or for men.

May I share with you the text of Scripture that a minister shared with me that turned my life around (if any one text could do so)?

> Know ye not that the unrighteous shall not inherit the kingdom of God? Be not deceived: neither fornicators, nor idolaters, nor adulterers, nor effeminate, nor abusers of themselves with mankind, Nor thieves, nor covetous, nor drunkards, nor revilers, nor extortioners, shall inherit the kingdom of God. [That list included me as I used to be several times over!] And such *were* some of you: but ye *are* washed, but ye *are* sanctified, but ye *are* justified in the name of the Lord Jesus, and by the Spirit of our God. (1 Corinthians 6:9–11,emphasis added)

This text pulled all the props out from under me. I had gone to this preacher just looking for information. He just quoted the Word, and I was speechless. That night, when confronted by my gay partner, my lover, I had to admit that I no longer had an excuse to remain gay. I loved my "Mr. Right" with all my heart, but my growing love for Jesus, who first loved me, soon outweighed that love and brought me to the point of a decision. It took time, but I chose Jesus, terminated my gay relationship, an act that was the one most traumatic experience in my entire life, and submitted myself to God's divine therapy, reconditioning, and re-creation.

In my book *That Kind Can Never Change! Can They...?*, I enumerate the sequential steps to victory that I discovered through the study of God's Word. By His grace I have never looked back, and I have never had any regrets. "Higher than the highest human thought can reach is God's ideal for His children" (*Education*, 18). I can testify to this. Also, "Eye hath not seen, nor ear heard, neither have entered into the heart of man, the things that God hath prepared for them that love Him" (1 Corinthians 2:9). This, too, I can vouch for. We don't have to wait for heaven to begin realizing this beautiful promise.

Jesus reaches out to all of us and pleads, "My son, give me thine heart" (Proverbs 23:26). I try daily to do just that, and then accept His promise to work in me "both to will and to do of His good pleasure" (Philippians 2:13), "being confident of this very thing, that he which hath begun a good work in [me] will perform it until the day of Jesus Christ" (Philippians 1:6).

I believe it is all a matter of surrender of the will, trusting that Father knows best.

Question: Why are Christians so homophobic?

Homophobia: An exaggerated and persistent dread of or aversion to those sexually attracted to persons of the same sex, or those having sexual relations with others of the same sex.

Reply: Let's look at Christian behavior toward gays.

Do Christians have an exaggerated and persistent dread of or aversion to homosexuals?

There are many people who do manifest a homophobic attitude toward gays, and that goes without question. But do Christians manifest this attitude? Are Christians homophobic?

First of all, it should be established what a Christian is, for, "Not every one that saith unto me, Lord, Lord, shall enter into the kingdom of heaven; but *he that doeth the will of my Father* which is in heaven" (Matthew 7:21).

A true Christian is one who not only accepts Jesus as the Savior but also accepts Him as Lord and Master over himself and lives according to the example and teachings of Jesus. He will, therefore, be Christ-like in his attitude and behavior toward the homosexual as toward any other of God's wayward children.

"What would Jesus do?" is a popular question of the day and is a good motto to live by. While hating sin, Jesus loved the sinner. How much? Enough to willingly lay down His own life in exchange for the life of even His own enemies.

But God commendeth his love toward us, in that, while we were yet sinners [yes, even homosexuals], Christ died for us ... For if, when we were enemies, we were reconciled to God by the death of his Son, much more, being reconciled, we shall be saved by his life." (Romans 5:8, 10)

Second, it should be stated that no homophobe is truly a Christian, and no true Christian is, nor can be, a homophobe. One characteristic automatically precludes the other. Notice what the apostle John says in 1 John 4: "God is love" (4:8), and if we are to be Christ-like, we will be God-like as loving and loveable Christians. "There is no fear [phobia] in love; but perfect love casteth out fear: because fear hath torment. He that feareth [i.e., the homophobe] is not made perfect in love" (4:18).

Study the context in which this is found:

Beloved, let us love one another: for love is of God; and every one that loveth is born of God, and knoweth God. *He that loveth not knoweth not God; for God is love.* In this was manifested the love of God toward us, because that God sent his only begotten Son into the world, that we might live through him. Herein is love, not that we loved God, but that he loved us, and sent his Son to be the propitiation for our sins. Beloved, *if God so loved us, we ought also to love one another.* ... If we love one another, God dwelleth in us, and his love is perfected in us. ... *There is no fear in love; but perfect love casteth out fear:* because fear hath torment. He that feareth is not made perfect in love... *If a man say, I love God, and hateth his brother, he is a liar:* for he that loveth not his brother whom he hath seen, how can he love God whom he hath not seen? And this commandment have we from him, That he who loveth God love his brother also." (1 John 4:7–12, 18, 20, 21, emphasis added)

Third, the attitude of the true Christian toward the homosexual will be one of loving compassion and concern. Since "perfect love casteth out fear," the true Christian cannot manifest homophobia, but rather, "homo-agape"—affection, benevolence, a love without benefit to self. Of God's two great commandments, the second one is to "love thy neighbour as thyself" (Matthew 22:39). The Christian's love toward the homosexual is a self-sacrificing love, even as God's is.

For God so loved the world, that he gave his only begotten Son, that whosoever believeth in him should not perish, but have everlasting life. For God sent not his Son into the world to condemn the world; but that the world through him might be saved. (John 3:16, 17)

The true Christian, likewise, in following the example and teaching of Jesus, is not to condemn the homosexual, but is to labor with selfless love that the homosexual might be saved from his sin. The promise is given that Jesus "shall save his people from their sins" (Matthew 1:21).

But even Christ could not, and cannot, force the will. He is the Way, the Truth, and the Life, but He will not coerce anyone against his will, and neither will the Christian force his will upon the gay community. However, the Christian has every right, indeed a responsibility, to proclaim the good news that there is a way out, so that the few who are seeking may find it.

In the words of Jesus, "Enter ye in at the strait gate: for wide is the gate, and broad is the way, that leadeth to destruction, and many there be which go in thereat: Because strait is the gate, and narrow is the way, which leadeth unto life, and few there be that find it" (Matthew 7:13, 14).

Revisiting the opening question, "Why are Christians so homophobic?" we find that in following the example and teaching of Jesus, the Christian will seek to save the lost. In pointing them to the Way, they are not manifesting "phobia" but "agape." True Christians are not homophobic at all. They are "homo-agapic."

Question: How do you justify picking and choosing which aspects of the Bible you follow? Remarriage is adultery and therefore a sin (Mark 10:11, 12). You yourself are remarried.

Reply: First of all, not all remarriage is adultery and sin according to the Bible. There are biblical grounds for divorce and remarriage, but that is another subject for another day.

That being said, I do not believe in self-justification. Nor do I believe in picking and choosing which aspects of the Bible I follow, though many Christians do. For example, most Christians accept nine out of 10 of God's commandments, but reject the fourth commandment dealing with the seventh-day Sabbath as irrelevant, as Jewish, as nailed to the cross, as old covenant, when they don't believe the same way about murder, stealing, adultery, idolatry and the rest of God's Ten Commandments (Exodus 20:1–17).

I agree that it is truly sad to see Christians pick and choose which aspects of the Bible they wish to follow, based upon their own biases, prejudices, and preferences. John tells us that "sin is the transgression of the law" (1 John 3:4). James tells us:

> For whosoever shall keep the whole law, and yet offend in one point, he is guilty of all. For he that said, Do not commit adultery, said also, Do not kill. Now if thou commit no adultery, yet if thou kill, thou art become a transgressor of the law. So speak ye, and so do, as they that shall be judged by the law of liberty. (James 2:10–12)

The good news is that Jesus promises new life to those who accept him. He told Nicodemus during that famous night visit, "Verily, verily, I say unto thee,

Except a man be born again, he cannot see the kingdom of God" (John 3:3). Through the apostle Paul God tells us, "And the times of this ignorance God winked at; but now commandeth all men every where to repent (Acts 17:30). And once one does repent He says, "Therefore if any man be in Christ, he is a new creature: old things are passed away; behold, all things are become new" (2 Corinthians 5:17).

My friend, the entire plan of salvation is about starting over, second chances, re-creation, restoration, reconditioning, and reconciliation. God delights in taking that which is broken and re-creating it into what it was meant to be in the first place. Isn't He amazingly merciful, patient, loving, and understanding?

When my wife divorced me those many years ago, I was not a Christian. From there I went into multiple relationships and affairs and civil unions. When I did accept Jesus many years later, I was born-again and started a new life as "a new creature." I was prepared to live the rest of my life in celibacy, but God had a different plan. As a professing ex-gay, living singly, I was always under the suspicion of the skeptics. I could not be seen with a man without being accused of still being gay. I could not be seen with a woman without being accused of impropriety. I was a minister under constant surveillance by the skeptics who believed that people like me could never be changed. The power of God was on trial.

I took my burden to the Lord. When He brought my present wife into my life, He brought someone I had known since childhood. She knew me before I led a gay lifestyle and after. Because she trusted the power of God to make His children whole, she willingly took the steps to develop a relationship with me. In our subsequent marriage and parenthood, we chose to build a solid, stable Christian home on the Rock. Thus, God continues to demonstrate to the skeptics on a daily basis His power to save the whosoevers (homosexuals included), *from* their sins, not *in* their sins, and that He can save to the uttermost.

I have much remorse for my past, for all the pain and suffering I then inflicted upon others through my self-centered way of life. However, there is nothing I can do to change the past, and God does not want me to dwell there. He wants me, and He wants you, dear friend, to go forward in newness of life. One of the purposes of salvation from sin is to give hope and courage to others who are tempted to give up in futility.

I agree with you that certain divorces and remarriages among Christians are sin. But I hope you can see that when an unbeliever becomes a believer he is given a new lease on life, newness of life, second chances, and grace to succeed where he had previously only met with failure.

God bless you in your endeavor to follow Him and to walk in the light of truth.

Victor

Chapter 25

ASSURANCE AND SUPPORT

Q**uestion:** Will God really come through for me? I will give it one more try, and then, who knows?

Reply: In short, let me answer your question this way: all God's promises are conditional. If you will read them carefully, you will see that many of these promises start out with that great big word "if." For example, "If my people, which are called by my name, shall humble themselves, and pray, and seek my face, and turn from their wicked ways; then will I hear from heaven, and will forgive their sin, and will heal their land" (2 Chronicles 7:14). Notice:

1) My people, which are called by my name: you must give yourself totally to Jesus, accepting Him as your Lord, your Master, your Teacher, and you as His disciple (follower in thought, word, and deed).

2) Shall humble themselves: in complete submission to His will for your life, become teachable and render unquestioning, unconditional obedience.

3) And pray: pray without ceasing, asking God daily for fresh supplies of His Spirit and His grace, understanding that grace is the divine influence working upon your heart and reflecting in your life, according to the Greek definition. Grace, in short, is divine, supernatural power. He promises you that His grace is sufficient for you, to give you victory and to sustain you in that victory.

4) Seek my face: not God's back of disfavor, but His face of favor and approval. Live in such a way as to make Him proud of you, for He loves you with all His heart and only wants that which is for your best, for your joy, peace, happiness, fulfillment, health, and eternal life.

5) And turn from their wicked ways: this is the meaning of repentance. Turn from the behavior of which you know He disapproves, or at least be willing to turn from it. He then promises to work within you to both will and to do of His good pleasure (Philippians 2:13). Denounce and renounce your old lifestyle, your gay lifestyle. Put your feet in the water, so to speak, and turn from it, trusting that He will be able to sustain you in that decision.

6) Then He promises to bring you healing. But you must step out in faith. That's what the *if* is all about. "If … then … "

My friend, I would encourage you to not give it just one more try. Keep trying until you get it right. In ice-skating, I always comforted myself after a bad fall with the thought that if I never fell, I was not pushing and stretching myself to new levels of ability. When learning to walk, a baby falls, but those falls decrease to the point that eventually the baby can not only walk without falling, but also run in the Olympics and take the gold medal! Get my point?

Be strong in the Lord! You can make it. I know you can. Just never, never, ever give up!

Victor

Follow-up Question: How do you or I handle it when seeing someone who is beautiful? How do I change that temptation into something good?

Thanks for telling me to keep on trying. Wow, I did it for 23 years in my marriage, which ended this year after telling my wife my story. So now I have to try and pick up the pieces and carry on. I just do not know, but I will try to follow your guidelines. I enjoy your website. Thank you so much for your honesty and helps. Have a wonderful Christ-filled season.

Reply: In answer to your questions, God created all that is beautiful. It is not a sin to recognize, appreciate, and enjoy the beauty in people. It is lusting after them that is the sin. Straight men have the same problem that gay men have in this area. It is just as wrong to lust after a woman as it is to lust after a man, but there's nothing wrong with appreciating the beauty in another person.

However, if we focus on what is truly beautiful, we will discover that true beauty is usually displayed in the behavior and character of a person, not in his or her outward appearance and genetic makeup. I think this is where we have to practice—learning to appreciate the genuine beauty of one's character more than the skin-deep beauty of one's appearance.

Have you ever found someone to be initially very beautiful only to later have that image tarnished by his personality, pride, or obnoxious behavior? But suppose you come across a person whose outward beauty is only enhanced by a beautiful personality and noble character. What then? One of the Ten Commandments states, "Thou shalt not covet."

In other words, God asks us to not crave something that does not belong to us and that is off-limits to us. I suppose it is like enjoying the beauty of the flowers without picking them, enjoying the aroma of the coffee beans in isle six without purchasing the coffee, admiring someone else's beautiful new car without going into depression because it is his and not yours, or being blessed by the musical talents of some great musician without getting all bent out of shape because he can sing and has all the fame and you don't.

We all are meant to be a blessing to others around us, through our talents, behavior, generosity, or attractiveness (should that exist). If everyone would focus on using their God-given gifts and talents to draw attention to their Creator instead of to themselves, what a wonderful world this would be, right?

Perhaps it would help to look at a beautiful person not as someone to desire, but as someone who also has problems, flaws, quirks, and is in great need of a Savior and Redeemer—someone you could possibly assist in that direction.

I hope these thoughts are helpful to you.

Another Follow-up Question: Thank you so much for replying. At the moment I am sitting in a deep, dark hole of depression. I'll not go into all the details, but I do enjoy reading what you have said. Somehow God will have to intervene and quickly. I really feel like giving up on everything in my life. I have come to the point where nothing matters anymore. Whether I die or live, live straight or gay, it really does not matter anymore. I am, in any case, just going through the motions of being alive. Yes, I know I should try and get out of it, but somehow life is a drag.

Please, if you feel like it, pray for me.

Reply: I do not know your religious affiliation. Are you by any chance Seventh-day Adventist? Whether you are or not, I would like to advise you to find the book *Prophets and Kings* by E. G. White and read chapter 13, "What Doest Thou Here?" It is the story of Elijah's discouragement after his Mt. Carmel high standing up against Ahab and the priests of Baal. You recall how discouraged he became by the threat of one woman!

Anyway, this chapter has some amazing insight into discouragement and how to overcome it. I know it will be a blessing to you as it has been for me in just the past few weeks. I, too, sometimes battle discouragement. Surprise, surprise! All of God's children have to fight back against it from time to time, because Satan is relentless in his attempts to bring us down!

Let me know what you think after reading it. God be with you, and yes, I will certainly be praying for you!

Victor

Question: What must I do to have assurance of true and complete victory over homosexuality?

Reply: This question reflects the cry of many a soul sin-sick and desperate for relief from the power of sin, its guilt, and its shame. In my own personal devotion this morning, I was reading in Romans 12 and was particularly struck by the impact of the first two verses:

> I beseech you therefore, brethren, by the mercies of God, that ye present your bodies a living sacrifice, holy, acceptable unto God, which is your

reasonable service. And be not conformed to this world: but be ye transformed by the renewing of your mind, that ye may prove what is that good, and acceptable, and perfect, will of God.

The commentary on this text in my Bible is profound. Let me share it with you:

Man, fallen man [even the homosexual] may be transformed by the renewing of the mind, so that he can "prove what is that good, and acceptable, and perfect, will of God." How does he prove this? *By the Holy Spirit taking possession of his mind, spirit, heart, and character.*

Where does the proving come in? "We are made a spectacle unto the world, and to angels, and to men." A real work is wrought by the Holy Spirit upon the human character, and its fruits are seen.

Just as a good tree will bear good fruit, so will the tree that is actually planted in the Lord's garden produce good fruit unto eternal life. Besetting sins [such as homosexuality] are overcome; evil thoughts [such as fantasizing and lusting] are not allowed in the mind; evil habits [homosexual behavior and activities] are purged from the soul temple. The [homosexual] tendencies, which have been biased in a wrong direction, are turned in a right direction. Wrong dispositions and feelings are changed, new principles of action supplied, and there is a new standard of character. Holy tempers and sanctified emotions are now the fruit borne upon the Christian tree. *An entire transformation has taken place.* This is the work to be wrought.

We see by experience that in our own human strength, resolutions and purposes are of no avail. Must we, then, give up our determined efforts? No; although our experience testifies that we cannot possibly do this work ourselves, help has been laid upon One who is mighty to do it for us. But the only way we can secure the help of God is to put ourselves wholly in His hands, and trust Him to work for us. As we lay hold of Him by faith, He does the work. The believer can only trust. As God works, we can work, trusting in Him and doing His will. (*Seventh-day Adventist Bible Commentary* Vol. 6, 1080)

What more can I say?
Blessed assurance to you!
Victor

Question: Do you believe that gays can become completely straight?

Reply: Based upon my own personal experience, yes! Based upon the word of God, yes. Notice: "Therefore if any man be in Christ, he is a new creature: old things are passed away; behold, all things are become new" (2 Corinthians 5:17).

This beautiful text of Scripture is telling us that the old nature, born of blood and the will of the flesh, cannot inherit the kingdom of God.

> The old ways, the hereditary tendencies, the former habits, must be given up; for grace is not inherited. The new birth consists in having new motives, new tastes, new tendencies. Those who are [born] unto a new life by the Holy Spirit have become partakers of the divine nature, and in all their habits and practices they will give evidence of their relationship to Christ. When men who claim to be Christians retain all their natural defects of character and disposition, in what [way] does their position differ from that of the [non-Christian]? They do not appreciate the truth as a sanctifier, a refiner. They have not been born again ... (*Review and Herald*, April 12, 1892)

> God makes no compromise with sin. A genuine conversion changes hereditary and cultivated tendencies to wrong...

> Christ's plan is the only safe one. He declares, "Behold, I make all things new." "If any man be in Christ, he is a new creature." Christ gives man no encouragement to think that He will accept a patchwork character, made up mostly of self, with a little of Christ. ... At first there seems to be some of self and some of Christ. But soon it is all of self and none of Christ. ... Christ looks with pitying tenderness on all who have combination characters. (*Seventh-day Adventist Bible Commentary* Vol. 6, 1101)

In the article at the end of this book, "A Rainbow of Promises," you may find many more exceeding great and precious promises giving assurance of victory over sin, of new birth, and new life.

Question: Having chosen to turn away from homosexuality, I still sometimes feel very weak, almost overwhelmed with temptation. How do I successfully maintain my new direction in life?

Tips for a consistent walk in the path of victory:
    Maintain an attitude of gratitude and praise.
    In Psalms 18:3, we read the words of David who, though at one time appeared to be a hopeless sinner, was referred to as a man after God's own heart. He

says, "I will call upon the LORD, who is worthy to be praised: so shall I be saved from mine enemies."

This can be personalized to, "So shall I be saved from my enemy Satan, for he is my chief enemy and the author of sin."

The apostle John counsels us, "And they overcame [the accuser of the brethren, Satan] by the blood of the Lamb, *and by the word of their testimony…* " (Revelation 12:11 emphasis added).

As you confess before men and women your confidence in the Lord, additional strength is given to you. Determine to praise Him. With firm determination comes increased willpower, and soon you will find that you cannot help praising Him, for with each victory comes new strength and cause for rejoicing.

"In everything give thanks: for this is the will of God in Christ Jesus concerning you" (1 Thessalonians 5:18).

"Rejoice in the Lord alway" (Philippians 4:4).

"But they that wait upon the LORD shall renew their strength; they shall mount up with wings as eagles; they shall run, and not be weary; and they shall walk, and not faint" (Isaiah 40:31).

Question: Does God really have the ability to heal me from my homosexuality? If so, then why am I still attracted to guys and to my lover Bob?

I have been trying for years to become straight, for I know what God's Word says. I'm at the point of just letting go of God and being true to myself, just accepting being gay, for He has not healed me. However, I know God won't let go of me, and that's the painful thing. I wish He would stop playing games with me and just deliver me from being gay, for I'm starting to lose faith in His ability to heal me. Maybe God likes me this way?

Reply: First of all, let me assure you that God *does* like you. In the words He spoke to Jeremiah, "Before I formed thee in the belly I knew thee" (Jeremiah 1:5). In other words, "I knew you from the point of conception. I loved you then, and I love you now. I knew what you would become in life, but I allowed you to be born anyway—knowing what you would become, but also knowing what you *could* become—and wanting to spend eternity with you, if you would allow me to be your Savior from sin, the wages of which, otherwise, is death."

Yes, my friend, He does like you very much, even though you are gay and presently out of sync with His ultimate plan for your life. You see, it is the sin he hates, not you the sinner. He loves you enough to give you the opportunity to choose to become other than what you may now be.

I can assure you that God is not playing games with you. He is deadly serious about reclaiming that which was taken from Him by Satan. Just look to the cross of Calvary, and you will see how serious He is about saving you from a life of sin

STRAIT ANSWERS TO THE GAY QUESTION

and its consequences. He gave His only Son that you, should you believe in Him, need not perish (the wages of sin), but that you might have life, and that more abundantly, even eternal life (See John 3:16; John 10:10).

God's ability to heal your homosexuality is limited only by your power of choice, which He created in you. I remember the time I pleaded with God to get me out of my gay relationship. It was a bad one, and I wanted Him to get me out of it. So I made a deal with Him. "If you will bring this relationship to an end, God, I promise that I will go straight; I will never enter into another gay relationship."

The relationship ended shortly thereafter by mutual agreement. And it wasn't even two weeks later that I was considering another fellow as a suitable replacement! My promise to God was completely forgotten—not that I could have kept it on my own anyway.

Several years later, under much conviction about the sinfulness of my life, I again promised God that if He would bring my relationship to an end, then I would go straight. I just couldn't bear the thought of breaking another heart.

God did not bring that relationship to an end, however. He just laid on an ever-increasing conviction until I knew that I had to step out in faith. I had to act upon my beliefs and convictions, realizing that His grace (divine strength) was sufficient for me. With explicit trust in Him, I terminated my "perfect" gay relationship with a man I dearly loved and entered into a covenant relationship with my Redeemer instead, whom I had learned to love, trust, and obey even more.

Our God is able, but we must trust Him enough to obey Him, regardless of the consequences. We cannot hang on to our "lover Bob" and wait for healing from homosexuality. We must act upon our convictions, trusting God for His promised strength and healing during the process.

I would just like to reiterate that there *is* something we can do to make the change in our lives. God says in Jeremiah 3, only to acknowledge your sin, your need, and He will heal you.

First we must acknowledge homosexuality to not be in harmony with God's will. Isn't knowing this the cause of the mental anguish and struggle? Then we can choose to allow Him to be Lord and Master. We then trust and obey Him with a complete surrender of our own will. Jesus rendered unquestioning obedience to His Father, according to Philippians 2, and practiced total self-denial when tempted to deviate from God's plan for His life. Paul tells us in Philippians 2:5, "Let this mind be in you, which was also in Christ Jesus."

These are just a few suggestions, not meant to be comprehensive at all. We do have our part to play, mainly to surrender the will, and make the right choices. He then can work in us to will and to do what is right.

Through the right exercise of the will, an entire change may be made in your life. By yielding up your will to Christ, you ally yourself with all the power [in heaven and earth]. You will have strength from above to hold you steadfast, and thus through constant surrender to God you will be enabled to live the new life, even the life of faith. (*Steps to Christ*, 48)

And, you are right, God won't let go of you, my friend, because He truly loves you and wants the very best for you. Look once again at the cross, and you will see why He will not let you go easily. Jesus died for you. Why not live for Him?

Victor

Question: Can "born-a-gay" be "born-again"? If so, what does God expect from me?

Reply: The concept of being born-again implies change, old things passing away, and resulting newness of life. The work of overcoming homosexuality must begin in the heart, and we must come into such a relation with God that Jesus can put His divine mold upon us. We must be emptied of self in order to give room to Jesus. But so often here's where the problem lies: we have our hearts so filled with idols that they have no room for the Redeemer of the world. The very thing we want to overcome quite often holds our hearts in captivity. While resisting overt behavior, we still center our thoughts and affections upon the desires of the flesh. In addition, we hold to our opinions and ways, and cherish them as idols in the soul. Self asserts itself, but we cannot afford to yield ourselves to the service of self, holding to our own ways and ideas, and excluding the truth of God.

We must be emptied of self, but this is not all that is required, for when we have renounced our idols, the vacuum must be filled. If the heart is left desolate, and the vacuum not filled, it will be in the condition of the one whose house was "empty, swept, and garnished" (Matthew 12:44), but without a guest to occupy it. The evil spirit then brought in "seven other spirits more wicked than himself, and they enter[ed] in and [dwelt] there; and the last state of that man [was] worse than the first."

You may feel that you cannot meet the approval of heaven. You may think and say, "I was born with a natural tendency toward homosexuality, and I cannot overcome," but every provision has been made by our heavenly Father whereby you may be able to overcome every unholy tendency. God expects you to overcome even as Christ overcame on your behalf. He says, "To him that overcometh will I grant to sit with me in my throne, even as I also overcame, and am set down with my Father in his throne" (Revelation 3:21).

It was sin that imperiled the human family, and before man was even created the provision was made that if man failed to bear the test, Jesus would become His sacrifice and surety, that through faith in Him, man might be reconciled to God, for Christ was the Lamb "slain from the foundation of the world" (Revelation 13:8).

Christ died on Calvary that you might have power to overcome your natural tendencies to sin—that you might overcome even your "natural tendency" toward homosexuality!

But you might say, "Why can't I have my own way and act myself? Can I not be a born-again homosexual, keep my gay relationship, and still serve the Lord?"

According to Scripture, no, you cannot have your way and enter the kingdom of heaven. No "my way" will be there. No human ways will find place in the kingdom of heaven. Our ways must be lost in God's ways. "Except a man be born again [of water and of the Spirit], he cannot see the kingdom of God" (John 3:3, 5).

Shall we continue in sin [transgressing God's law], that grace may abound? God forbid. How shall we, that are dead to sin, live any longer therein? Know ye not, that so many of us as were baptized into Jesus Christ were baptized into his death? Therefore we are buried with him by baptism into death: that like as Christ was raised up ... even so we also should walk in newness of life ... Knowing this, that our old man is crucified with him, that the body of sin might be destroyed, that henceforth we should not serve sin. For he that is dead is freed from sin. (Romans 6:1–7)

He that is truly born-again will yield his homosexuality over to Christ, painful though it may be, for to continue therein is to continue in sin, placing one's homosexuality above allegiance to Christ. Jesus says, "Thou shalt have no other gods before me" (Exodus 20:3). "If ye love me, keep my commandments" (John 8:42).

The basis for finding an effective church and support group.

Question: With so many Christians believing homosexuality cannot be overcome, how do I find a safe haven in a church for support and nurture?

Reply: It is true that many Christians do not believe that the homosexual can be changed. To them, God is not really *omnipotent*, but rather, *impotent*; not really able to save the "whosoevers," nor is He able to save "to the uttermost" (Hebrews 7:25), as the gospel really teaches. Too many Christians, sadly, are "Having a form of godliness, but denying the power thereof: from such turn away," warns the apostle Paul in 2 Timothy 3:5.

This tells us something about the necessity of being carefully selective about forming spiritual relationships with church groups or any other support group.

In light of this counsel, I must acknowledge that my message is not the most popular one, for so many people wanting to be saved do not understand what salvation is saving us from. Many people want to be saved from the penalty of sin and to receive the gift of eternal life. But Jesus came to save His people from their sins, not just from the penalty of their sins (Matthew 1:21). Actually, being saved from the penalty of sin is only the first of three phases of salvation.

1) As the all-sufficient atoning Lamb of God, Jesus does promise to save us from the penalty of sin, if we will allow Him to do so.

2) And, as King of Kings and Lord of Lords, Jesus promises to save His people from the very presence of sin when He comes to take His children home at His soon second coming.

3) However, as Priest and High Priest ministering in the heavenly sanctuary (see the book of Hebrews), illustrated through the entire Jewish economy of old, Jesus also promises to save His people from the power of sin itself, by cleansing them and giving them grace (divine strength) to overcome.

Isn't He amazing? Offering to save us from the penalty of sin, the presence of sin, and the power of sin itself!

But as stated above, too many Christians want only to be saved from the penalty of sin. Therefore, they do not have the promised enmity or hatred for sin in their hearts (Genesis 3:15), and they want to cling to it still, though claiming to be saved. To these I simply ask, "What has He been able to save you from?"

To fully understand what Jesus offers to do for us, we must accept the Bible definition of sin, which is "the transgression of the law" (1 John 3:4). To reject any portion of God's great moral law, the Ten Commandments, is to practice transgression of the law, equaling sin, the wages of which is death (Romans 6:23). James tells us in James 2:10, 11:

For whosoever shall keep the whole law, and yet offend in one point, he is guilty of all. For he that said, Do not commit adultery, said also, Do not kill. Now if thou commit no adultery, yet if thou kill, thou art become a transgressor of the law.

James is obviously talking here about the Ten Commandments, and we must realize that no one commandment is the law. The law is composed of 10 commandments, based upon two great principles: supreme love to God and love to man. This is also referred to as the first and second commandments:

Master, which is the great commandment in the law? Jesus said unto him, Thou shalt love the Lord thy God with all thy heart, and with all thy soul, and with all thy mind. This is the first and great commandment. And the second is like unto it, Thou shalt love thy neighbour as thyself. On these two commandments hang all the law and the prophets. (Matthew 22:36–40)

Yet, so many Christians, when faced with one commandment which they do not wish to accept, then turn around and say that the law was nailed to the cross.

What they really mean is, the fourth commandment of the law was nailed to the cross! Nowhere in the Bible can that be substantiated.

What am I getting at? For me to be consistent in my message of victory over the sin of homosexuality, I must teach victory over sin, period. Therefore, I must be able to accept the Bible's definition of sin. If I am then consistent in my belief in the legitimacy of all of the Ten Commandments, not just nine of them, and if I practice keeping all 10, then I can expect the Lord to supply me sufficient grace to keep the seventh one as well, which, in the past, was the area of my habitual sin of homosexuality. If I choose to reject one point of the law, then I have no assurance that God will grant me the grace I need to consistently keep any other point of the law, or to teach anyone else how to, either.

Paul counsels us in Romans 6:1, 2: "What shall we say then? Shall we continue in sin [in transgression of the law, the Ten Commandments], that grace may abound? God forbid. How shall we, that are dead to sin, live any longer therein?" And in 1 Corinthians 9:27, he says, "But I keep under my body, and bring it into subjection: lest that by any means, when I have preached to others, I myself should be a castaway."

Anyway, this is all said in order to answer the question of how to find a safe haven in a church for support and nurture. I have chosen a church group that seems to be most consistent in its theology of sin being the transgression of the law, the Ten Commandments, the law spoken by God and written with His own finger as an expression of His own character. When I came to the Lord in 1992, I came to Him for salvation from sin, not in sin. For the promise is that Jesus came to save His people from their sins.

In accepting what sin was, not only did I have to die to the sin of homosexuality and adultery of any kind (which is transgression of the seventh commandment), but in all honesty, I had to also acknowledge the validity of His fourth commandment as well. The fourth commandment has to be just as valid today as thou shalt not steal, kill, bear false witness, dishonor your parents, covet, have any other gods, worship idols, or take the Lord's name in vain. Indeed, the fourth commandment is in the very heart of the 10. To omit it would be to cut out the very heart of God's law!

Much ado is being made in Christian circles today about the phrase "under God" in our pledge of allegiance, yet we tend to rebel against God ourselves when it comes to consistently keeping His law, which is but a reflection of His own character. Are we under God or not? Are we under God, or under the traditions of men?

God tells us in various places in the Bible that the Sabbath was to be a sign between Himself and us that *He*, the creator God, is our God, and we, in keeping His Sabbath, are His people (see Ezekiel 20:12, 19, 20). Not only is He the creator God, He is the re-creator God, the Redeemer, the Restorer, and the Renewer.

Revelation 2 and 3 give a number of promises to those who understand the definition of sin and then become overcomers. Revelation 21:7 says, "He that overcometh shall inherit all things; *and I will be his God, and he shall be my son.*" And in John 1:12, "But as many as [did receive] him, to them gave he power [grace] to become the sons of God, even to them that believe on his name."

I thank God that through His grace, His divine strength, not through my own strength, I can be an overcomer and be restored as one of His sons—one of His children! Don't you?

Chapter 26

"BY THE WORD OF
THEIR TESTIMONY"

Question: How do I, or should I, come out to my fellow believers as an ex-gay who has been born-again and recently rebaptized because I believed God wanted my love for Him (and also for my wife of 30 years), to be a witness to all sinners, gay or straight, that God can "change that kind"? Someday, if He wills, all sinners here where I live (with the help of the Holy Spirit) can hear how God can heal and cleanse one such as I, once and completely for all time.

Reply: Thanks for your question. It is a good one, but somewhat difficult for me to answer.

I have been sharing my testimony now for a number of years. But even though I have published my story with details and have a website, which specifically addresses the issue of my past, until recently in my public appearances and testimony I only spoke of my life as one of self-destruction and degradation. In this way people knew that I had been saved from something really bad, but I avoided offending people with the specifics that may make them uncomfortable or turned off to the testimony, which really is about what God has done in my life, not what Satan did all those years.

It was nine years after leaving the gay lifestyle that I was finally called to write my book and start sharing openly my testimony, which, as I said, I still do with great discretion. The Lord saw fit to hold me back until I had years of victory so that I would be a credible witness when called upon to be more open. Up to that point I shared my testimony everywhere I went, but still referring to self-destruction and degradation, not homosexuality. If people knew about, or found out about, the gay issue in my past, they would have to admit that I had been honest in my testimony, because gay fits within the parameters of self-destruction and degradation.

Does that make sense? When sharing with others about Christ in your life, be quick to admit that your past was really bad, but don't be so quick to share details. Spend your time sharing the power of Christ who is mighty to save, the whosoevers from whatsoever, even to the uttermost, you being a prime example. In this way, your testimony can be a blessing not only to people who are struggling with the gay issue, but those dealing with other major sin issues as well.

The Holy Spirit seems to make it very clear to me when I am to share the nature of my life of self-destruction and degradation. Usually it is with someone privately. And always it has then been made clear that my revelation was exactly what that person needed at that time. By sharing privately under the leading of the Holy Spirit, the other person was not embarrassed, but rather greatly impressed that the Lord had spoken directly to him or her about their need of Christ, or about His power to help their loved one or friend for whom they were concerned.

As you stay really close to Jesus, He will make the times and places for giving your testimony very clear to you. Don't think it a denial of your witness to use the better part of discretion. On the other hand, don't hesitate to share if under conviction. Psalm 107:2 says, "Let the redeemed of the LORD say so whom he hath redeemed from the hand of the enemy." But even then, it does not say that you need to share sordid details. You can share what the Lord has done without shining too much light on what Satan has done. You can talk about how He has brought new meaning into your marriage and made it a blessed relationship after years of stormy seas, for example, acknowledging that you were the cause of the unrest without going into detail.

Too often, people get up to share their testimonies and go on and on about the sin in their lives which tends to glorify the sin. Young people can come away from such a session thinking, "Wow! That man spent years in the fast lane, sowing his wild oats, getting it all out of his system, and then came back to the Lord before it was too late! He got to have his cake and eat it, too! Perhaps I have time to spend the years of my youth and my prime that way, too. Then I can come back to the Lord when I'm older, and after I've gotten all this stuff out of my system!"

Do you see how we can be a stumbling block to others, especially the young, if we are not very careful how we reveal the sins of our youth and the details of our testimonies?

I hope these thoughts will be of some help to you. Thank you for sharing with me.

Victor

P.S. As I have been called to do more and more public speaking over the past several years, I now state openly that homosexuality was the sin of my past. However, I still avoid going into detail, but rather focus upon the transforming power of God.

Testimony of Michelle Slade

I was born to a woman who was told she'd never have children and to a man who never thought he wanted any. My father was a Christian and my mother a convert from Catholicism, so I was raised in an Adventist family. I grew up about half in northern and half in southern California. The majority of my schooling was of Adventist education with public schooling a year here and there, and I remember a very happy early childhood.

A volatile relationship developed between my mother and me as she started physically and verbally abusing me around the age of 11. I started experimenting with members of the opposite sex at around age 12 or 13 and had boyfriends from time to time like most young teenagers. I used alcohol periodically at around age 15 with drugs to follow soon after. As time went on the abuse from my mother increased to my detriment, as did my use of alcohol and drugs. I started to sample more, and of course, they were of the stronger variety.

I was 16 when I had my first feelings toward a member of the same sex. It wasn't so much an outright, realized crush, but one day, lost in thought, I realized I wanted to kiss my then best friend. I thought, "If I could kiss her and no one would know, not even she would remember, would I?" The answer was yes. I was then saying to myself, "What?! What am I thinking? I can't be a lesbian; that's a sin!" However, I didn't really dwell on this but kind of forgot about the incident and went on with my day-to-day life.

A couple years passed, years of abuse, ditching school, drinking, and drug use. I even willingly left the academy I loved toward the end of my junior year! I thought I wanted to go to the public high school my brother was attending, and once that happened we proceeded to ditch every day for the remainder of that school year. We would go to a girl's house whose parent was at work during the day and indulge in drug use with quite a few friends. It really was a daily ritual. My senior year I realized my mistake in leaving academy, and to this day it's a great regret in my life. I neither graduated in a school I loved, nor with friends.

Later that year, in a hysterical state because of an abusive fight with my mother, I tried to commit suicide. Thankfully, I was unsuccessful. The incident made me realize how much of a mistake it was. I did not want to die.

Sometime later a friend of mine "came out" to me as being bisexual. She started flirting with me, and I then realized I was bisexual as well. Not too long after, I had my first experience, and, due to the Internet, I easily embraced my new sexuality in AOL chat rooms and met my first love. Instantly, being with a woman felt more natural to me—like I had been missing something all along. While I was still involved with said first love, I woke up one night as a good male friend of mine was basically raping me. This incident happened the week before my parents left California for a new home in Tennessee. The ordeal was never reported to authorities, and, unfortunately, I just learned to deal with what had happened.

So in 1995 my parents moved out of state. I went with them for the holidays, leaving my vehicle and belongings in a California storage facility. Plans were in place for me to later return and live with a friend in the Los Angeles area. Fast forward. I had left Tennessee, moved to Moreno Valley, then to Burbank, Van Nuys, Hollywood, San Francisco, Long Beach, Glendale, and Hollywood again. On September 10, 2001, I left LAX on an American Airlines flight for Bluefield, West Virginia where I later moved in with my parents. While living there my father died in 2004. Then my mother, brothers, and I moved to Las Vegas, Nevada, my mother's hometown.

Fast-forward again to 2007. I was still in Vegas, and, by the grace of God, I finally reached a point where I did not want to be romantically involved with anyone. All my life I had had the dream of wanting to find "the one." But finally, I realized that I had had enough heartbreak. I had been in many relationships and was just done. It was a welcome blessing. Through these adventures I had always called myself a Christian, though I now know I wasn't. I was living my life for myself alone. I did not really know God, but yet, He had always been calling me, waiting patiently for the day my heart would start to answer.

My roommate and youngest brother had found that 3ABN came in through the TV antenna. I already wanted to return to church and keep the Sabbath again, so this was an amazing, providential blessing.

Sabbath, June 30, 2007, the fourth day of Operation Global Rain[32] I was watching 3ABN on a rabbit-eared TV when *It Is Written* with Shawn Boonstra came on. The subject was of a homosexual man (Ron Woolsey) who had lived the life for 16 years, but the Lord had changed him.[33]

When the program was over I solemnly walked into my bedroom, fell to my knees, and pled, "Lord, are you trying to tell me something?" Enormously convicted of what I had just seen, I *knew* the Lord had set this appointment especially for me.

I don't recall if I asked the Lord to show me the answer through the Word, or if I just opened my Bible to a random page, but what I landed on was page 962, where I found the passage that changed my life forever.

"Your own wickedness will correct you, And your backslidings will rebuke you. Know therefore and see that it is an evil and bitter thing That you have forsaken the LORD your God, And the fear of Me is not in you," Says the Lord GOD of hosts. (Jeremiah 2:19, NKJV)

This was an evil and bitter thing! I had forsaken the Lord my God! It was as if this passage was just for me.

"How can you say, 'I am not polluted; I have not gone after the Baals [other gods]'? See your way in the valley; know what you have done: You are a swift dromedary [camel] breaking loose in her ways [in the uncontrollable violence of her brute passion]." (Jeremiah 2:23 NKJV)

It was almost beyond belief. The Word was speaking directly to me.

"Withhold your foot from being unshod, and your throat from thirst. But you said, 'There is no hope. No! For I have loved aliens, and after them I

---

32 Operation Global Rain was a movement in that summer of 2007 to pray for the latter rain of the Holy Spirit. Adventists all over the world were specifically praying for certain subjects each day for a week or two. On that June thirtieth they were praying for confession and repentance. How awesome is that?

33 This was the four-part series "Compassion without Compromise" featuring Ron Woolsey, available on DVD through the website: www.victorjadamson.com.

will go.' Why do you beautify your way to seek love? Therefore you have also taught the wicked women your ways." (Jeremiah 2:25, 33 NKJV)

In one of my relationships, I was a young woman's first.

"Yet you say, 'Because I am innocent, Surely His anger shall turn from me.' Behold, I will plead My case against you, Because you say, 'I have not sinned.'" (Jeremiah 2:35)

My excuse for my homosexuality was, "It's just love. How can it be wrong?" I was fooling myself into believing it wasn't a sin.

"Lift up your eyes to the desolate heights and see: Where have you not lain with men? By the road you have sat for them [eager for idolatry], like an Arabian [desert tribesman who waits to plunder] in the wilderness; and you have polluted the land with your harlotries and your wickedness.

Therefore the showers have been withheld, and there has been no latter rain. You have had a harlot's forehead; you refuse to be ashamed." (Jeremiah 3:2, 3 NKJV)

I was amazed that the Word was answering me and bringing conviction, yet I was in frightened turmoil. Overwhelmed, I repeated, "What do I do? What do I do?"

Time stood still, but I had found my answer; I didn't need to search any further. I just stared at the words and cried out to the Lord. Then there was an occurrence so small I almost missed it. The top right hand corner of the page curled, as if someone had started to curl it, or as if the page wanted me to turn it. The fan was blowing, but I realized if the breeze was to catch the page it would have started to flip. Turning the page, Jeremiah 3:13–15 stared back at me:

> "'Only acknowledge your iniquity, That you have transgressed against the LORD your God, and have scattered your charms to alien deities under every green tree, and you have not obeyed My voice,' says the LORD. "Return, O backsliding children," says the LORD; "for I am married to you. I will take you, one from a city and two from a family, and I will bring you to Zion. And I will give you shepherds according to My heart, who will feed you with knowledge and understanding."

That was it! I knew I had to leave this life and my very identity behind.

I got a trash bag and starting at my DVD rack, grabbed every lesbian film, every love story, and tossed them in. I went to my bookshelf threw out the lesbian almanac an old roommate had given me, a lesbian photography book from my best friend, and anything else that was tied to who I thought I was. And then I just stood there, with this bag hanging from my clasped fist. So much more than just possessions, this bag was symbolically my whole life, and my resolve started to wane.

"I don't have to throw this away now," I told myself. "I can just put it in the closet."

I returned to my Bible and skimmed through those verses again and progressed to chapter four. Verse one called to me:

"If you will return, O Israel," says the LORD, "Return to Me; and if you will put away your abominations out of My sight, then you shall not be moved."

Here I stood with this bag of gods, and all of a sudden I had the resolve! I had a supernatural strength! I picked up that trash bag and, as if on autopilot, walked right out my front door, over to the dumpster and tossed it in. It was amazing really; I felt like I was being driven by something, as if I was along for the ride. I know now it was the Holy Spirit.

Her Prayers, My Freedom
By Linda Carter

The Saturday morning I said to myself, "I am so tired of going through this," was the morning my mother's prayers caught up to me. She knew I was struggling with lesbianism, and she never stopped praying for me. That morning I fell down at the foot of my bed, lifted my hands up to God, and totally surrendered. In that moment, at the age of 33, I was saved.

For as long as I can remember I found myself attracted to women. I didn't know how to explain what I was feeling inside, and because I thought that sexual and other "worldly" matters were never to be discussed, I never talked about what was going on inside of me. Even though I was raised in a strong and loving Christian home, I carried around this secret for years.

I wanted so badly to be "normal" like all my friends were. In high school, they all had boyfriends. They felt comfortable dressing up and wearing makeup, something I did not do except on Sundays. I was comfortable in blue jeans and t-shirts. When I did end up having my first boyfriend in eleventh grade, I still felt attracted to other girls and tried to fight these feelings.

My first sexual encounter with a woman was in the fall of 1980 when I enrolled in a junior college. Everything I wanted in a man, I found in her. Everything started out so wonderful, but she soon betrayed me. She began having affairs. The committed relationship I wanted was not enough for her. She wanted to try it all: other women, drugs, and alcohol. I never wanted that kind of life. We went our separate ways. I was completely devastated.

The pain I felt after our breakup began to show itself as I began drinking and partying obsessively. Though I did not want another love, I started going to gay bars and house parties. I met a lot of other women but was afraid to get seriously involved with any of them. Eventually I had relationships with six other women, but none of them lasted more than one year. I was living the gay life now, but instead of feeling good about it, I felt trapped.

During those years I prayed to God, "When is this roller-coaster ride going to end? Are you ever going to change me?" No matter how hard I prayed, it seemed as if God did not hear me. Finally, I stopped praying altogether. Though I had given up, my mother persevered in her prayers for me. I didn't know it, but she "stood in the gap" for me. She was a real woman of God and a true and loving mother.

When my mother passed away in the spring of 1985, I became aware of a huge void in my life. It was then I realized that something important was missing. I entered a time of great depression, though God was really beginning to help me come to terms with my desire for women.

Things in my life began to change. My attraction to women began to decrease. When my lesbian friends called me to ask if I would go out with them, I turned them down. I went from being a woman who always went to gay parties and clubs to being a woman whose interest in these activities was disappearing. Eventually I even stopped taking calls from my old friends, and I changed my phone number.

I began to seek the Lord in every way I knew how: through Christian television, prayer, and by reading the Bible. God also led me to a Bible-teaching church. I was hungry for the Lord, and as I focused on Him my desires for women continued to fade.

I started dating a man whose company I enjoyed; he seemed different from any man I had ever met. I thought we could end up getting married. We had a long-distance relationship because I was away at college, but we traveled back and forth to see each other. I began to feel more strongly that he was the man for me. It was at this time, however, that we became sexually involved. When I got pregnant, he broke off our relationship, destroying all my hopes; I was alone again and very disillusioned. After the birth of my son, I went back into the lesbian lifestyle. Thankfully, the Lord did not let me go. Instead, He pursued me and brought me out.

Now I have such peace and joy in my heart. God is working in my life with all His power. I have even had the opportunity to share my past on different occasions. After sharing my story one night at my church, my son said to me, "Mom, I am so proud of you!"

I want the world to see and know that I am glad to be free, and I want to give hope to those who feel hopeless. I also want to encourage those who know people struggling with their sexual identity to continue praying. "The effectual fervent prayer of a righteous man availeth much" (James 5:16), as seen from the power my mother's prayers had in my life.

That Saturday morning her prayers were answered: I repented and asked God to help me. He has. God created me to be a woman, and deep inside of me He has assured me that this is what I am. God comes to give us life, joy, and peace. He wants us to experience freedom. What He has done in my life I believe He can do in your life as well. To God be the glory for redeeming my life from destruction!

Linda D. Carter graduated from Alabama State University with a BA in Communications. She is the Executive Director of Restoration Ministry of Mobile and a member of Nazaree Full Gospel Church. Linda is the proud single parent of one teenage son; they reside in Mobile, Alabama.

Two from California: "My husband and I were at the It Is Written Monterey Partnership this past weekend. We bought your book, and we each read it separately—not being able to put it down after starting it. We saw in print for the first time that someone else in the world was feeling exactly how my husband had felt for 20 years, being addicted to pornography and self-abuse. He had promised God for years that he would stop this behavior after each fall from grace, but the promises were empty promises; after a while he said he felt that there was no hope for him and no hope for eternal life, because he surely must have committed the unpardonable sin by now!

Life was empty, sad, and hopeless. Then I (the wife) found out about his addiction! Counseling was a helpful start, but your book has been the assurance that we both needed that there is hope for any kind of sinner, that God is mourning the separation that choosing sin causes for any of His dear children, that we can choose to live every moment His way, and that He wants us back still.

Thank you for writing your book and sharing your feelings in such depth. The last chapter with the list of suggestions for overcoming are also much appreciated.

Sincerely,

Two from California.

Daniel's Story

Question from Julio: My son Daniel is 22 years old. Born into a Christian family, he attended church all his life and even served in kids' ministries during his high school years. A year ago he told us he was gay. A few days ago he went further, telling us that he doesn't necessarily believe in the Word of God, that he doesn't consider himself saved, and that he doesn't believe God condemns homosexuality.

We live in Mexico City, and I pay for his studies at one of the best culinary institutes outside of New York City. I already told him that I could not accept homosexuality but that my love for him is unconditional. He, of course, tells me that if I love him I need to accept him just as he is and with the lifestyle that he has chosen. He even wants me to meet his boyfriend.

My wife and I, as well as his four older siblings, have firmly opposed his lifestyle but have not cut contact or communication with him at all. He has been looking for churches that accept the homosexual lifestyle.

I am about to tell him that I have made the decision to stop all financial support, both for his schooling and any other need he might have. It might strike you as odd that I still support him financially 100%, but this is completely normal in Mexican culture, and it has been like that with all my children. We are very well-off, and he has never lacked for any material thing.

Do you believe this is a wise decision? My fear is that this will cause him to act out even more. I'm not even sure how, but I am afraid that he will do something worse out of rebellion. He cannot work in the states legally until he gets his degree because he is under a student visa right now. I am reluctant to do this because my reasoning is that if I cut him off financially, he will have to move in with his boyfriend and find a way to make money, and this might spiral him deeper into more sin.

What would be your advice? My wife and I are desperate and only want to do God's will. We will be visiting our son in a couple of weeks for spring break, and that is when we plan to tell him about this decision.

Thank you in advance, and let me just say that your site has been a tremendous blessing for us.

God bless you,

Julio

Reply: Hello, Julio:

First of all, let me say that my heart goes out to you and your family as you are dealing with this heartbreaking situation. And let me commend you for assuring your son of your unconditional love for him.

However, unconditional love does not require you to condone sinful behavior, to participate in it, or to support it financially. You can accept him without accepting his gay lifestyle. As a Christian, you do not want to push your lifestyle upon him, and he should respect his family enough to not push his lifestyle upon you.

If you are uncomfortable meeting his boyfriend, just tell him that you do love him (your son), but that you are not comfortable meeting his boyfriend. You are presently trying to come to grips with his being gay, and you are just not ready to meet his boyfriend. Of course, it would not be wrong for you to meet him. But if your son loves you, he should not push upon you something you are not comfortable with, and you can tell him so.

Now, about the financial support you are giving him. I would advise you to continue giving him the same financial support you would give any other of your children, especially to get him through school. Otherwise he might perceive partiality on your part toward his siblings and come to believe that you do not love and accept him. You do not have to support sinful behavior financially, but it is probably the right thing to do to continue supporting him through his education. In this way, you are demonstrating unconditional love, patience, and mercy. Once he finishes his education, you can allow him to be on his own.

While you are doing this, you can also make it very clear that he needs to respect your family and household standards when visiting your home. You are the priest of the family, and you are expected by God to protect the sanctity of your home environment. What your son chooses to do outside the home is his business. But he needs to be informed that what goes on inside your Christian home is your business, but you still love him with all your heart.

This principle is actually revealed in the fourth commandment, for example, where God says about the Sabbath, "In it thou shalt not do any work, thou, nor thy son, nor thy daughter, thy manservant, nor thy maidservant, nor thy cattle, nor thy stranger that is within thy gates" (Exodus 20:10).

Not allowing open sin to be conducted within your domain is not unloving or unkind. It is simply stating that you do not condone, or participate in it, and you will not sanction it by allowing it to go on in your house. The issue that I'm warning about here is that of allowing your son to bring his boyfriend into your home for a visit where they might expect to share the bedroom and the bed, etc. You do not need to allow that.

However, visiting him and his friend on their turf would be doing what Jesus did in mingling with sinners while not participating in their sins. He was criticized for that, you know. But it was His practice, nevertheless.

I do hope that my thoughts are helpful to you. And, again, may I say how sorry I am that you are going through this disappointment within your family. Don't give up on your son, but remember that Jesus loves him more than you do and will do everything possible to turn him around. Keep interceding for him in your prayers, keep loving him unconditionally, and …

Keep looking up,

Victor

Julio: Hi Victor:

I don't have the words to express how grateful I am for your advice. It was like a huge load taken off my shoulders. I am convinced that finding you through an e-mail that a friend sent me with a link to your story and web page was God's providence in response to our prayers. We will be visiting our son in New York for Easter, and hopefully, we will be able to share a good time with him. And we will persevere in prayer trusting that our Lord will finish what he started in our son.

Thank you again for your advice, and I will keep you informed and maybe will be asking some more advice as things go forward. I hope to be able to meet you in the near future, and I will be praying for your amazing ministry.

May God keep blessing you abundantly.

In Christ's Love,

Julio

From these few e-mails, the correspondence from Julio advanced to frequent phone calls asking for continued advice and counsel. Eventually Julio suggested that he and Daniel fly to Little Rock, Arkansas, reserve a couple hotel rooms, and spend several days counseling together.

I accepted the invitation, and we had several days of very intense visitation. I spent time with Julio alone, then with Daniel alone, then with both of them together. Probably more time was spent with the father than with the son, for he needed just as much, if not more, counseling.

Daniel was very polite and talked openly with me about his feelings, his desires, his love for his family, and his desire to not hurt them, but he was very much in love with his boyfriend and could not see his way clear to turn from the gay life.

We had a very cordial parting a few days later, and I continued to hear from Julio with reports on Daniel's life and adventures in Europe and his committed relationship with his boyfriend.

Two years later I received the following e-mail. If ever I feel discouraged with my ministry, thinking that my efforts are insufficient and pointless, it is letters like this that spur me on to continue fighting the good fight of faith as we war against the enemy of souls in these perilous times of the great controversy between good and evil, between Christ and Satan.

The Letter: Victor:

I hope this message finds you well.

We met in Little Rock, Arkansas in the fall of 2009. My father and I went to see you for two days looking for counseling on the subject of my rebellion against my family and ultimately against God. Although I imagine that you have ministered to many young men like me, I hope that you remember my story and me. I am sorry that I never wrote to you and thanked you formally for your help. At the time, you see, I was determined to justify my life of sin and knew very well that contact with you would surely not help my determination. So for that I apologize.

I write to you now because I finished reading your book for the second time. The first time my heart was clouded with stubbornness to not let anything deter me from my mission. But today, reading it again, your story took on a whole new life and meaning. I can tell you now with such happiness that I, like you so long ago, have returned home (to Mexico City). I have confessed my sins to Jesus, I have asked for His forgiveness, and He has been faithful and just to forgive my sins and cleanse me of all wickedness.

My parents and family have seen their prodigal son return and have been nothing but amazingly kind and gracious toward me. Their prayers, advice, and encouragement throughout these years will forever be a testament to me of true faith in the Lord. I cannot express how happy my return has made my family and me. I wanted to share this with you because your life and your story were very helpful in my return to Jesus. I thank God for bringing you into our lives, particularly mine.

My story is incredibly similar to yours. So I now find *myself* in the "wilderness." I returned from the hustle and bustle of New York City to the wonderful home and family with which God blessed me. I truly don't understand how I could have stayed away for so long from the wonderful life He gave me. So like you, I now find myself asking Him for my very own "second chances and double portions."

From the moment I decided to leave my life of sin behind and accept God's purpose, I have felt the burden of ministering in some way, shape, or form. I cannot deny that I feel every day more and more urgency to serve God somehow and perhaps make up for the time I lost serving my sin and myself. Nevertheless, I have committed to wait for His guidance in every step I take from now on. So I have yet to discover how that ministry will come, but I have faith that it will.

Aside from thanking you and sharing my story with you, I wanted to ask you, if I may, for your prayers. I certainly do not feel exempt from temptation yet, and I know that the devil is roaming like a lion in my life waiting for me to fall again. So if you could keep me in your prayers, I would be so thankful.

I want so badly to serve the Lord and to fulfill the purpose He has for my life, but I do admit that I have fears and am uneasy about what the future holds. I want my life and story to glorify Him, but sometimes I wish I could seclude myself from the entire world in case I should fall into any sin again and shame Him. I know that God does not want me to be afraid, but as I'm sure you can sympathize, it comes from not having feelings of great strength in the Lord yet after living in rebellion for so long.

I thank God for you, for your ministry, and for the example you are to me and other people struggling with homosexual sin. I hope that you and your entire family are doing wonderfully. I hope that God continues to bless you.

Warm regards,

Daniel

It was a number of months later that I received a call from Julio telling me that Daniel's older brother had now come out as gay. The family was reeling.

241

Would I be able to visit with this brother the way I had with Daniel several years earlier? He was willing to visit with me, but this time the family would fly me to Mexico City for a week. After all, the entire family was anxious to meet me.

Off to Mexico City I went and had a wonderful time with this very special family. Daniel's brother was just as gracious and attentive as was Daniel several years earlier, and I was able to plant many seeds of truth into his mind and heart for the Holy Spirit to water, nurture, and bring to fruition.

One day Daniel took me for a long walk in the central park bringing me up to speed on all that was happening in his life. He was so excited about his newfound faith and the full life ahead of him.

"Ron," he said, "I want to tell you something. I have met this girl. I really like her and wonder if the Lord is leading me in that direction. My pastor, however, has told me to leave her alone, that I should not move in that direction until I know for sure that I am 'cured.' What do you think?"

"Daniel," I asked, "how will you ever know you are cured? Take that girl out to dinner! Get to know her! You don't have to make any commitments, just move forward one step at a time and see how the Lord leads, and how the chemistry works."

"Thank you, Ron! I was hoping you would say that!"

December, One Year Later:

Dearest Victor!

This is Daniel. I am sitting here with my mom and dad, and we wanted to send you an e-mail wishing you and your family a Merry Christmas! We hope that the Lord is doing wonderful things in your life and family, and is continuing to use you and your ministry to bless people the way you blessed our family. Even though we do not stay in touch as much as we should, you are always in our family's prayers. And we are so thankful to have met you. You are a HUGE blessing in our lives.

Victor, I am very sorry I have been so bad at keeping in touch, but I promise I will make a better effort next year. There is so much to tell you. First off, the Lord has blessed my life in the most extraordinary way. If I may refresh your memory, when you were here in February, I told you that I was starting to have feelings for this girl named Paulina. You advised me to make my feelings known and to pray for this relationship.

Well, I did, Victor, and the Lord has taken all matters into His own hands and made things so, so wonderful with her. We have shared an incredible relationship for the past year and things could not be better. The Lord sent me the most wonderful woman; she is such an enormous blessing.

Furthermore, the Lord has given me a restaurant, something small. It's a café, mostly sandwiches, salads, and such. We opened recently, but things have been wonderful. The Lord has provided for every need and has blessed it beyond what I could imagine. He has also healed every single wound that I in my rebellion inflicted upon my parents and our relationship. The Lord has made our relationship wonderful again. There is so much love between us, and I have never felt so lucky to have the parents that I do.

My relationship with the Lord has also grown so much this year. I cannot imagine how I strayed so far from my Creator. Walking with Him this year has filled me with so much peace and purpose, He has been faithful and just to restore every single thing that I destroyed in my rebellion. I cannot stress more how blessed I feel, and how the Lord has redeemed and healed me in every way possible.

But it doesn't end there. There's even more exciting news. Today I picked up the engagement ring that I bought for Paulina. I have asked her father for her hand and he, knowing my story entirely, has said that he would be so happy to have me as his son-in-law. I am planning to give the ring to her on New Year's.

I have fallen in love like I never had before. And I cannot imagine my life without her anymore. Hopefully I won't have to. And every step of the way has been guided by Him. My physical attraction to her has also grown by leaps and bounds from what it was when we first started, and I have experienced on a personal level how beautiful God's creation is, that he made us men to have feelings like this when things are done His way that are pure and shameless and so beautiful.

The Lord has been so, so, so good to me. I am so happy that I can share this joyous news with you. I remember you telling me that you had your church praying for Daniel, and that they were so happy to hear that I had returned. If I could send you something for you to read to them all, I would be so thankful. So here it is:

To the wonderful congregation that kept me in their prayers:

Hello. I know that we have never met, and you know very little about me. But Ron has told me that you kept me and my life in your prayers. I just wanted to tell you that every single one of those prayers was heard by our Almighty Father. He has restored and redeemed my heart and life, and I live now in his faithful ways. I have walked with the Lord for over a year now, and it has been the most beautiful journey. I would not have returned if it weren't for the prayers of people like you.

I know that my life is no coincidence and that the Lord had everything in his hands. I am so happy that He found me when I was most lost and desperate and that His love and grace overwhelmed my brokenness. I walk now in obedience with Him and keep discovering at every corner I turn how much greater His plans are.

Even though I doubt that I will meet all of you on this earth, I know for certain that we will meet on that great day when we go home to our Creator, and on that day I will thank all of you for taking part in my salvation. From the bottom of my heart I send the warmest regards and wish all of you happy holidays.

Hope to hear from you soon, Victor

Much Love,

Daniel

May, Five Months Later:

Dear Victor,

It is so nice to hear from you! My father forwarded your e-mail to me. How have you been? How is your family? Ministry?

Well, as for me, I am doing wonderfully! The Lord has just showered me with His grace and His blessings, and I just could not be more thankful. The wedding plans are going wonderfully well. We finally have an official date, which is November 2. We would be so honored and blessed if you were there. It's in the Lord's hands, but I personally would just be thrilled.

As for Paulina and me, we are doing wonderfully as well. To be quite honest, it's been an interesting ride. I've come to realize this time, pre-wedding, is really a cleansing and maturing time when the Lord really gives us a nice trimming of things He does not want in our marriage. That's putting it optimistically!

Paulina and I have grown so much in this time and have really matured in our walk with the Lord. It has been an amazing, though tiring, process. I am so thankful for this stage that I am living in.

The restaurant is going well. It's also been a big process of trusting the Lord and not leaning on my own strength. It is just truly amazing to see all that the Lord has done for me in this, my return to Christ. I feel so very blessed and loved by Him. I truly have never felt more close to Him and His ways, Victor. I am truly overwhelmed by His grace.

Please do keep in touch, and keep me posted!

Warmest regards, Victor!

Daniel

Driving to church one Sabbath I received a phone call from Mexico City. It was Daniel's mother Jennifer. "Ron, Daniel is getting married in November, and it would not be right for him to get married without you being here. Julio and I want to bring you and your wife Claudia to Mexico City for a one-week all-expenses-paid vacation so you can come to Daniel's wedding!"

Needless to say, I cleared my calendar.

The wedding was phenomenal! Hundreds of guests were at the courtyard wedding at the family hacienda. Daniel and Paulina had planned it to be an outreach event for all their friends and family. They each gave their testimonies to a very receptive audience. Daniel introduced my wife and me, announcing that had it not been for us and for our church praying for him over the past four years this day would never have happened.

The entire event was very spiritual with scriptural placards all around the courtyard and being carried down the aisle during the wedding processional. God was the center of the day, the ceremony, and the new life pledged together. Everywhere we turned during the reception, family members were thanking us for all we had done to make this day a reality.

How wonderful it is to be a part of the family of God!

Three months after the wedding:

My dear friends,

Sorry it has taken me so long to write, but better late than never! Words cannot describe the joy it was to see the two of you sitting there as I walked down the aisle with my mother on that very special day. It was just the biggest treat to have you both there sharing that miraculous day. We were just so overjoyed that you could be there, and meeting your wife just sealed every promise from the Lord that Paulina and I could aspire to one day have a marriage like yours. It gave us, and my entire family, such joy to have you both there!

I can tell you now, three months later, that I am truly living a dream. Marriage was definitely designed by our great and wonderful God, and it is good! I am still in awe of the woman the Lord had for me, and I am still wondering how he deemed me worthy of such a mate. Paulina is the most wonderful thing the Lord has given me. She is truly my help and confidante and the utmost joy in my life. I can only imagine how great and awesome are the plans that He has for me. If marrying Paulina is only the first step, I cannot imagine how much better this will get!

It is sad, however, the amount of time we got to spend with the two of you. It was just too short! I can't wait to see both of you again and get some more time to talk with you. We hope so much that you enjoyed yourselves and had a nice time at our wedding. There were so many people there that it really felt like the blink of an eye for both of us, but it really was everything we asked the Lord.

Our ceremony and our testimonies had a great impact on our friends and family, and we are just so thankful that the Lord used us as a vessel to manifest His undying fidelity and overwhelming grace. We think back on that day and are just so thankful for every small detail and for every person who attended.

In reality, you both were just the cherry on top of it all! Thank you so much for all your wonderful presents. We have used most all of them as we settle into our new home. You are so thoughtful, Claudia, for giving us all those things, and we are so thankful!

We hope to see you again soon, and we are so happy to have you in our lives. We look forward to spending eternity with friends like you.

With all the love in our hearts,
Daniel and Paulina

Chapter 27
EXCEEDING GREAT AND PRECIOUS PROMISES

A **Thought for the Day:** The perversity of the human mind [is] ingenious in evading truth. (*Seventh-day Adventist Bible Commentary* Vol. 7, 945)

Words of wisdom from Peter
A reference is made to the knowledge of Jesus Christ:

> Whereby are given unto us exceeding great and precious promises: that by these ye might be partakers of the divine nature, having escaped the corruption that is in the world through lust. (2 Peter 1:4)

> The Lord knoweth how to deliver the godly out of temptations. (2 Peter 2:9)

What wonderful promises! We must realize, dear friend, that through belief in Jesus it is our privilege to be partakers of the divine nature and in this way to escape the corruption that is in the world through lust. Then we can be cleansed from *all* sin, from *all* defects of character. We really need not retain one sinful propensity, tendency, bent, or habit.

As we partake of the divine nature, hereditary and cultivated tendencies to wrong are cut away from the character, and we are made a living power for good. Ever learning of the divine Teacher, daily partaking of His nature, we cooperate with God in overcoming Satan's temptations. (*The Review and Herald*, April 24, 1900)

In His Word God reveals what He can do for human beings. He molds and fashions after the divine likeness the characters of those who will wear His yoke. Through His grace [through His divine influence and power working on the heart and reflecting in the life] they are made partakers of the divine nature, and are thus enabled to overcome the corruption that is in the world through lust. It is God who gives us power to overcome. Those who hear His voice and obey His commandments are enabled [and empowered by Him] to form righteous characters [to overcome the sin that so easily overcomes them]. (*Seventh-day Adventist Bible Commentary* Vol. 7, 943)

What possibilities are opened up to the youth who lay hold of the divine assurances of God's Word! Scarcely can the human mind comprehend what is the breadth and depth and height of the spiritual attainments that can be reached by becoming partakers of the divine nature. The human agent who daily yields obedience to God, who becomes a partaker of the divine nature, finds pleasure daily in keeping the commandments of God; for he is one with God. It is essential that he hold as vital a relation with God as does the Son to the Father. (Ibid.)

Temptation must be met and resisted, friend. Day by day the spiritual battle goes on. Day by day we are to work out our own salvation from sin with fear and trembling, for it is God who works in us, to will and to do of His good pleasure. With Him all things are possible. His grace, His divine power, is sufficient for, yes, even you! (See Philippians 2:12, 13; Mark 10:27; 2 Corinthians 12:9.)

Never Again
By Anonymous

Never again will I profess, "I can't" for "I can do all things through Christ which strengtheneth me" (Philippians 4:13).

Never again will I profess lack for "my God shall supply all [my] need according to his riches in glory by Christ Jesus" (Philippians 4:19).

Never again will I profess fear for "God hath not given us the spirit of fear; but of power, and of love, and of a sound mind" (2 Timothy 1:7).

Never again will I profess doubt or lack of faith for "God hath dealt to every man the measure of faith" (Romans 12:3).

Never again will I profess weakness for "the Lord is the strength of my life" (Psalm 27:1).

Never again will I profess defeat for God "always causeth us to triumph in Christ" (2 Corinthians 2:14).

Never again will I profess lack of wisdom for "[Christ Jesus] is made unto us wisdom" (1 Corinthians 1:30).

Never again will I profess worries and frustrations, for I am "casting all [my] care upon him; for he careth for [me]" (1 Peter 5:7).

Never again will I profess bondage, for "where the Spirit of the Lord is, there is liberty" (2 Corinthians 3:17).

Never again will I profess condemnation, for "there is therefore now no condemnation to them which are in Christ Jesus, who walk not after the flesh, but after the Spirit" (Romans 8:1).

Never again will I profess loneliness, for Jesus said, "lo, I am with you always, even unto the end of the world" (Matt. 28:20), and "I will never leave thee, nor forsake thee" (Hebrews 13:5).

Never again will I profess discontent "for I have learned, in whatsoever state I am, therewith to be content" (Philippians 4:11).

Never again will I profess unworthiness "for he hath made him to be sin for us, who knew no sin; that we might be made the righteousness of God in him" (2 Corinthians 5:21).

Never again will I profess confusion "for God is not the author of confusion, but of peace" (1 Corinthians 14:33).

Never again will I profess persecution, for "if God be for us, who can be against us?" (Romans 8:31).

Never again will I profess the domination of sin over my life "for the law of the Spirit of life in Christ Jesus hath made me free from the law of sin and death" (Romans 8:2). And "as far as the east is from the west, so far hath he removed our transgressions from us" (Psalm 103:12).

Never again will I profess anxiety for "thou wilt keep him in perfect peace, whose mind is stayed on thee: because he trusteth in thee" (Isaiah 26:3).

A Rainbow of Promises
by Victor J. Adamson

A thought to ponder: "All [God's] biddings are enablings" (*Christ's Object Lessons*, 333).

Grace and peace be multiplied unto you through the knowledge of God, and of Jesus our Lord, According as his divine power hath given unto us all things that pertain unto life and godliness, through the knowledge of him that hath called us to glory and virtue: Whereby are given unto us exceeding great and precious promises: that by these ye might be partakers of the divine nature, having escaped the corruption that is in the world through lust. (2 Peter 1:2–4)

We must realize that through belief in [Jesus] it is our privilege to be partakers of the divine nature, and so escape the corruption that is in the world through lust. Then we can be cleansed from all sin, all defects of character. We really need not retain one sinful propensity [or tendency, bent, or habit]. (*The Review and Herald*, April 24, 1900)

As we partake of the divine nature, hereditary and cultivated tendencies to wrong are cut away from the character, and we are made a living power for good. Ever learning of the divine Teacher, daily partaking of His nature, we cooperate with God in overcoming Satan's temptations. (Ibid.)

In His Word God reveals what He can do for human beings. He molds and fashions after the divine similitude [or likeness] the characters of those who will wear His yoke. Through His grace [through His divine influence and power working on the heart and reflecting in the life] they are made partakers of the divine nature, and are thus enabled to overcome the corruption that is in the world through lust. It is God who gives us power to overcome. Those who hear His voice and obey His commandments are enabled [and empowered by Him] to form righteous characters. (Seventh-day Adventist Bible Commentary Vol. 7, 943)

It is by [personally applying] the great and precious promises of God's Word that we are to become partakers of the divine nature, having escaped the corruption that is in the world through lust ... The [person] who daily yields obedience to God, who becomes a partaker of the divine nature, finds pleasure daily [in obeying God], in keeping the commandments of God; for he is one with God. It is essential that he hold as vital a relation with God as does the Son to the Father. (Ibid.)

Temptation must be met and resisted. Day by day the spiritual battle goes on. Day by day we are to work out our own salvation [from sin] with fear and trembling. [For] it is God that works in us, to will and to do of His good pleasure. (Ibid.)

With God all things are possible. His grace, (His divine, transforming power) is sufficient for, yes, even you.

Wherefore, my beloved, as ye have always obeyed, not as in my presence only, but now much more in my absence, work out your own salvation with fear and trembling. For it is God which worketh in you both to will and to do of his good pleasure. (Philippians 2:12, 13)

And Jesus looking upon them saith, With men it is impossible, but not with God: for with God all things are possible. (Mark 10:27)

And he said unto me, My grace is sufficient for thee: for my strength is made perfect in weakness. Most gladly therefore will I rather glory in my infirmities, that the power of Christ may rest upon me. (2 Corinthians 12:9)

Therefore leaving the principles of the doctrine of Christ, let us go on unto perfection. (Hebrews 6:1)

Be ye therefore perfect, even as your Father which is in heaven is perfect. (Matthew 5:48)

For I am not ashamed of the gospel of Christ: for it is the power of God unto salvation to every one that believeth; to the Jew first, and also to the Greek. (Romans 1:16)

That as sin hath reigned unto death, even so might grace reign through righteousness unto eternal life by Jesus Christ our Lord. (Romans 5:21)

Being then made free from sin, ye became the servants of righteousness. (Romans 6:18)

But now being made free from sin, and become servants to God, ye have your fruit unto holiness, and the end everlasting life. (Romans 6:22)

That the righteousness of the law might be fulfilled in us, who walk not after the flesh, but after the Spirit. (Romans 8:4)

And be not conformed to this world: but be ye transformed by the renewing of your mind, that ye may prove what is that good, and acceptable, and perfect, will of God. (Romans 12:2)

There hath no temptation taken you but such as is common to man: but God is faithful, who will not suffer you to be tempted above that ye are able; but will with the temptation also make a way to escape, that ye may be able to bear it. (1 Corinthians 10:13)

Therefore if any man be in Christ, he is a new creature: old things are passed away; behold, all things are become new. (2 Corinthians 5:17) (See the Pot of Gold at the end of the "A Rainbow of Promises.")

The old nature, born of blood and the will of the flesh, cannot inherit the kingdom of God. The old ways, the hereditary tendencies, the former habits, must be given up; for grace is not inherited. The new birth consists in having new motives, new tastes, new tendencies. Those who are begotten unto a new life by the Holy Spirit have become partakers of the divine nature, and in all their habits and practices they will give evidence of their relationship to Christ. When men who claim to be Christians retain all their natural defects of character and disposition, in what does their position differ from that of the worldling? They do not appreciate the truth as a sanctifier, a refiner. They have not been born again." (*The Review and Herald*, April 12, 1892).

God makes no compromise with sin. A genuine conversion changes hereditary and cultivated tendencies to wrong. The religion of God is a firm fabric, composed of innumerable threads, and woven together with tact and skill. Only the wisdom which comes from God can make this fabric complete. There are a great many kinds of cloth which at first have a fine appearance, but they cannot endure the test. They wash out. The colors are not fast. Under the heat of summer they fade away and are lost. The cloth cannot endure rough handling.

So it is with the religion of many. When the warp and woof of character will not stand the test of trial, the material of which it is composed is worthless. The efforts made to patch the old with a new piece do not better the condition of things; for the old, flimsy material breaks away from the new, leaving the rent much larger than before. Patching will not do. The only way is to discard the old garment altogether, and procure one entirely new.

Christ's plan is the only safe one. He declares, "Behold, I make all things new." "If any man be in Christ, he is a new creature." Christ gives man no encouragement to think that He will accept a patchwork character, made up mostly of self, with a little of Christ. This is the condition of the Laodicean church. At first there seems to be some of self and some of Christ. But soon it is all of self and none of Christ. The root of selfishness is revealed. It continues to grow, striking its roots deeper and deeper, till its branches are covered with objectionable fruit. Christ looks with pitying tenderness on all who have combination characters. Those with such a character have a connection with Christ so frail that it is utterly worthless.

The patchwork religion is not of the least value with God. He requires the whole heart. No part of it is to be reserved for the development of hereditary or cultivated tendencies to evil. To be harsh, to be severe, too self-important, selfish, to look out for one's own selfish interest and yet be zealous that others shall deal unselfishly is a religion which is an abomination to God. Many have just such an experience daily, but it is a misrepresentation of the character of Christ. (*Seventh-day Adventist Bible Commentary* Vol. 6, 1101)

Having therefore these promises, dearly beloved, let us cleanse ourselves from all filthiness of the flesh and spirit, perfecting holiness in the fear of God. (2 Corinthians 7:1)

Casting down imaginations, and every high thing that exalteth itself against the knowledge of God, and bringing into captivity every thought to the obedience of Christ. (2 Corinthians 10:5)

I am crucified with Christ: nevertheless I live; yet not I, but Christ liveth in me: and the life which I now live in the flesh I live by the faith of the Son of God, who loved me, and gave himself for me. (Galatians 2:20)

According as he hath chosen us in him before the foundation of the world, that we should be holy and without blame before him in love. (Ephesians 1:4)

Now unto him that is able to do exceeding abundantly above all that we ask or think, according to the power that worketh in us, Unto him be glory. (Ephesians 3:20, 21)

That ye put off concerning the former conversation the old man, which is corrupt according to the deceitful lusts; And be renewed in the spirit of your mind; And that ye put on the new man, which after God is created in righteousness and true holiness. (Ephesians 4:22–24)

That he might sanctify and cleanse it with the washing of water by the word, That he might present it to himself a glorious church, not having spot, or wrinkle, or any such thing; but that it should be holy and without blemish. (Ephesians 5:26, 27)

Let this mind be in you, which was also in Christ Jesus. (Philippians 2:5)

That ye may be blameless and harmless, the sons of God, without rebuke, in the midst of a crooked and perverse nation, among whom ye shine as lights in the world. (Philippians 2:15)

I can do all things through Christ which strengtheneth me. (Philippians 4:13)

And you, that were sometime alienated and enemies in your mind by wicked works, yet now hath he [Jesus] reconciled in the body of his flesh through death, to present you holy and unblameable and unreproveable in his sight: If ye continue in the faith grounded and settled, and be not moved away from the hope of the gospel, which ye have heard. (Colossians 1:21–23)

And the Lord make you to increase and abound in love one toward another, and toward all men, even as we do toward you: To the end he may stablish your hearts unblameable in holiness before God, even our Father, at the coming of our Lord Jesus Christ with all his saints. (1 Thessalonians 3:12, 13)

Furthermore then we beseech you, brethren, and exhort you by the Lord Jesus, that as ye have received of us how ye ought to walk and to please God, so ye would abound more and more. (1 Thessalonians 4:1)

For God hath not called us unto uncleanness, but unto holiness. (1 Thessalonians 4:7)

And the very God of peace sanctify you wholly; and I pray God your whole spirit and soul and body be preserved blameless unto the coming of our Lord Jesus Christ. (1 Thessalonians 5:23)

But we are bound to give thanks alway to God for you, brethren beloved of the Lord, because God hath from the beginning chosen you to salvation through sanctification of the Spirit and belief of the truth. (2 Thessalonians 2:13)

That thou keep this commandment without spot, unrebukeable, until the appearing of our Lord Jesus Christ. (1 Timothy 6:14)

Nevertheless the foundation of God standeth sure, having this seal, The Lord knoweth them that are his. And, Let every one that nameth the name of Christ depart from iniquity. (2 Timothy 2:19)

Flee also youthful lusts: but follow righteousness, faith, charity, peace, with them that call on the Lord out of a pure heart. (2 Timothy 2:22)

All scripture is given by inspiration of God, and is profitable for doctrine, for reproof, for correction, for instruction in righteousness: That the man of God may be perfect, thoroughly furnished unto all good works. (2 Timothy 3:16, 17)

The aged women likewise, that they be in behaviour as becometh holiness, not false accusers, not given to much wine, teachers of good things. (Titus 2:3)

Teaching us that, denying ungodliness and worldly lusts, we should live soberly, righteously, and godly, in this present world; Looking for that blessed hope, and the glorious appearing of the great God and our Saviour Jesus Christ; Who gave himself for us, that he might redeem us from all iniquity, and purify unto himself a peculiar people, zealous of good works. (Titus 2:12–14)

Therefore leaving the principles of the doctrine of Christ, let us go on unto perfection; not laying again the foundation of repentance from dead works, and of faith toward God. (Hebrews 6:1)

Now the God of peace, that brought again from the dead our Lord Jesus, that great shepherd of the sheep, through the blood of the everlasting covenant, Make you perfect in every good work to do his will, working in you that which is wellpleasing in his sight, through Jesus Christ; to whom be glory for ever and ever. Amen. (Hebrews 13:20, 21)

But let patience have her perfect work, that ye may be perfect and entire, wanting nothing. (James 1:4)

Wherefore lay apart all filthiness and superfluity of naughtiness, and receive with meekness the engrafted word, which is able to save your souls. (James 1:21)

Submit yourselves therefore to God. Resist the devil, and he will flee from you. Draw nigh to God, and he will draw nigh to you. Cleanse your hands, ye sinners; and purify your hearts, ye double minded. (James 4:7, 8)

But as he which hath called you is holy, so be ye holy in all manner of conversation; Because it is written, Be ye holy; for I am holy. (1 Peter 1:15, 16)

Seeing ye have purified your souls in obeying the truth through the Spirit unto unfeigned love of the brethren, see that ye love one another with a pure heart fervently. (1 Peter 1:22)

Dearly beloved, I beseech you as strangers and pilgrims, abstain from fleshly lusts, which war against the soul; Having your conversation honest among the Gentiles: that, whereas they speak against you as evildoers, they may by your good works, which they shall behold, glorify God in the day of visitation. (1 Peter 2:11, 12)

But the God of all grace, who hath called us unto his eternal glory by Christ Jesus, after that ye have suffered a while, make you perfect, stablish, strengthen, settle you. (1 Peter 5:10)

Seeing then that all these things shall be dissolved, what manner of persons ought ye to be in all holy conversation and godliness. (2 Peter 3:11)

He that saith he abideth in him ought himself also so to walk, even as he walked. (1 John 2:6)

If ye know that he is righteous, ye know that every one that doeth righteousness is born of him. (1 John 2:29)

And every man that hath this hope in him purifieth himself, even as he is pure. (1 John 3:3)

Little children, let no man deceive you: he that doeth righteousness is righteous, even as he is righteous. (1 John 3:7)

And whatsoever we ask, we receive of him, because we keep his commandments, and do those things that are pleasing in his sight. (1 John 3:22)

Ye are of God, little children, and have overcome them: because greater is he that is in you, than he that is in the world. (1 John 4:4)

For this is the love of God, that we keep his commandments: and his commandments are not grievous. For whatsoever is born of God overcometh the world: and this is the victory that overcometh the world, even our faith. (1 John 5:3, 4)

Now unto him that is able to keep you from falling, and to present you faultless before the presence of his glory with exceeding joy, To the only wise God our Saviour, be glory and majesty, dominion and power, both now and for ever. Amen. (Jude 1:24, 25)

To him that overcometh will I grant to sit with me in my throne, even as I also overcame, and am set down with my Father in his throne. (Revelation 3:21)

Here is the patience of the saints: here are they that keep the commandments of God, and the faith of Jesus. (Revelation 14:12)

He that overcometh shall inherit all things; and I will be his God, and he shall be my son. (Revelation 21:7)

Blessed are they that do his commandments, that they may have right to the tree of life, and may enter in through the gates into the city. (Revelation 22:14)

The Pot of Gold: Through all ages and in every nation those that believe that Jesus can and will save them personally from sin, are the elect and chosen of God; they are his peculiar treasure. They obey his call, and come out of the world and separate themselves from every unclean thought and unholy practice. (*The Review and Herald*, August 1, 1893)
